SAVOR SANTA BARBARA

WATERFRONT TO WINE COUNTRY

A COLLECTION OF RECIPES FROM ASSISTANCE LEAGUE® OF SANTA BARBARA

Tom and Pat DeBerry

Yoshiharu and Yoshie Ohara

Photograph © Kirk Irwin

Savor Santa Barbara

WATERFRONT TO WINE COUNTRY

A COLLECTION OF RECIPES FROM ASSISTANCE LEAGUE® OF SANTA BARBARA

Published by ASSISTANCE LEAGUE® of Santa Barbara

Library of Congress Control Number: 2002101232
ISBN: 0-9710029-0-8

Edited, Designed, and Manufactured by
Favorite Recipes® Press
An imprint of

FRP

P.O. Box 305142
Nashville, Tennessee 37230
800-358-0560

Art Director: Steve Newman
Book Design: Jim Scott
Project Editor: Linda Jones

Manufactured in the United States of America
First Printing: 2002
20,000 copies

Dedicated to the people who make it possible for us to serve the community by their contributions to our projects.

Completed in 1929, the Santa Barbara County Courthouse (pictured on the cover and below) is a stunning example of Spanish-Moorish architecture. Inside this graceful structure you'll find historic murals, intricately carved doors, imported tile and elegant wrought-iron chandeliers. The building is surrounded by beautifully landscaped grounds and crowned with an eighty-foot clock tower, which offers magnificent mountain and ocean views.

contents

This symbol denotes wine suggestions.

I was delighted to be asked to contribute a foreword to this collection of recipes, which has been compiled, tested, tasted, and refined by members of the ASSISTANCE LEAGUE® of Santa Barbara.

I've lived in Santa Barbara twice in the past thirty-five years; the first time from 1964 until 1972, the second time from 1982 to the present. What I noticed early on is that almost everyone in Santa Barbara comes from somewhere else. Most of us are torn between a desire to brag about the advantages of living in this community and an ever-so-crafty urge to keep our big mouths shut so the town won't be overrun with "riffraff," which is to say, anyone not us. After all, we got here first and it's natural to feel protective of the beauty and serenity that epitomize the Santa Barbara experience. At the same time, most of us feel so blessed by circumstance we can't help wanting to share the wealth. Okay, well maybe not the actual wealth, but at least a "taste" of the lifestyle we've come to enjoy.

These recipes are testimony to the generosity, skill, diversity, and talent of local food enthusiasts, whose appreciation of good food and good wine form yet another common denominator besides our basic chauvinism. We hope you'll savor these dishes in your own homes, not necessarily right here in Santa Barbara between Labor Day and Memorial Day. Summer is open season. Bon appétit!

Sue Grafton

Sue Grafton

Sue Grafton is an international best-selling author of detective novels with readership in the millions. She makes her home in Santa Barbara.

The proceeds from the sale of this book will enable ASSISTANCE LEAGUE® of Santa Barbara to expand and improve our facilities, resulting in greater service to our community.

introduction

ASSISTANCE LEAGUE® of Santa Barbara is one of 108 chapters of NATIONAL ASSISTANCE LEAGUE®. With its auxiliary Las Aletas, the chapter has a combined membership numbering over 300. Members of this nonprofit, all volunteer, service organization identify, develop, implement, and fund the following projects in order to serve the specific needs of children and adults in the greater Santa Barbara area.

HILLSIDE HOUSE:

Residential home for persons with cerebral palsy or brain injuries. Generous financial support and various activities are provided by members.

OPERATION SCHOOL BELL® and TEEN SCHOOL BELL:

Provides area children in need with appropriate new clothing for the school year.

FUN IN THE SUN:

Appropriate new clothing is provided for disadvantaged children chosen to attend summer day camp.

H.U.G.S. (Helping Us Give Service):

Provides teddy bears to local agencies for comfort to injured or traumatized children.

THE LITTLE COTTAGE:

Offers housing for out-of-area families in need whose relatives are in the hospital.

V.I.P. (Very Improved Performers):

Hosts luncheons honoring middle school students who have shown improvement in attendance, attitude, and citizenship.

FRIENDSHIP LUNCHEONS:

Provides lunch and entertainment to local senior citizens.

FOSTERING FRIENDS:

Offers mentoring and assistance to young adults leaving the foster care system.

OPERATION BOOK SHELF:

Provides library service to shut-ins.

KIDS ON THE BLOCK:

Puppet programs designed to raise awareness in dealing with current issues are made available to local school-age children.

SAVOR THE SPIRIT

beverages and appetizers

PRAWNS WITH FETA, LIME
AND MINT VINAIGRETTE

SWEET CHINESE PORK (CHAR SIU)

OLIVE STICKS

SUN-DRIED TOMATO AND FETA TORTA

MARGARITAS ESPAÑOLAS

BABY VEGETABLES WITH
CREAMY CAESAR DIP

(shown left to right)

Yacht Basin *Photograph © David Muench*

Brandy Alexander Extraordinaire

6 tablespoons brandy
3 tablespoons Kahlúa or crème de cacao
3 tablespoons cream or half-and-half
2 or 3 ice cubes
Vanilla ice cream to taste

Blend the brandy, Kahlúa, cream and ice cubes in a blender until smooth and frosty. Add the ice cream and blend well. Serve in chilled or frosted glasses.

YIELD: 2 SERVINGS

Cosmopolitan

2 tablespoons vodka
2 tablespoons Triple Sec
Juice of 1/2 lime
2 tablespoons cranberry juice cocktail

Combine the vodka, Triple Sec, lime juice and cranberry juice cocktail in a blender or shaker and blend or shake to mix well.

YIELD: 1 SERVING

KAHLÚA (KAH-LOO-AH)

Kahlúa is a coffee-flavored product of Mexico. Here's a simple recipe for homemade coffee liqueur:

Blend 2 1/2 cups sugar, 1/4 cup instant coffee powder and 4 cups water in a saucepan. Bring to a boil and reduce the heat. Simmer for 1 1/2 hours. Remove from the heat to cool. Add 1 broken vanilla bean and 3 cups vodka. Pour into a bottle with a tight-fitting lid; secure the lid. Shake once a day for 3 to 4 weeks. Store in a dark place until ready to serve.

LEMON DROP MARTINI

¹/₄ cup sugar
2 lemon wedges
Ice
¹/₄ cup Absolut Citron vodka

2 tablespoons Cointreau
2 tablespoons fresh lemon juice
1 teaspoon sugar

Place ¹/₄ cup sugar in a saucer. Rub the rim of each martini glass with a squeezed lemon wedge. Dip lightly into the sugar in the saucer to coat the rim of each glass. Fill a shaker with ice. Add the vodka, Cointreau, lemon juice and 1 teaspoon sugar. Shake for 30 seconds. Pour into the prepared glasses. Garnish each glass with a lemon slice.

YIELD: 2 SERVINGS

STRAWBERRY DAIQUIRI

4 cups crushed ice
8 fresh or frozen whole
    strawberries
4 ounces frozen limeade
    concentrate

1 teaspoon vanilla extract
2 tablespoons confectioners' sugar
¹/₄ cup milk
³/₄ cup light rum

Fill a blender halfway with crushed ice. Add the strawberries, limeade concentrate, vanilla, confectioners' sugar, milk and rum. Add enough water to fill 1¹/₂ inches from the top of the blender. Blend until slushy. Pour immediately into chilled glasses to serve.

YIELD: 4 TO 6 SERVINGS

MARGARITAS ESPAÑOLAS

Photograph for this recipe is shown on page 12.

Kosher salt
Lime wedges
2 cups tequila
1 cup Triple Sec
1 cup fresh lime juice

3/8 cup simple syrup (see note
  below), or 1 tablespoon light
  corn syrup
3 cups crushed ice

Place the kosher salt in a saucer. Rub margarita glasses with lime wedges. Dip in the kosher salt to coat. Remove the excess salt from inside of each glass. Blend the tequila, Triple Sec, lime juice, simple syrup and 1 cup of the ice in a blender. Serve over the remaining ice in the prepared glasses.

Note: For simple syrup, mix equal parts sugar and water in a saucepan. Bring almost to a boil to dissolve the sugar completely.

YIELD: 8 SERVINGS

For Frozen Margaritas, blend the tequila, Triple Sec, lime juice and simple syrup with 3 cups crushed ice.

SANTA BARBARA SUMMER COOLER

2 cups fresh orange juice, chilled
1 (6-ounce) can frozen lemonade
  concentrate, thawed
1 cup Triple Sec, chilled

1 (750-milliliter) bottle dry white
  wine, chilled
1 (33-ounce) bottle club soda,
  chilled

Combine the orange juice, lemonade concentrate, Triple Sec, wine and club soda in a punch bowl and mix well just before serving. Garnish with a frozen ice ring with fresh strawberries and mint or thin slices of lime, orange or lemon floating on top.

YIELD: 20 (4-OUNCE) SERVINGS

TRIPLE SEC

Triple Sec, a clear, orange liqueur dating from the sixteenth century, originally was made from bitter oranges grown on the island of Curaçao. The name means "triple-sweet" after the three-stage processing method. Curaçao, Cointreau, and Grand Marnier are all Triple Secs, and often can be substituted for one another.

FANDANGO SANGRIA

Photograph for this recipe is shown on page 70.

4 cups burgundy
¹/₂ cup orange liqueur
¹/₄ cup sugar
2 tablespoons lemon juice
2 cups club soda

Combine the burgundy, orange liqueur, sugar and lemon juice in a large pitcher and blend well. Chill, covered, until ready to serve. Add the club soda and blend well. Serve over ice cubes in glasses. Garnish with lemon and orange slices.

YIELD: 10 SERVINGS

SUNRISE RAMOS FIZZ

4 ounces frozen orange juice concentrate
2 ounces frozen lemonade concentrate
³/₄ cup vodka
1 cup vanilla ice cream, softened
¹/₂ teaspoon orange flower water
2 egg whites
Ice cubes

Combine the orange juice concentrate, lemonade concentrate, vodka, ice cream, orange flower water and egg whites in a blender. Add enough ice cubes to fill and blend well.

Note: To avoid raw eggs that may carry salmonella, we suggest using an equivalent amount of pasteurized egg substitute.

YIELD: 4 SERVINGS

LIQUEURS

Sweet and syrupy, liqueurs are spirits that have been flavored with a wide range of ingredients such as fruits, seeds, nuts, spices, coffee, or chocolate. The spirit base is usually brandy, rum, or whiskey. Liqueurs are generally sipped as an after-dinner drink or used to flavor sauces and desserts. Add liqueurs cautiously, since the concentrated sweetness and intense flavor can overwhelm your dish.

Frosty Fruit Punch

1 gallon Ocean Spray Cran-Raspberry Juice
2 (46-ounce) cans pineapple juice
2 cups sugar
1 cup water
2 (33-ounce) bottles club soda
2 (33-ounce) bottles ginger ale

Bring the cran-raspberry juice, pineapple juice, sugar and water to a boil in a saucepan over medium heat. Remove from the heat and cool slightly. Pour into sealable plastic bags. Freeze until firm.

To serve, thaw the frozen juice mixture for 5 hours or until slushy. Spoon into a punch bowl. Add the club soda and ginger ale. Ladle into punch cups.

Note: Use only the Ocean Spray brand of cran-raspberry juice or the punch will turn dark gray in color.

YIELD: 40 SERVINGS

Baked Brie with Kahlúa

¼ cup packed brown sugar
¼ cup Kahlúa
1¼ cups chopped roasted pecans
1 (14-ounce) miniature wheel Brie cheese

Bring the brown sugar and Kahlúa to a boil in a small saucepan over medium heat and reduce the heat. Cook for 5 minutes, stirring occasionally. Remove from the heat and stir in the pecans.

Remove the rind from the cheese using a sharp knife. Arrange in a 9-inch glass pie plate or similar microwave-safe dish. Pour the Kahlúa mixture over the cheese. Microwave on High for 1½ to 2 minutes or until the cheese softens. Watch carefully so the cheese will not overheat and melt. Serve with toasted French bread rounds or sliced fruit.

YIELD: 8 SERVINGS

BRIE (BREE)

The traditional soft-ripening cheeses, which include Brie and Camembert, are fully ripened and ready to eat when they have a consistent buttery-soft interior surrounded by an edible white rind. Brie, a product of France dating back to the eighth century, can be made from uncooked or pasteurized whole or skim milk and contains fifty to sixty percent butterfat. When shopping for Brie, look for a wheel that is plump and firm.

MARINATED FETA IN OLIVE OIL

SUN-DRIED TOMATOES

Drying fresh tomatoes,
either in the sun or
by artificial means,
intensifies the flavor
and modifies the
texture. Sun-dried
tomatoes have a
dark red, somewhat
shriveled appearance,
a deep, rich taste,
and a dense, chewy
texture. They are
available oil- or dry-
packed, and add a
unique dimension to
sauces and salads.

8 ounces feta cheese
5 (3-inch) sprigs each of fresh
    rosemary, oregano and thyme,
    or 2 tablespoons each of dried
    rosemary, oregano and thyme

4 garlic cloves, peeled
5 or 6 niçoise or salt-cured olives
    or Spanish-style green olives
1/2 cup olive oil

Cut the cheese into large chunks. Pack into a 1 1/2-cup jar or crock. Add the herbs, garlic and olives. Pour the olive oil over the top to cover the cheese. Chill, covered, for 5 days before serving. Serve at room temperature with crackers. You may store in the refrigerator for up to 6 weeks.

YIELD: 1 1/2 CUPS

SUN-DRIED TOMATO AND FETA TORTA

Photograph for this recipe is shown on page 12.

1 cup (2 sticks) unsalted butter,
    cut into pieces
12 ounces feta cheese
8 ounces cream cheese, softened
2 garlic cloves, minced
1 shallot, minced
2 to 4 tablespoons vermouth

White pepper or hot pepper sauce
    to taste
1/2 cup pine nuts, toasted
8 ounces sun-dried tomatoes,
    softened, minced
1 cup pesto

Process the butter, feta cheese, cream cheese, garlic, shallot and vermouth in a food processor until smooth. Season with white pepper. Oil a 4- to 5-cup straight-sided mold or springform pan. Line with plastic wrap. Alternate layers of the pine nuts, sun-dried tomatoes, pesto and cheese mixture in the prepared mold until all of the ingredients are used and the mold is full. Fold the plastic wrap over the top and press to compact the layers. Chill for 1 hour or until firm before serving.

    Note: You may layer the ingredients in any order.

YIELD: 20 SERVINGS

BLEU CHEESE DIP

6 cups mayonnaise
  (1 quart plus 1 pint)
2 cups sour cream
1/4 teaspoon onion powder
1/4 teaspoon garlic powder

Salt and pepper to taste
8 ounces bleu cheese, crumbled
1 tablespoon ketchup
1 tablespoon Worcestershire sauce

Combine the mayonnaise, sour cream, onion powder, garlic powder, salt and pepper in a bowl and mix well. Add the cheese, ketchup and Worcestershire sauce and mix well. Store, covered, in the refrigerator until ready to serve.

YIELD: 8 CUPS

A good choice to have on hand as a dip, but it also makes a delicious salad dressing.

CREAMY CAESAR DIP

Photograph for this recipe is shown on page 12.

2 medium garlic cloves, peeled
1/2 cup grated Parmesan cheese
1/4 cup packed chopped fresh
  parsley

6 canned anchovy fillets
3 tablespoons fresh lemon juice
1/2 cup (or more) sour cream
1/2 cup mayonnaise

Process the garlic in a food processor until minced. Add the cheese, parsley, anchovies and lemon juice and process to form a paste. Spoon into a bowl. Add the sour cream and mayonnaise and mix well, adding additional sour cream if needed for the desired consistency. Serve with fresh baby vegetables.

YIELD: 2 CUPS

Santa Barbara "Caviar"

1 (15-ounce) can black-eyed peas,
    rinsed, drained
1 (15-ounce) can white beans,
    rinsed, drained
1 tablespoon minced garlic
1/2 small sweet onion, minced
1/2 small red bell pepper,
    minced
1/4 cup chopped fresh cilantro

1 (4-ounce) can chopped green
    chiles, drained
3 tablespoons chopped jalapeño
    chiles
3 tablespoons fresh lime juice
2 teaspoons olive oil
1 teaspoon salt
1/4 to 1/2 teaspoon pepper
1 avocado

Combine the black-eyed peas, white beans, garlic, onion, bell pepper, cilantro, green chiles, jalapeño chiles, lime juice, olive oil, salt and pepper in a bowl and mix well. Chill, covered, for 3 to 12 hours to enhance the flavor. Chop the avocado and stir into the pea mixture just before serving. Serve with tortilla chips.

YIELD: 4 CUPS

Spoon "caviar" onto fresh lettuce leaves, roll up, and you have a tasty lettuce wrap.

Hot Crab Dip

24 ounces cream cheese, softened
1 (4-ounce) can chopped green
    chiles, drained
3 scallions, chopped

3 tablespoons minced parsley
2 teaspoons Worcestershire sauce
2 (6-ounce) cans crab meat,
    drained, flaked

Combine the cream cheese, green chiles, scallions, parsley and Worcestershire sauce in a bowl and mix well. Fold in the crab meat. Spoon into a 1 1/2-quart baking dish. Bake at 350 degrees for 30 minutes or until heated through and bubbly around the edges. Serve with crackers or thinly sliced baguettes.

YIELD: 24 SERVINGS

CRAB SPREAD

2 (7-ounce) cans crab meat
1 envelope unflavored gelatin
1 (10-ounce) can tomato soup
8 ounces cream cheese, softened
1 cup mayonnaise

1/2 cup chopped scallions
1/2 cup chopped celery
10 to 20 drops of Tabasco sauce,
   or to taste

Drain and flake the crab meat, reserving 1/4 cup of the liquid. Soften the gelatin in the reserved liquid in a bowl. Heat the soup and cream cheese in a double boiler until the cream cheese melts, whisking until smooth. Remove from the heat. Add the gelatin mixture and whisk until dissolved. Add the mayonnaise, scallions, celery and Tabasco sauce and mix well. Spoon into an oiled mold. Chill, covered, for 6 to 8 hours or until firm. Unmold onto a serving plate. Serve with crackers.

YIELD: 20 SERVINGS

CURRY GINGER DIP

1/2 cup mayonnaise
1/2 cup sour cream
1/4 cup minced onion
1 garlic clove, minced
1/4 cup minced water chestnuts
1/4 cup minced candied ginger

1 tablespoon soy sauce
1 teaspoon curry powder
1 tablespoon finely chopped
   chutney
Salt to taste

Combine the mayonnaise, sour cream, onion, garlic, water chestnuts, ginger, soy sauce, curry powder, chutney and salt in a bowl and mix well. Chill, covered, for up to 4 days before serving. Serve with crackers, chips or fresh vegetable sticks.

YIELD: 12 SERVINGS

CURRY POWDER

Curry powder is a blend of spices consisting mainly of chiles, cloves, coriander, fennel seeds, nutmeg, mace, cayenne pepper, sesame seeds, saffron, and turmeric (which is responsible for its yellow color). *Indian* curry powder is mild, while *Madras* is hot. It's advisable to use sparingly, since the spice is capable of overwhelming other flavors and may add too much "heat."

FIESTA GUACAMOLE

AVOCADO

Although Californians would like the distinction, Florida grew the first United States avocado trees in the 1830s. Today, almost eighty percent of the crop comes from California. Sometimes referred to as *alligator pears*, avocados range from bright green to black, round to pear-shaped, and smooth to pebbly. Placing avocados in a paper bag for two to four days will hasten the ripening process. Once cut, the flesh will brown rapidly, but adding lemon or lime juice will help prevent this.

7 Haas avocados	**1 teaspoon lemon pepper**
2/3 cup chopped onion	**1/4 teaspoon Tabasco sauce, or**
1/4 teaspoon salt	**to taste**
1/8 teaspoon black pepper	**2 tablespoons lemon juice**

Mash the avocados in a large bowl. Add the onion, salt, black pepper, lemon pepper, Tabasco sauce and lemon juice and mix well. Chill, covered, for at least 1 hour. Serve with tortilla chips.

Note: Chopped tomato, chopped green chiles, cilantro and garlic are welcome additions to this popular dip.

YIELD: 7 CUPS

 For a special treat, serve with Fandango Sangria on page 18. If you are adventurous, try a white zinfandel or a white merlot to balance the spice and still show the fruit.

STUFFED SHEEPHERDER'S BREAD

1 round loaf unsliced	**1/4 teaspoon garlic salt**
sheepherder's bread	**1/4 teaspoon pepper**
32 ounces cream cheese, softened	**6 scallions, chopped**
1 (5-ounce) package chipped beef,	**3 or 4 tablespoons mayonnaise**
finely chopped	**2 teaspoons lemon juice**

Cut 5 or 6 inches from the top of the bread loaf, reserving the top. Hollow out the center of the loaf to form a shell. Combine the cream cheese, beef, garlic salt, pepper, scallions, 3 tablespoons mayonnaise and lemon juice in a bowl and mix well. Add the remaining 1 tablespoon mayonnaise if needed for the desired consistency. Spoon the cream cheese mixture into the bread shell. Replace the reserved bread top. Cover the entire bread loaf with foil and place on a baking sheet. Bake at 300 degrees for 1 1/2 to 1 3/4 hours. Serve with fresh vegetables and chips and chop the bread top for dipping.

YIELD: 12 SERVINGS

EL PRESIDIO BEEF DIP

2 pounds lean ground beef
1 cup finely chopped onion
2 or 3 garlic cloves, minced
2 (8-ounce) cans tomato sauce
1/2 cup ketchup

1 1/4 teaspoons crushed oregano
2 teaspoons sugar
16 ounces cream cheese, softened
2/3 cup grated Parmesan cheese

Brown the ground beef with the onion in a skillet, stirring until the ground beef is crumbly and the onion is tender; drain. Stir in the garlic, tomato sauce, ketchup, oregano and sugar. Simmer, covered, for 10 minutes. Remove from the heat. Add the cream cheese and Parmesan cheese and stir until the cream cheese is melted. Serve warm with corn chips.

YIELD: 6 CUPS

SUPER MACHO NACHOS

8 ounces chorizo sausage or
    Italian sausage
8 ounces ground beef
1 large onion, chopped
Liquid hot pepper to taste
Salt to taste
1 (16-ounce) can refried beans

1 (4-ounce) can chopped green
    chiles, drained
2 or 3 cups (8 or 12 ounces)
    shredded Monterey Jack
    cheese
1 (6-ounce) jar taco sauce

Remove the casings from the sausage and crumble into a skillet. Add the ground beef and onion. Cook until the sausage and ground beef are brown and crumbly, stirring frequently; drain. Add the liquid hot pepper and salt and mix well. Spread the refried beans in a shallow glass baking dish. Layer the ground beef mixture, green chiles and cheese in the prepared dish. Drizzle with the taco sauce. Bake at 375 degrees for 30 minutes or until bubbly and heated through. Serve with tortilla chips.

YIELD: 8 TO 10 SERVINGS

CHORIZO (CHOR-EE-SOH)

Chorizo, popular throughout the Southwest, is a spicy, coarsely ground pork flavored with garlic, chili powder, onion, cumin, and other spices. Be sure to remove the casing and crumble before cooking. To add pizzazz to nachos, top with chopped scallions, chopped ripe olives, sour cream, and guacamole.

RANCHERO DIP

BLACK-EYED PEAS

Also called cowpeas, black-eyed peas are small and beige with a distinctive black "eye" in the middle. To cook, place the fresh peas in a large saucepan and cover with water. Bring to a boil and reduce the heat. Simmer for about one to two hours or until tender. Dried peas need to be soaked for four to twelve hours before cooking. According to Southern tradition, eating black-eyed peas, hog jowls, and corn bread on New Year's Day will bring good luck.

1 (15-ounce) can black-eyed peas, rinsed, drained
1 cup canned white beans
1 tablespoon minced fresh garlic
1 cup chopped tomatoes
1/2 cup finely chopped green bell pepper
1/2 cup chopped scallions
2 tablespoons chopped fresh cilantro
1 tablespoon chopped fresh parsley
1 tablespoon chopped jalapeño chile
1 teaspoon salt
1 tablespoon lemon juice
3/4 cup zesty Italian salad dressing
1 large avocado, chopped

Combine the black-eyed peas, white beans, garlic, tomatoes, bell pepper, scallions, cilantro, parsley, jalapeño chile, salt, lemon juice and salad dressing in a bowl and mix well. Add the avocado and mix gently. Chill, covered, for 3 to 12 hours to enhance the flavor before serving.

YIELD: 4 CUPS

LIVER PÂTÉ

8 ounces chicken livers
2 tablespoons butter
2 tablespoons Cognac
6 ounces cream cheese, softened
2 tablespoons finely chopped onion
1 tablespoon chopped fresh parsley or cilantro
1 teaspoon Worcestershire sauce
3/4 teaspoon salt
1/4 teaspoon pepper

Sauté the chicken livers in the butter in a skillet for 10 minutes or until tender. Add the Cognac gradually. Cook for 1 minute; cool slightly. Process in a food processor until the chicken livers are finely chopped.

Beat the cream cheese in a mixing bowl until light and fluffy. Add the chicken livers, onion, parsley, Worcestershire sauce, salt and pepper and mix well. Serve with crackers.

YIELD: 8 SERVINGS

 A perfect accompaniment would be a pinot noir or a dry pinot grigio.

MUSHROOM TAPENADE

1 pound finely chopped brown
   mushrooms
1/3 cup minced sweet onion
1 1/2 teaspoons minced garlic
1 tablespoon drained capers
1/2 teaspoon white pepper

1 teaspoon basil
1/4 cup balsamic vinaigrette
1/3 cup dry sherry
Several dashes of liquid Maggi
   Seasoning

Combine the mushrooms, onion, garlic, capers, white pepper and basil in a bowl and mix well. Add the vinaigrette and sherry. Season with the liquid Maggi Seasoning. Marinate, covered, in the refrigerator for 24 hours. Drain about 1 cup of the liquid from the mushroom mixture before serving. Serve with baguette slices.

YIELD: 2 CUPS

OLIVE TAPENADE

1 1/2 cups chopped pimento-stuffed
   green olives
1 tablespoon finely chopped garlic
1/3 cup finely chopped red onion
1 large red bell pepper, finely
   chopped

1/2 cup chopped toasted pine nuts
1/4 cup grated Parmesan cheese
6 tablespoons olive oil and vinegar
   salad dressing

Process the green olives, garlic, onion, bell pepper, pine nuts and cheese in a food processor until smooth. Add the salad dressing and mix well. Serve with baguette slices or crackers.

YIELD: 12 SERVINGS

TAPENADE (TA-PUH-NAHD)

This award-winning mushroom blend was developed for a Paul Newman recipe contest and placed in the top fifty. A traditional tapenade is a thick paste made from a base of green or black olives, to which anchovies, capers, olive oil, lemon juice, spices, and tuna are added. The puréed mixture is commonly spread on crostini, dabbed on salads, or tossed into pasta.

MINIATURE BLINI

2 cups small curd cottage cheese
1 tablespoon sour cream
1 teaspoon vanilla extract
1/2 teaspoon sugar
3 tablespoons butter, melted
3 eggs
1/2 cup baking mix

Process the cottage cheese, sour cream, vanilla, sugar and butter in a food processor until well mixed. Add the eggs 1 at a time, processing constantly after each addition. Add the baking mix and mix well. Pour into greased miniature muffin cups, filling each cup 3/4 full. Bake at 350 degrees for 20 to 25 minutes or until golden brown. Remove from the muffin cups to cool. Serve with a dollop of sour cream and top with gold or black caviar.

Note: Blini may be frozen after baking and thawed before adding the toppings and serving.

YIELD: 12 SERVINGS

CHEESE STICKS

1 loaf unsliced dry white bread
3 ounces cream cheese, softened
12 ounces sharp Cheddar cheese, shredded (3 cups)
1/2 cup (1 stick) butter or margarine
2 egg whites, stiffly beaten

Trim the crusts from the bread. Cut the bread into 1 1/2-inch-long sticks. Melt the cream cheese, Cheddar cheese and butter in a double boiler over hot water until of a rarebit consistency. Remove from the heat to cool. Fold in the stiffly beaten egg whites. Dip the bread sticks into the mixture, coating all sides. Arrange on a baking sheet and freeze. Store the frozen cheese sticks in sealable plastic freezer bags until ready to serve. To serve, arrange the frozen cheese sticks on a baking sheet. Bake at 400 degrees for 10 to 15 minutes or until golden brown.

YIELD: 8 TO 10 SERVINGS

GRUYÈRE CHEESE PUFFS

1 cup water
1/2 cup (1 stick) butter or margarine
Dash of salt
1 cup all-purpose flour
4 eggs
1/2 cup finely chopped prosciutto
1/2 cup (2 ounces) shredded Gruyère cheese

Combine the water, butter and salt in a small saucepan. Bring to a boil and remove from the heat. Add the flour and whisk vigorously. Return the pan to medium heat. Cook until the batter thickens and pulls away from the side of the pan, stirring constantly. Remove from the heat. Add the eggs 1 at a time, beating well after each addition until the batter is smooth and shiny. Stir in the prosciutto and cheese. Drop by teaspoonfuls 1 inch apart onto a large greased baking sheet. Bake at 400 degrees for 20 to 25 minutes or until golden brown.

Note: You may freeze the puffs. Reheat at 350 degrees for 15 to 20 minutes to serve.

YIELD: 9 DOZEN

GRUYÈRE (GROO-YEHR) CHEESE

A moderate-fat cow's milk cheese, Gruyère is named for the valley in Switzerland. Also produced in France and other countries, this firm, pale yellow cheese is usually aged for ten to twelve months and then formed into 100-pound wheels. Gruyère has a rich, sweet, nutty flavor and is delicious eaten fresh or used in cooking.

CHEESE-STUFFED MUSHROOMS

36 mushrooms, 1 inch in diameter
3 tablespoons melted butter
Salt and pepper to taste
3 tablespoons minced onion
2 tablespoons butter
1 tablespoon vegetable oil
3 tablespoons minced scallions
$1/3$ cup madeira
3 tablespoons fine white dry bread crumbs

$1/4$ cup shredded Swiss cheese
$1/4$ cup grated Parmesan cheese
$1/4$ cup chopped fresh parsley or cilantro
$1/2$ teaspoon tarragon
2 to 3 tablespoons cream
3 tablespoons shredded Swiss cheese

Rinse the mushrooms and pat dry. Remove the stems from the mushroom caps. Chop the mushroom stems finely. Dip the mushroom caps in 3 tablespoons melted butter and arrange cup side up in a shallow baking dish. Season with salt and pepper.

Sauté the onion in 2 tablespoons butter and the oil in a skillet for 3 to 4 minutes; do not brown. Add the scallions and mushroom stems. Sauté until light brown. Add the wine. Boil until almost all of the liquid has evaporated.

Mix the bread crumbs, $1/4$ cup Swiss cheese, Parmesan cheese, parsley, tarragon and salt and pepper to taste in a bowl. Add the mushroom mixture and mix well. Add the cream a spoonful at a time, stirring until the mixture is moistened but stiff enough to hold its shape on a spoon. Adjust the seasonings if necessary. Fill each mushroom cap with the stuffing and place on a baking sheet. Top each with a pinch of the remaining Swiss cheese. Chill, covered, until ready to bake. Place on an oven rack in the upper third of the oven. Bake at 375 degrees for 15 to 20 minutes or until the mushroom caps are tender and the tops are light brown.

YIELD: 36 SERVINGS

MONTECITO MARINATED MUSHROOMS

1 pound small or medium fresh mushrooms
$3/4$ cup vegetable oil
$1/3$ cup red wine vinegar
2 tablespoons lemon juice
1 tablespoon chopped fresh chives
1 teaspoon chopped fresh tarragon
1 garlic clove, crushed
1 teaspoon salt
$1/2$ teaspoon sugar
$1/8$ teaspoon pepper

Place the mushrooms in a sealable plastic bag. Combine the oil, vinegar, lemon juice, chives, tarragon, garlic, salt, sugar and pepper in a bowl and mix well. Pour over the mushrooms and seal the bag. Marinate in the refrigerator for 8 to 12 hours, turning the bag once or twice.

YIELD: 8 SERVINGS

FRESH FIGS WITH PROSCIUTTO

Rinsed fresh figs
Balsamic vinegar
Olive oil
Freshly ground pepper
$1/2$ slice prosciutto per fig

Cut the figs into halves and sprinkle with balsamic vinegar, olive oil and pepper. Wrap each fig half with prosciutto and secure with wooden picks. Place each wrapped fig on a fig leaf and arrange on a serving tray. Garnish with whole figs.

YIELD: VARIABLE

MONTECITO

Approaching Montecito you'll immediately be captivated by this charming community of approximately ten thousand residents. Located just east of Santa Barbara, Montecito is the reputed home of the rich and famous, and has attracted vacationers such as John and Jacqueline Kennedy, Jean Harlow, and Katharine Hepburn to its elegant resorts. Gated mansions dot the foothills overlooking beautiful Butterfly Beach, named for the Monarch butterflies attracted to the area.

OLIVE STICKS

Photograph for this recipe is shown on page 12 and below.

KALAMATA OLIVES
(KAL-UH-MAH-TUH)

An almond-shaped
Greek delight, kalamata
olives have a dark,
eggplant-purple color
and an extraordinary
rich, salty taste. The
flesh is often cut
during the soaking
process so that the red
wine vinegar marinade
can more effectively
penetrate the olive.
They are firm and fruity
and an ideal choice for
Mediterranean dishes
from salads to entrées.

8 ounces feta cheese, drained, crumbled
$1/3$ cup minced fresh parsley
$2/3$ cup olive paste
2 egg whites
1 (17-ounce) package frozen puff pastry sheets, thawed

Mix the cheese, parsley, olive paste and egg whites with a fork in a small bowl until thoroughly blended. Unfold 1 pastry sheet on a lightly floured surface, keeping the remaining pastry sheet in the refrigerator. Roll the pastry sheet into a 14×16-inch rectangle.

Cut the rectangle crosswise into halves. Spread $1/2$ of the olive paste mixture evenly over 1 pastry half; top with the remaining pastry half. Roll over the top with a rolling pin to seal the layers together. Cut the rectangle crosswise into strips $1/2$ inch wide, taking care not to tear the pastry. Twist each strip 3 or 4 times and arrange 1 inch apart on a large greased baking sheet. Repeat the procedure with the remaining pastry sheet and olive paste mixture. Bake at 400 degrees for 12 to 15 minutes or until the pastry is puffed and light brown. Remove to a wire rack to cool. Store at room temperature in a tightly covered container.

Note: You may make your own olive paste by puréeing 1 cup pitted kalamata olives with 2 tablespoons olive oil in a blender or food processor.

YIELD: 6 TO 8 SERVINGS

Sweet Chinese Pork (Char Siu)

Photograph for this recipe is shown on page 12.

3 tablespoons brown sugar
1¹/₂ to 2 pounds boneless pork
    tenderloin
¹/₃ cup water
¹/₄ cup honey
3 tablespoons hoisin sauce
1 tablespoon white wine

1 tablespoon red food coloring
1 teaspoon soy sauce
¹/₂ teaspoon salt
¹/₈ teaspoon five-spice powder
Mustard Dipping Sauce (below)
Toasted sesame seeds

Rub the brown sugar into the pork. Let stand for 5 minutes. Place in a 9×13-inch glass baking dish. Combine the water, honey, hoisin sauce, wine, red food coloring, soy sauce, salt and five-spice powder in a bowl and blend well. Pour over the pork. Marinate, covered, in the refrigerator for 8 to 12 hours.

Drain the pork, reserving the marinade. Arrange the pork on a rack and place over a roasting pan of hot water. Roast at 350 degrees for 30 minutes. Turn the pork and baste with the reserved marinade. Discard any remaining marinade. Roast for 30 minutes longer. Cut into slices ¹/₈ inch thick. To serve, dip the pork in the Mustard Dipping Sauce and then in the sesame seeds.

YIELD: 10 TO 12 SERVINGS

Our first choice is a light-bodied white wine such as a riesling or a gewürztraminer.

Mustard Dipping Sauce

Dry mustard
Beer

2 or 3 drops of soy sauce

Mix enough dry mustard and beer in a bowl until the mixture is of a sauce consistency. Pour the sauce into a shallow bowl. Add the soy sauce in the center of the sauce.

WINE COUNTRY HAM BALLS

2 pounds cooked country ham, ground	1¹/₂ to 2 cups milk
1 pound bulk pork sausage	2 cups packed brown sugar
2 cups dry bread crumbs	1 cup water
2 eggs	1 cup white vinegar
	1 tablespoon prepared mustard

Combine the ground ham, sausage, bread crumbs and eggs in a bowl and mix well. Stir in enough of the milk to moisten the mixture. Shape into 1-inch balls. You may freeze at this point.

Arrange the ham balls in a baking dish. Bring the brown sugar, water, vinegar and mustard to a boil in a saucepan, stirring to mix well. Pour over the ham balls. Bake at 350 degrees for 45 minutes, basting frequently with the sauce.

YIELD: 8 TO 10 SERVINGS

ASIAN MEATBALLS

2¹/₂ pounds ground pork	¹/₂ cup cornstarch
1 (8-ounce) can water chestnuts, drained, finely chopped	1 cup cold water
1¹/₄ cups bread crumbs	1 cup vinegar
6 scallions, chopped	³/₄ cup sugar
3 eggs	2 tablespoons soy sauce
2 tablespoons soy sauce	2 cups pineapple juice
1¹/₂ teaspoons salt	2 cups beef consommé
Cornstarch for coating	3 tablespoons chopped fresh
Vegetable oil for browning	gingerroot

Combine the ground pork, water chestnuts, bread crumbs, scallions, eggs, 2 tablespoons soy sauce and the salt in a bowl and mix well. Shape into balls. Roll in cornstarch to coat. Cook the meatballs in oil in a skillet until brown and cooked through; drain.

Dissolve ¹/₂ cup cornstarch in the cold water in a large saucepan. Add the vinegar, sugar, 2 tablespoons soy sauce, pineapple juice, beef consommé and gingerroot. Cook over low heat until thickened, stirring constantly. Add the meatballs. Cook until warm and bubbly. Serve hot.

YIELD: 8 TO 10 SERVINGS

CHICKEN IN PEANUT SAUCE

4 boneless skinless chicken breasts
1 tablespoon cornstarch
1 tablespoon soy sauce
2 garlic cloves, minced
2 tablespoons white wine
1/2 teaspoon hot pepper paste
1 teaspoon grated fresh gingerroot
2 tablespoons lemon juice
3 tablespoons dark soy sauce
2 tablespoons honey
3 to 6 tablespoons peanut butter
1/2 cup water

Cut the chicken into 1-inch pieces. Combine the cornstarch, 1 tablespoon soy sauce, garlic and wine in a bowl and mix well. Add the chicken. Marinate, covered, in the refrigerator for 30 minutes. Brown in a skillet until cooked through.

Combine the pepper paste, gingerroot, lemon juice, 3 tablespoons soy sauce, honey, peanut butter and water in a saucepan and mix well. Bring to a boil and reduce the heat. Add the chicken mixture. Simmer for 10 minutes. Serve warm using wooden picks or serve over white rice as a main course.

Note: The peanut sauce will yield enough for 1 pound of chicken breasts.

YIELD: 12 APPETIZER SERVINGS

 With this hot and spicy dish serve a riesling, chardonnay, or zinfandel.

PEANUT BUTTER

Peanut butter was first introduced as a health food at the 1904 St. Louis World's Fair. Homemade peanut butter is not only more healthful than commercial, since it doesn't contain additives, but it is also considered tastier. To make your own, chop peanuts in a food processor and add just enough vegetable oil until you get the right consistency. Be sure to refrigerate homemade peanut butter or it may become rancid.

CHICKEN DRUMETTES

2 cups (4 sticks) butter	$^1/_2$ (10-ounce) bottle
Juice of 1 lemon	Worcestershire sauce
1 (14-ounce) bottle ketchup	1 cup sugar
1 (6-ounce) bottle prepared	1 cup vinegar
mustard	4 to 5 pounds chicken drumettes

Combine the butter, lemon juice, ketchup, mustard, Worcestershire sauce, sugar and vinegar in a saucepan. Bring to a boil and reduce the heat. Simmer for 10 minutes. Arrange the chicken in a shallow baking dish. Pour the sauce over the chicken. Bake at 350 degrees for 30 to 45 minutes or until the chicken is cooked through, basting frequently.

YIELD: 8 TO 10 SERVINGS

CEVICHE

1 pound (about) fresh halibut fillets	1 large sweet onion, finely chopped
1 teaspoon cracked black	2 jalapeño chiles, seeded, finely
peppercorns	chopped
1 teaspoon coarse salt	$^1/_4$ cup olive oil
$^1/_4$ teaspoon oregano	Chopped fresh parsley or cilantro
Juice of 6 limes	to taste
4 tomatoes, seeded, minced	

Cut the uncooked fish into thin strips and place in a dish. Crush the peppercorns, salt and oregano in a mortar with a pestle. Add the lime juice and mix well. Pour over the fish. Marinate, covered, in the refrigerator for 2 to 4 hours, turning occasionally. Add the tomatoes, onion, jalapeño chiles, olive oil and parsley. Adjust the seasonings to taste. Marinate, covered, in the refrigerator for 24 hours, mixing gently 2 or 3 times. Serve in a bowl or individually on lettuce leaves. Garnish with avocado and lime slices.

YIELD: 4 SERVINGS

Uncooked fresh fish that has marinated in lime juice and herbs for several hours tenderizes the flesh of the fish and turns it from translucent to white.

CLAM PUFFS

24 ounces cream cheese, softened
1¹/₂ teaspoons Tabasco sauce
1¹/₂ teaspoons Worcestershire sauce
1¹/₂ teaspoons dry mustard
5 to 6 (7-ounce) cans clams, drained
¹/₂ cup chopped scallions
¹/₂ cup chopped fresh parsley
1 tablespoon chopped garlic
3 (17-ounce) packages frozen puff pastry

Beat the cream cheese in a mixing bowl until light and fluffy. Add the Tabasco sauce, Worcestershire sauce and dry mustard and mix well. Stir in the clams, scallions, parsley and garlic.

Thaw the puff pastry slightly. Do not thaw too much or the dough will become sticky; thaw too little and the pastry will not roll out properly. Roll 1 puff pastry sheet at a time into a 12×15-inch rectangle. Cut each rectangle into 3-inch squares. Place 1 teaspoon of the clam mixture onto each square and fold up the edges to form a small puff. Arrange on a baking sheet and freeze immediately. Place frozen puffs into sealable plastic freezer bags and return to the freezer until ready to use.

To bake, arrange the frozen puffs on a baking sheet. Bake at 425 degrees for 11 to 12 minutes or until puffed and golden brown.

YIELD: 120 PUFFS

Once you've tried these you'll be hooked. They'll keep in the freezer for up to six months (if you can resist them that long) and can be ready in twelve minutes for those unexpected guests.

BAKED CRAB CAKES

1/2 cup minced red bell pepper
1 teaspoon vegetable oil
1/2 cup mayonnaise
1 egg
11/2 tablespoons Dijon mustard
1 to 2 teaspoons fresh lemon juice
1 teaspoon tarragon
1 pound lump jumbo crab meat, flaked
Salt and pepper to taste
11/2 cups panko (Japanese flaked bread crumbs)
1/4 cup (1/2 stick) unsalted butter, melted

Sauté the bell pepper in the oil in a small nonstick skillet over medium-high heat for 2 minutes or until tender and golden brown. Whisk the mayonnaise, egg, Dijon mustard, lemon juice, tarragon and sautéed bell pepper in a bowl. Stir in the crab meat. Season with salt and pepper. Chill, covered, for 1 hour or up to 24 hours.

Spread the panko in an even layer in a large shallow baking pan. Bake at 350 degrees for 10 minutes or until toasted and golden brown, stirring occasionally. Remove from the oven to cool.

Shape rounded teaspoonfuls of the crab meat mixture into slightly flattened 1-inch rounds. Coat gently with the toasted panko. Arrange in a shallow baking pan. Chill, loosely covered with waxed paper, for at least 2 hours. Drizzle a scant 1/4 teaspoon butter over each crab cake. Bake at 450 degrees on the middle oven rack for 10 to 12 minutes or until crisp and cooked through.

YIELD: 42 MINIATURE CRAB CAKES

 Excellent served with a chardonnay or a fruity sauvignon blanc.

BACON AND AVOCADO QUESADILLAS

2 avocados
1¹/₂ cups (6 ounces) shredded Monterey Jack cheese
¹/₂ cup chopped scallions
8 slices bacon, crisp-cooked, crumbled
Salt and pepper to taste
4 to 6 (8-inch) flour tortillas
Butter or margarine

Mash the avocados in a bowl. Stir in the cheese, scallions and bacon. Season with salt and pepper. Spread the avocado mixture over half of each tortilla and fold over. Spread butter on the outside of the tortillas. Fry in a hot nonstick skillet until golden brown and the cheese is melted. Cut the quesadillas into wedge-shaped pieces and serve immediately.

YIELD: 4 TO 6 SERVINGS

QUESADILLA
(KEH-SAH-DEE-YAH)

Take a flour tortilla, top with your choice of fillings, fry or broil, fold in half, and you have a quesadilla. The fillings can be as varied as your imagination— cheese, beef, pork, chicken, and refried beans are popular choices. Quesadillas are usually cut into strips or quartered and can be served as an appetizer, side dish, or main dish.

SMOKED SALMON QUESADILLAS

SMOKED SALMON

There are two methods for smoking salmon— hot and cold. Hot-smoked fish is processed for six to twelve hours in temperatures ranging from 120 to 180 degrees. Cold-smoked fish is placed in a smokehouse anywhere from one day to three weeks at a temperature of seventy to ninety degrees. Lox is brine-cured cold-smoked salmon and has a slightly saltier taste and a less flaky texture than other smoked salmon.

4 ounces cream cheese, softened
4 ounces feta cheese
3 garlic cloves, crushed
3 tablespoons chopped green chiles
1 tablespoon olive oil
6 (8-inch) flour tortillas
8 ounces smoked salmon or small cooked shrimp
1 small red onion, thinly sliced
$^1/_2$ cup coarsely chopped fresh cilantro
3 tablespoons olive oil

Combine the cream cheese, feta cheese, garlic, green chiles and 1 tablespoon olive oil in a bowl and mix well. Divide the cheese mixture into 6 portions. Spread each portion on $^1/_2$ of each tortilla. Arrange the salmon, onion and cilantro over the cheese mixture. Fold the uncoated half of the tortillas over the filling. Heat 1 tablespoon olive oil in a skillet over medium-high heat. Add 2 of the filled tortillas. Cook for 3 minutes being careful not to burn. Turn and cook for 2 minutes longer, reducing the heat if necessary. Repeat with the remaining tortillas and olive oil. Serve warm.

YIELD: 12 SERVINGS

 A chardonnay or white zinfandel would pair nicely with these quesadillas.

CROSTINI WITH BAY SHRIMP AND FETA CHEESE

1 pound fresh bay shrimp, cooked, peeled
8 ounces feta cheese
1 cup chopped scallions
2 garlic cloves, chopped
1/4 cup finely chopped fresh basil
Juice of 1 lemon
1/2 cup olive oil
1/2 teaspoon kosher salt, or to taste
1 French baguette
Olive oil

Combine the shrimp, cheese, scallions, garlic, basil, lemon juice, 1/2 cup olive oil and kosher salt in a medium bowl and toss to mix well. Marinate, covered, in the refrigerator for 2 to 3 hours or longer to enhance the flavors.

Cut the baguette into thin slices and brush with olive oil. Arrange on a baking sheet lined with parchment paper. Bake at 325 degrees for 5 minutes or until the bread is dry and slightly crisp, but not brown.

To serve, spoon the shrimp mixture on top of each crostini.

YIELD: 4 TO 8 SERVINGS

This is a versatile mixture that can be served cold as a salad, over hot pasta as a topping, or on toasted French bread crostini as an appetizer.

EL PRESIDIO

The historic Santa Barbara Royal Presidio sits in the middle of the busy downtown area. The whitewashed adobe buildings with red tile roofs were built in 1782 by the Spanish as a military fortress and governmental center. Surrounded by a wall supporting two cannon bastions, the buildings of the Presidio formed a quadrangle encircling a parade ground. El Cuartel, the guard's house, is the oldest building in Santa Barbara and the second oldest in California.

PRAWNS WITH FETA, LIME AND MINT VINAIGRETTE

Photograph for this recipe is shown on page 12 and below.

1/2 cup extra-virgin olive oil
3 tablespoons chopped fresh mint
1/2 teaspoon salt
1/2 teaspoon freshly ground pepper

1 pound fresh medium prawns,
  peeled, deveined
Lime and Mint Vinaigrette (below)

Combine the olive oil, mint, salt and pepper in a bowl and mix well. Add the prawns. Marinate, covered, in the refrigerator for 30 minutes. Drain the prawns. Place in a fish basket or thread onto skewers. Grill or broil for 1 to 2 minutes or until the shrimp turn pink, turning once. Cool slightly. Chill in a bowl for 30 minutes. Add the Lime and Mint Vinaigrette and toss to coat. Let stand for 15 minutes. Arrange the prawns on serving plates. Garnish with lime halves and mint sprigs.

YIELD: 8 SERVINGS

LIME AND MINT VINAIGRETTE

1/2 cup extra-virgin olive oil
Juice of 2 or 3 limes
2 tablespoons crumbled feta
  cheese

3 tablespoons chopped fresh mint
1 1/2 teaspoons salt
1 1/2 teaspoons freshly ground
  pepper

Combine the olive oil, lime juice, cheese, mint, salt and pepper in a bowl and mix well.

PICKLED SHRIMP

2 pounds fresh unpeeled shrimp
3 or 4 bay leaves
6 small white onions, thinly sliced
1/2 teaspoon salt
1/2 teaspoon dry mustard
1/2 teaspoon confectioners' sugar

1 cup vegetable oil
1/2 cup tarragon vinegar
1/4 cup pickling spices
Juice of 1/2 lemon
Salt to taste

Boil the shrimp in water to cover in a saucepan until the shrimp turn pink; drain. Peel and devein the shrimp. Alternate layers of the shrimp, bay leaves and onions in a deep dish until all of the ingredients are used. Mix 1/2 teaspoon salt, the dry mustard and confectioners' sugar together in a bowl. Add to a mixture of the oil and vinegar in a bowl and blend well. Pour over the shrimp. Add the pickling spices and lemon juice. Marinate, covered, in the refrigerator for at least 24 hours, stirring occasionally. Season with salt to taste. To serve, drain the shrimp mixture and arrange on a serving platter, discarding the bay leaves.

Note: If more marinade is needed to cover the shrimp, keep the proportions 2 parts oil to 1 part vinegar.

YIELD: 8 SERVINGS

PEPPY ALMONDS

1/4 cup (1/2 stick) butter, melted
2 teaspoons salt
2 teaspoons celery salt

2 teaspoons chili powder
1/3 teaspoon cayenne pepper
3 cups shelled whole almonds

Combine the butter, salt, celery salt, chili powder and cayenne pepper in an 8×10-inch baking pan and mix well. Stir in the almonds. Bake at 375 degrees for 15 minutes, stirring occasionally. Drain on paper towels. Store in an airtight container. Serve hot or cold.

YIELD: 3 CUPS

ALMONDS

Versatile and delicious, almonds are tiny nutritional powerhouses containing protein, calcium, fiber, vitamins, and minerals. California is the only state where almonds are grown commercially; six thousand growers cultivate almonds on more than 480 thousand acres of fertile land. To blanch almonds, place them in boiling water in a saucepan and immediately remove the pan from the heat. Drain the water, pinch off the skins, and dry the almonds on a baking sheet in a 200-degree oven for ten minutes.

SAVOR THE DAWN

breakfast, brunch and breads

GRAPE CLUSTER BREAD

SUNRISE CINNAMON ROLLS

DELICIOUS FRUIT MUFFINS

FIESTA BREAD

CINNAMON FRENCH TOAST

BRANDIED ORANGE BUTTER

SWISS OMELET ROLL

QUICHE CUPS OLÉ

(shown left to right)

Douglas and Francesca Deaver

Nicholas and Sue Vincent

Photograph © Michael Brown

Pacific Sunrise *Photograph © David Muench*

Chiles Rellenos

1 cup half-and-half	**1 (4-ounce) can whole green**
2 eggs	**chiles, drained**
1/3 cup all-purpose flour	**8 ounces Monterey Jack cheese,**
1/2 teaspoon cumin	**shredded (2 cups)**
1 teaspoon salt	**8 ounces Cheddar cheese,**
1/4 teaspoon pepper	**shredded (2 cups)**

Whisk the half-and-half, eggs, flour, cumin, salt and pepper in a large bowl until blended. Alternate layers of the egg mixture, chiles, Monterey Jack cheese and Cheddar cheese in a greased 8×8-inch baking pan until all ingredients are used. Bake at 350 degrees for 1 hour.

YIELD: 4 TO 6 SERVINGS

Chilaquiles (chil-a-kye-les)

2 tomatoes, peeled	**4 to 6 tablespoons vegetable oil**
2 to 4 green or yellow chiles	**for frying**
6 tomatillos	**6 eggs**
2 garlic cloves	**3/4 cup shredded mozzarella,**
Salt and pepper to taste	**Monterey Jack or Cheddar**
8 corn tortillas, cut into wedges	**cheese**

Combine the tomatoes, green chiles and tomatillos in a large saucepan. Add enough water to cover. Bring to a boil. Boil until tender; drain. Process with the garlic, salt and pepper in a blender or food processor until blended.

Fry the tortillas in the oil in a skillet until crisp. Add the eggs. Scramble the eggs with the tortillas until the eggs are set. Add the salsa. Sprinkle with the cheese and serve.

YIELD: 4 SERVINGS

In many Spanish homes, this snappy dish is often served for breakfast with refried beans.

Cumin (KUH-mihn)

Cumin, the dried seed of a plant in the parsley family, was used as a food preservative by the early Greeks and Romans. It has an earthy, nutty flavor and is popular in Middle Eastern, Asian, Mexican, and Mediterranean cooking. Cumin is the principal ingredient in both chili powder and curry powder.

HUEVOS PICANTE (SPICY EGGS)

PIMENTO (PIH-MEN-TOH)

Pimento, the Spanish word for "pepper," is a scarlet, heart-shaped, sweet pepper that measures about four inches in length. A large portion of the pimento crop is used to make paprika, a staple of Hungarian cooking. Fresh peppers are available from late summer to early fall, but canned and jarred pimentos can be found year-round, whole, chopped, or sliced.

1 pound bulk pork sausage,
   crumbled
4 ounces sliced mushrooms
1 medium onion, chopped
Salt and freshly ground pepper
   to taste
6 eggs

3 tablespoons sour cream
3 tablespoons Mexican hot sauce
16 ounces (4 cups) shredded
   Cheddar cheese
8 ounces (2 cups) shredded
   mozzarella cheese

Brown the sausage with the mushrooms and onion in a large skillet over medium-high heat, stirring until the sausage is crumbly; drain. Season with salt and pepper.

Blend the eggs and sour cream in a blender for 1 minute. Pour into a greased 9×13-inch baking dish. Bake at 400 degrees for 4 to 7 minutes or until the eggs are softly set. Drizzle with the hot sauce. Top with the sausage mixture, Cheddar cheese and mozzarella cheese. Broil until the cheese melts.

YIELD: 8 SERVINGS

QUICHE CUPS OLÉ

Photograph for this recipe is shown on page 44.

6 eggs, well beaten
1/2 cup light cream
1/3 cup minced onion
1 (4-ounce) can chopped green
   chiles, drained
1 (2-ounce) jar chopped pimento,
   drained
1/4 teaspoon seasoned salt

1/8 teaspoon garlic powder
1/4 teaspoon cumin
Dash of seasoned pepper
2 1/2 cups (10 ounces) shredded
   Monterey Jack cheese
4 (8-inch) flour tortillas
Vegetable oil for brushing

Blend the eggs and cream in a large bowl. Add the onion, green chiles, pimento, seasoned salt, garlic powder, cumin and seasoned pepper and mix well. Stir in the cheese. Brush the tortillas lightly with oil. Arrange in 4 soufflé or custard cups. Pour about ¾ cup of the egg mixture into each cup. Bake, uncovered, at 325 degrees for 20 to 30 minutes or until set.

YIELD: 4 SERVINGS

QUICK CRAB QUICHE

1/2 cup mayonnaise	8 ounces Swiss cheese, sliced,
2 tablespoons all-purpose flour	chopped (2 cups)
2 eggs, beaten	1/3 cup sliced scallions
1/2 cup milk	1/4 teaspoon thyme (optional)
1 (7-ounce) can crab meat,	1 unbaked (9-inch) pie shell
drained, flaked	

Mix the mayonnaise, flour, eggs and milk in a bowl. Stir in the crab meat, cheese, scallions and thyme. Pour into the pie shell. Bake at 350 degrees for 40 to 45 minutes or until set.

YIELD: 6 SERVINGS

WINE AND CHEESE OMELETS FOR A CROWD

1 large loaf dry French or Italian	16 eggs
bread, torn into small pieces	3 1/4 cups milk
6 tablespoons unsalted butter,	1/2 cup dry white wine
melted	4 large scallions, minced
12 ounces Swiss cheese, shredded	1 tablespoon Dijon mustard
(3 cups)	1/2 teaspoon black pepper
8 ounces Monterey Jack cheese,	1/8 teaspoon red pepper
shredded (2 cups)	1 1/2 cups sour cream
1 pound bulk pork sausage,	1/3 to 1 cup grated Parmesan
cooked, crumbled	cheese

Butter two 9×13-inch shallow ceramic or glass baking dishes. Arrange the bread over the bottom of the dishes and drizzle with the melted butter. Sprinkle the cheeses and sausage in each dish. Beat the eggs, milk, wine, scallions, Dijon mustard, black pepper and red pepper in a bowl until foamy. Pour over the sausage. Cover the dishes with foil, crimping the edges to seal. Chill for 12 to 24 hours. Remove from the refrigerator 30 minutes before baking. Bake, covered, at 325 degrees for 1 hour. Uncover and spread with the sour cream. Sprinkle with the Parmesan cheese. Bake, uncovered, for 10 minutes or until the tops are crusty and light brown.

Note: This recipe may be prepared ahead and frozen. Remove from the freezer 2 to 3 hours before baking.

YIELD: 16 TO 24 SERVINGS

CRAB

Crab, second only to shrimp in popularity among shellfish in the United States, can be found in either fresh or saltwater. Live crabs should be cooked the day they are purchased, and kept covered with a damp cloth in the refrigerator until cooking time. Leftover crab meat will last for two days if stored in a tightly covered container and refrigerated.

Swiss Omelet Roll

Photograph for this recipe is shown on page 44.

1 cup mayonnaise	$1/2$ teaspoon salt
2 tablespoons prepared mustard	$1/8$ teaspoon pepper
2 tablespoons chopped scallions	$1 1/2$ cups finely chopped ham
$1/2$ cup (about) mayonnaise	1 cup (4 ounces) shredded Swiss
2 tablespoons all-purpose flour	cheese
12 eggs, separated	$1/4$ cup chopped scallions
1 cup milk	

Mix 1 cup mayonnaise, the prepared mustard and 2 tablespoons scallions in a bowl. Let the sauce stand at room temperature until ready to serve.

Line a 10×15-inch baking pan with waxed paper. Brush with mayonnaise. Combine ½ cup mayonnaise and the flour in a saucepan. Beat the egg yolks in a small bowl. Add the milk and egg yolks to the saucepan gradually, stirring constantly. Cook over low heat until thickened, stirring constantly. Remove from the heat and cool for 15 minutes. Beat the egg whites in a mixing bowl until stiff peaks form. Fold in the egg yolk mixture, salt and pepper. Pour into the prepared pan. Bake at 425 degrees for 20 minutes. Invert onto a clean towel. Remove the waxed paper. Cover with a mixture of the ham, Swiss cheese and ¼ cup scallions. Roll up from the narrow end, lifting with the towel while rolling. Arrange seam side down on a serving platter. Top with the mayonnaise sauce. Garnish with watercress.

YIELD: 6 TO 8 SERVINGS

Dutch Babies

4 medium apples, peeled, sliced	1 cup all-purpose flour
6 tablespoons butter	Dash of salt
6 eggs, beaten	4 to 6 tablespoons butter
1 cup milk	Confectioners' sugar

Sauté the apples in 6 tablespoons butter in a skillet until tender. Beat the eggs, milk, flour and salt in a bowl. Melt 4 to 6 tablespoons butter in a cast-iron skillet. Add the egg mixture. Bake at 400 degrees for 20 minutes. Remove from the oven and sprinkle with confectioners' sugar. Spoon the sautéed apples into the middle.

Note: You may also serve with syrup and lemon wedges instead of the sautéed apples.

YIELD: 6 SERVINGS

CINNAMON FRENCH TOAST

Photograph for this recipe is shown on page 44 and below.

2 eggs
1/4 cup milk
1/4 cup all-purpose flour
1/4 teaspoon baking powder
1/2 teaspoon cinnamon

1/4 teaspoon vanilla extract
Vegetable oil
1 loaf thick-sliced cinnamon swirl
   bread or specialty bread
Confectioners' sugar

Beat the eggs in a mixing bowl until smooth. Add the milk, flour, baking powder, cinnamon and vanilla and blend well. The batter should be the consistency of heavy cream. Brush a skillet with oil. Dip the bread slices into the batter, coating both sides. Fry in the prepared skillet until brown on each side. Sprinkle with confectioners' sugar. Serve with fresh fruit and whipped cream.

YIELD: 8 SERVINGS

Serve with Brandied Orange Butter (below) for a special treat.

BRANDIED ORANGE BUTTER

Photograph for this recipe is shown on page 44.

1/2 cup (1 stick) butter, softened
1 cup sifted confectioners' sugar
2 tablespoons brandy

1 teaspoon finely grated orange
   zest

Whip the butter, confectioners' sugar, brandy and orange zest in a bowl until light and fluffy. Chill, covered, until firm.

YIELD: 1 CUP

BRANDY

Brandy is a by-product of wine that has been fermented, stored in barrels, and later distilled. The most prized brandies, Cognac and Armagnac, are products of France. Cognac, considered the finest, comes from the Grande Champagne region, and is distilled twice before it is aged in Limousin oak barrels. Armagnac is the pride of the Gascony region and dates back to the twelfth century.

STUFFED FRENCH TOAST

8 ounces cream cheese, softened	**1/2 teaspoon vanilla extract**
1 teaspoon vanilla extract	**1/2 teaspoon nutmeg**
1/2 cup chopped walnuts	**1 loaf dry French bread**
4 eggs	**11/2 cups apricot preserves**
1 cup milk	**1/2 cup orange juice**

Mix the cream cheese, 1 teaspoon vanilla and the walnuts in a bowl. Beat the eggs, milk, 1/2 teaspoon vanilla and nutmeg in a bowl until blended. Cut the bread into 3/4-inch slices.

Spread 1/2 of the bread slices with the cream cheese mixture. Top with the remaining bread. Dip in the egg mixture and arrange on a baking sheet. Bake at 375 degrees for 10 to 12 minutes or until golden brown.

Mix the apricot preserves and orange juice in a bowl. Drizzle over the French toast to serve.

Note: The French toast may be made a day ahead and chilled in the refrigerator.

YIELD: 8 SERVINGS

BERRY GOOD BUCKLE

22/3 cups all-purpose flour	**1 (16-ounce) package frozen**
1 cup sugar	**blackberries, blueberries or**
31/4 teaspoons baking powder	**boysenberries**
1 teaspoon salt	**2/3 cup sugar**
1/3 cup butter, softened	**1/2 cup all-purpose flour**
1 cup milk	**1 teaspoon cinnamon**
2 eggs	**1/3 cup butter**

Combine 22/3 cups flour, 1 cup sugar, baking powder, salt, 1/3 cup butter, milk and eggs in a bowl and mix well. Stir in the blackberries. Pour into a greased 9×13-inch baking dish. Mix 2/3 cup sugar, 1/2 cup flour and the cinnamon in a bowl. Cut in 1/3 cup butter until crumbly. Sprinkle over the blackberry mixture. Bake at 375 degrees for 50 to 55 minutes or until the top is golden brown.

YIELD: 16 SERVINGS

APPLE CINNAMON COFFEE CAKE

5 tablespoons sugar
2 teaspoons cinnamon
3 cups all-purpose flour
1 tablespoon baking powder
2 cups sugar
1/2 teaspoon salt

1 cup vegetable oil
1/4 cup orange juice
4 eggs
1 1/2 teaspoons vanilla extract
4 large apples, peeled, sliced

Mix 5 tablespoons sugar and the cinnamon in a small bowl. Combine the flour, baking powder, 2 cups sugar and salt in a large bowl and mix well. Add the oil, orange juice, eggs and vanilla and beat until smooth. Layer the batter, apples and cinnamon mixture 1/2 at a time in a greased and floured bundt or tube pan. Bake at 350 degrees for 1 1/4 hours or until a wooden pick inserted in the center comes out clean.

YIELD: 16 SERVINGS

SOUR CREAM COFFEE CAKE

2 cups all-purpose flour
1 teaspoon baking powder
1 teaspoon baking soda
1/8 teaspoon salt
1/2 cup (1 stick) butter, softened
1 cup sugar
2 eggs

1 teaspoon vanilla extract
1 cup sour cream
1/2 cup chopped nuts
1 teaspoon cinnamon
1/4 cup packed brown sugar
1 apple, peeled, chopped

Sift the flour, baking powder, baking soda and salt together. Cream the butter and sugar in a mixing bowl until light and fluffy. Add the eggs and vanilla and mix well. Add the flour mixture and sour cream alternately, beating well after each addition. Mix the nuts, cinnamon, brown sugar and apple in a bowl. Layer the batter and apple mixture 1/2 at a time in a buttered and floured bundt pan. Bake at 350 degrees for 45 minutes.

YIELD: 8 TO 10 SERVINGS

Tied with a ribbon, this coffee cake makes an ideal teacher's gift.

EGGS—HOW MARKETED

Most eggs on the market are graded according to USDA specifications and sorted by size based on weight. Eggs are graded AA, A, and B, and sized jumbo, extra large, large, medium, and small. The USDA requires eggs to be washed and sanitized. Producers spray the eggs with a natural mineral oil to seal the shells' pores, which adds protection from bacteria and prevents moisture loss.

HOLIDAY COFFEE CAKE

MARASCHINO CHERRIES

Maraschino cherries used to be soaked in maraschino liqueur, hence the name. They are made from light-colored or white cherries that are pitted and preserved in sugar syrup, then dyed red or green and packed in syrup. Maraschinos are used in cocktails and as a garnish. What would an ice cream sundae be without a cherry on top?

³/₄ cup (1¹/₂ sticks) butter	¹/₂ cup sliced almonds
1 cup water	10 to 12 red maraschino cherries,
1 cup sifted all-purpose flour	cut into thirds or quarters
4 eggs	5 or 6 green maraschino cherries,
Almond Icing (below)	cut into thirds or quarters

Bring the butter and water to a boil in a saucepan. Boil until the butter melts. Remove from the heat. Beat in the flour gradually. Add the eggs 1 at a time, beating well after each addition. Shape some of the dough into a ring on an ungreased 12×18-inch baking pan. Spoon large spoonfuls of the remaining dough around the top of the circle to form a wreath. Bake at 400 degrees for 20 to 25 minutes or until golden brown. The dough will rise like cream puffs. Drizzle Almond Icing over the puffs and sprinkle with the almonds. Decorate with the maraschino and green candied cherries. The puffs will fall slightly when served.

YIELD: 8 SERVINGS

ALMOND ICING

1¹/₄ cups confectioners' sugar	1 tablespoon almond extract
2 tablespoons cream or milk	

Combine the confectioners' sugar, cream and almond extract in a bowl and mix until smooth.

DELICIOUS FRUIT MUFFINS

Photograph for this recipe is shown on page 44.

1^1/$_2$ cups all-purpose flour
2 teaspoons baking powder
1 teaspoon baking soda
^{1}/$_2$ (scant) teaspoon salt
1 teaspoon cinnamon
^{1}/$_3$ cup boiling water
1 cup chopped dried apricots, cranberries, cherries or currants
2 eggs
^{3}/$_4$ cup plus 1 or 2 tablespoons sugar
2 cups coarsely grated or finely chopped peeled apples
^{1}/$_2$ cup (1 stick) unsalted butter, melted
^{1}/$_2$ cup chopped pecans
2 teaspoons vanilla extract

Mix the flour, baking powder, baking soda, salt and cinnamon in a large bowl. Pour the boiling water over the dried fruit in a bowl. Let stand until the fruit is softened. Whisk the eggs, sugar and apples in a glass or stainless steel bowl. Let stand for at least 10 minutes. Add the melted butter, pecans and vanilla and mix well. Stir the apple mixture and dried fruit mixture into the flour mixture. Do not overmix. The mixture should not be moist enough to slide off a spoon, but if it appears too dry, add ^{1}/$_4$ cup juice compatible with the dried fruit being used. Spoon the batter into 12 greased or paper-lined muffin cups. Bake at 400 degrees for 14 to 16 minutes or until a wooden pick inserted in the center comes out clean. Cool in the pan for 2 to 3 minutes. Remove to a wire rack to cool completely.

Note: The crisp sweet varieties of apples work best in this recipe.

YIELD: 1 DOZEN

CURRANTS

If you've wondered why you can't get fresh currants at the market, it's because they are highly perishable. Dried currants, although easier to find, actually are not currants at all, but are a type of miniature grape that is distinctive for its tart-sweet taste. They are ideal for cakes, breads, and desserts, adding a rich, succulent flavor and texture.

NUTTY LEMON MUFFINS

1³/₄ cups all-purpose flour
1 cup chopped walnuts or pecans
¹/₃ cup sugar
2 teaspoons baking powder
2 teaspoons grated lemon zest
¹/₂ teaspoon salt

1 egg
¹/₂ cup milk
¹/₃ cup margarine, melted
¹/₄ cup sour cream
Streusel Topping (below)

Mix the flour, walnuts, sugar, baking powder, lemon zest and salt in a large bowl. Beat the egg with a fork in a small bowl. Beat in the milk, margarine and sour cream. Add to the flour mixture and stir until blended. Fill greased muffin cups ²/₃ full. Sprinkle with Streusel Topping. Bake at 400 degrees for 15 to 25 minutes or until a wooden pick inserted in the center comes out clean.

YIELD: 2 DOZEN

STREUSEL TOPPING

3 tablespoons all-purpose flour
3 tablespoons sugar
3 tablespoons chopped walnuts or pecans

2 tablespoons margarine, softened
2 teaspoons grated lemon zest

Combine the flour, sugar, walnuts, margarine and lemon zest in a bowl and mix well.

SUNRISE CINNAMON ROLLS

Photograph for this recipe is shown on page 44.

1 envelope dry yeast	1/2 cup (1 stick) butter, melted
1 teaspoon sugar	2 teaspoons cinnamon
1/2 cup warm water	1/4 cup sugar
3/4 cup (11/2 sticks) butter, softened	1/4 cup packed brown sugar
1/2 cup sugar	1 cup walnuts, chopped
2 eggs	1 cup raisins
1 cup milk, scalded, cooled	1/4 cup (1/2 stick) butter
1 cup mashed cooked potatoes	1 cup packed brown sugar
5 to 6 cups all-purpose flour	1 tablespoon water
1 teaspoon salt	1 teaspoon vanilla extract

Dissolve the yeast and 1 teaspoon sugar in ½ cup warm water in a bowl. Cream ¾ cup butter and ½ cup sugar in a mixing bowl until light and fluffy. Add the yeast mixture and mix well. Add the eggs, milk and potatoes and mix well. Beat in the flour and salt until smooth. Store, covered, in the refrigerator for 8 to 12 hours.

Divide the batter into 2 equal portions. Roll each portion into a 9×13-inch rectangle on a lightly floured surface. Brush each rectangle generously with ¼ cup melted butter. Sprinkle with the cinnamon, ¼ cup sugar and ¼ cup brown sugar. Sprinkle with the walnuts and raisins. Roll each as for a jelly roll. Cut each roll into 12 equal slices.

Bring ¼ cup butter, 1 cup brown sugar, 1 tablespoon water and the vanilla to a boil in a saucepan, stirring frequently. Boil for 1 minute; do not stir. Remove from the heat to cool. Pour into two 9×13-inch baking pans.

Arrange the rolls in the prepared pans. Let rise for 4 hours. Bake at 350 degrees for 30 minutes. Invert the rolls immediately and cool on a wire rack.

YIELD: 2 DOZEN

POTICA (PO-TEE-SA)

1/2 cup milk, scalded	1/4 cup warm water
1/4 cup (1/2 stick) butter, cut into 4 pieces	1 egg
1/4 cup sugar	3 cups unbleached all-purpose flour
1 teaspoon salt	2 tablespoons butter, melted
1 envelope dry yeast	Walnut Filling (below)

Combine the milk, 1/4 cup butter, sugar and salt in a mixing bowl and stir until dissolved. Cool until warm. Dissolve the yeast in the warm water in a bowl. Stir into the milk mixture. Add the egg and 1½ cups of the flour and beat until smooth. Add 1 to 1½ cups of the remaining flour gradually, stirring to form a soft dough. Scrape the dough from the side of the bowl. Let rise, covered, for 45 to 60 minutes or until doubled in bulk.

Punch the dough down with a wooden spoon. Do not knead, as this dough should be relaxed. Toss the dough on a lightly floured surface until no longer sticky. Divide the dough into 2 equal portions. Roll each portion into a 16- to 18-inch circle on a lightly floured surface, preventing the dough from sticking by continuing to lightly flour the surface while rolling the dough. If the dough should become too springy to roll, cover lightly with a towel and let the dough relax. Brush the circles of dough with 2 tablespoons butter. Spread with Walnut Filling. Roll up gently as for a jelly roll. Arrange each roll to form a coil or snail shape on a buttered baking sheet, placing about 2 inches apart. Let rise, covered, for 1 hour or until doubled in bulk. Bake at 350 degrees for 35 to 40 minutes or until brown. Cool on a wire rack.

YIELD: 2 LOAVES

WALNUT FILLING

2 cups walnuts, finely chopped	1/2 cup sugar
1/2 teaspoon cinnamon	1/3 cup honey
1/2 cup evaporated milk	1 teaspoon vanilla extract

Place the walnuts in a saucepan. Stir in the cinnamon, evaporated milk, sugar and honey in the order listed. Cook over medium heat until thickened, stirring constantly. Remove from the heat. Stir in the vanilla. Cool to room temperature.

APPLESAUCE DATE NUT BREAD

³/₄ cup chopped walnuts
1 cup chopped dates
1¹/₂ teaspoons baking soda
¹/₂ teaspoon salt
1 cup applesauce
3 tablespoons shortening
2 eggs
1 teaspoon vanilla extract
1 cup sugar
1¹/₂ cups all-purpose flour

Mix the walnuts, dates, baking soda and salt in a medium bowl. Microwave the applesauce in a microwave-safe bowl until heated through. Add the shortening and stir until melted. Add to the walnut mixture and mix well. Let stand, loosely covered, for 20 minutes.

Beat the eggs in a large mixing bowl using a fork. Add the vanilla, sugar and flour and mix well. The mixture will be quite dry. Add the walnut mixture ¼ at a time, mixing gently after each addition. Do not overbeat. Spoon into a greased 5×9-inch loaf pan. Bake at 350 degrees for 65 minutes or until a wooden pick inserted in the center comes out clean. Cool in the pan for 10 minutes. Invert onto a wire rack to cool completely. Wrap in foil and store for 8 to 12 hours before slicing.

YIELD: 1 LOAF

This recipe took first prize at the Santa Cruz County Fair seven years in a row until the author finally felt sorry for the other entrants and stopped submitting it.

MAPLE OAT BANANA BREAD

Rolled oats
2 cups all-purpose flour
1 cup (or more) rolled oats
2 teaspoons baking soda
1 cup shortening
2 cups sugar
2 cups mashed bananas (about 4 or 5 bananas)
4 eggs
1 cup chopped walnuts
Maple Glaze (below)

Grease a 2½-quart tube pan and sprinkle with rolled oats. Mix the flour, 1 cup oats and the baking soda together. Cream the shortening and sugar in a mixing bowl until light and fluffy. Add the bananas, eggs and walnuts and mix well. Add the flour mixture. Beat at low speed until mixed. Pour into the prepared pan. Bake at 350 degrees for 1 hour and 20 minutes or until a wooden pick inserted in the center comes out clean. Begin checking for doneness after 1 hour. Cool in the pan for 5 minutes. Invert onto a wire rack to cool completely. Drizzle with Maple Glaze.

YIELD: 12 SERVINGS

MAPLE GLAZE

1 cup confectioners' sugar
1 tablespoon lemon juice
1/2 teaspoon maple extract

Combine the confectioners' sugar, lemon juice and maple extract in a medium bowl and mix well. Add enough water gradually to form a smooth glaze consistency, stirring constantly.

BANANA CHOCOLATE CHIP BREAD

2 cups all-purpose flour	1 cup sugar
1 teaspoon baking powder	1 egg
1/2 teaspoon baking soda	1/2 cup (1 stick) butter, softened
1 cup mashed banana	1 cup (6 ounces) chocolate chips
3 tablespoons milk	1/2 cup finely chopped pecans

Mix the flour, baking powder and baking soda together. Mix the banana and milk in a small bowl. Cream the sugar, egg and butter in a large mixing bowl until light and fluffy. Add the flour mixture and banana mixture alternately, beating just until moistened after each addition. Stir in the chocolate chips and pecans. Pour into a greased 5×9-inch loaf pan. Bake at 350 degrees for 1 hour or until a wooden pick inserted in the center comes out clean. Cool in the pan for 10 minutes. Invert onto a wire rack to cool completely.

YIELD: 1 LOAF

HARVEST PUMPKIN BREAD

2 1/2 cups all-purpose flour	5 eggs
2 teaspoons baking soda	2 cups cooked pumpkin
1/2 teaspoon salt	1 1/2 cups vegetable oil
1 teaspoon cinnamon	2 (4-ounce) packages coconut
1 teaspoon nutmeg	instant pudding mix
1/2 teaspoon ground cloves	1 cup chopped nuts
2 cups sugar	

Sift the flour, baking soda, salt, cinnamon, nutmeg and cloves together. Combine the sugar, eggs, pumpkin and oil in a large bowl and mix well. Add the flour mixture and mix well. Add the pudding mix and nuts and mix well. Pour into 3 greased and floured 5×9-inch loaf pans. Bake at 350 degrees for 1 hour. If the pans are deep, the baking time will be 15 minutes longer.

YIELD: 3 LOAVES

Spicy Beer Bread

2¹/₂ cups all-purpose flour
¹/₄ cup sugar
¹/₂ teaspoon baking powder
Pinch of salt
1 (9-ounce) bottle pale ale beer
¹/₂ cup (2 ounces) shredded Cheddar cheese
Green tops of 2 scallions, thinly sliced
10 ounces jalapeño chiles, finely chopped (optional)
1 tablespoon melted butter

Sift the flour, sugar, baking powder and salt into a mixing bowl. Add the beer and mix well. Add the cheese, scallions and jalapeño chiles and mix well. The batter will be stiff. Spoon evenly into a 5×9-inch loaf pan sprayed with nonstick cooking spray. Brush the top with the melted butter. Bake at 300 degrees for 45 minutes or until light brown. Remove from the oven to cool. Cut into ¹/₄-inch-thick slices. To serve, arrange the bread slices on a baking sheet. Broil for 1 minute or until brown.

YIELD: 12 SERVINGS

LIMPA (SWEDISH RYE BREAD)

1 envelope dry yeast
1/2 teaspoon sugar
1/2 cup warm water
1/4 cup sugar
11/2 teaspoons salt
2 tablespoons butter, melted
11/2 teaspoons caraway seeds
1 cup warm water
1/4 cup dark molasses
1 tablespoon grated orange zest
11/4 cups sifted rye flour
4 cups sifted all-purpose flour
Butter

Dissolve the yeast and 1/2 teaspoon sugar in 1/2 cup warm water in a bowl. Let stand for 20 minutes. Combine 1/4 cup sugar, salt, 2 tablespoons butter, caraway seeds, 1 cup warm water, molasses and orange zest in a large bowl and mix well. Add the yeast mixture and mix well. Add the rye flour and all-purpose flour and mix until the dough leaves the side of the bowl. Turn onto a lightly floured surface. Knead until smooth and satiny. Place in a greased bowl, turning to coat the surface. Let rise, covered, for 1½ hours or until doubled in bulk. Punch the dough down. Divide the dough into 2 equal portions. Shape into round loaves. Arrange on a greased baking sheet. Let rise for 45 to 60 minutes or until doubled in bulk. Bake at 350 degrees for 30 minutes. Spread the top of each loaf with additional butter. Cool on a wire rack.

YIELD: 2 LOAVES

FIESTA BREAD

Photograph for this recipe is shown on page 44 and below.

1 cup quick-cooking or old-fashioned oats
1¹/₄ cups all-purpose flour
2 teaspoons baking powder
³/₄ teaspoon baking soda
¹/₂ teaspoon cumin
¹/₂ teaspoon chili powder
¹/₂ teaspoon salt (optional)
2 tablespoons butter or margarine
¹/₄ cup sliced scallions (about 2)
1 tablespoon finely chopped seeded jalapeño chile (about 1 medium)
1 cup nonfat plain yogurt
2 egg whites, lightly beaten

Process the oats at high speed in a blender for 1 minute. Combine the oats, flour, baking powder, baking soda, cumin, chili powder and salt in a bowl and mix well. Cut in the butter until crumbly. Add the scallions, jalapeño chile, yogurt and egg whites and mix until moistened. Knead gently on a lightly floured surface 6 times. Shape the dough into a 9-inch circle. Place in a 10-inch ovenproof skillet sprayed with nonstick cooking spray. Bake at 425 degrees for 15 minutes or until golden brown.

YIELD: 8 SERVINGS

In 1924, Santa Barbara planned a celebration to mark the opening of the new Lobero Theatre, as well as to increase tourism. The first *Fiesta* included an equestrian parade, cultural events, and extravagant feasts. Today, the five-day festival celebrates and preserves the city's heritage from Spanish, Mexican, and North American pioneers. Musical performances, parades, traditional cuisine, and special events are enjoyed in the spirit of friendship and hospitality.

GRAPE CLUSTER BREAD

Photograph for this recipe is shown on page 44.

2 envelopes dry yeast
$1/2$ cup warm (110-degree) water
$6^1/4$ cups all-purpose flour
$1^1/4$ cups warm (100-degree) milk
$1/4$ cup sugar
3 eggs
5 tablespoons butter
$1/2$ teaspoon salt
$1/2$ teaspoon vanilla extract
$1/2$ teaspoon almond extract
$1/2$ teaspoon lemon extract
Egg wash (optional)

Dissolve the yeast in $1/2$ cup warm water in a large mixing bowl. Add the flour, warm milk, sugar, 3 eggs, butter, salt and flavorings. Beat with an electric mixer fitted with a dough hook for 10 minutes. Place in an oiled bowl, turning to coat the surface. Let rise, covered, for 1 hour or until doubled in bulk. Punch the dough down. Let rise for 30 minutes. Shape the dough into 1 or 2 grape clusters on a baking sheet. Let rise until doubled in bulk. Brush with egg wash. Bake at 400 degrees for 25 to 30 minutes or until the loaf sounds hollow when tapped. Cool on a wire rack.

Note: An egg wash is a mixture of egg yolk or egg white beaten with a small amount of water or milk. Brushing with an egg wash before baking gives the baked loaves color and gloss.

YIELD: 1 OR 2 LOAVES

An eye-popping presentation. Superb bread to serve during a wine tasting, at a dinner party, or on a picnic.

Santa Ynez Corn and Cheese Bread

Santa Ynez Valley

A forty-five-minute drive north of Santa Barbara brings you to the heart of one of California's premier wine regions. Oak-studded rolling hills, orchards, and vineyards weave scenic tranquility into this rich landscape. Here the mountains and coastline run east to west, an unusual occurrence on the West Coast, resulting in hot, sunny days and cool evenings. This excellent balance of geology and climate creates a vintner's paradise.

2 (8-ounce) packages corn bread mix	1 cup cottage cheese
1 teaspoon salt	3/4 cup (1 1/2 sticks) butter or margarine, melted
1 cup chopped scallions	9 eggs, lightly beaten
1/2 cup chopped fresh cilantro	1 (16-ounce) package frozen corn with red and green bell peppers
3 tablespoons chopped green chiles	1 cup (4 ounces) shredded Cheddar cheese
1 cup sour cream	

Combine the corn bread mix, salt, scallions, cilantro, green chiles, sour cream, cottage cheese, butter, eggs, corn and cheese in a large bowl and mix well. Spread in a greased 9×13-inch baking dish. Bake at 400 degrees for 34 to 42 minutes or until a deep golden brown and a wooden pick inserted in the center comes out clean. Cool in the pan for 10 minutes. Cut into squares.

YIELD: 12 SERVINGS

Toasted Cheezy Bread

1 cup mayonnaise	2 tablespoons chopped bell pepper
3/4 cup (3 ounces) shredded Cheddar cheese	2 or 3 garlic cloves, chopped
3 tablespoons chopped red onion	1 loaf French bread, cut into halves

Combine the mayonnaise, cheese, onion, bell pepper and garlic in a bowl and mix well. Let stand for 1 hour. Spread on the bread. Arrange on a baking sheet. Broil for 2 to 5 minutes or until golden brown.

YIELD: 8 SERVINGS

ONION LOVER'S TWIST

1 envelope dry yeast	1/2 cup hot water
1/4 cup warm (100- to 115-degree) water	1/2 cup milk
	1/4 cup (1/2 stick) margarine
2 cups all-purpose flour	1 egg
1/4 cup sugar	2 cups all-purpose flour
1 1/2 teaspoons salt	Onion Filling (below)

Dissolve the yeast in 1/4 cup warm water in a large mixing bowl. Add 2 cups flour, the sugar, salt, 1/2 cup hot water, milk, margarine and egg. Beat at low speed until moistened. Beat at medium speed for 2 minutes. Stir in 2 cups flour by hand to form a soft dough. Let rise, covered, in a warm place for 45 to 60 minutes or until doubled in bulk.

Punch the dough down. Toss on a floured surface until the dough is no longer sticky. Roll into a 12×18-inch rectangle. Cut evenly into 3 long strips. Spread the Onion Filling down the center of each strip. Fold each strip over from each side and seal along the strip and on the ends. Braid the 3 sealed strips together on a greased baking sheet. Form into a crescent shape. Let rise, covered, until doubled in bulk. Bake at 350 degrees for 30 to 45 minutes or until golden brown. Best served hot from the oven.

YIELD: 1 LOAF

ONION FILLING

1/4 cup (1/2 stick) butter or margarine	2 tablespoons sesame seeds or poppy seeds
1 cup finely chopped onion	1 teaspoon garlic salt
2 tablespoons grated Parmesan cheese	1 teaspoon paprika

Melt the butter in a saucepan. Add the onion. Sauté until the onion is tender. Add the cheese, sesame seeds, garlic salt and paprika and mix well. Cover and keep warm until ready to use. Leave the mixture uncovered if there is excess liquid so some of the moisture can evaporate.

ARTICHOKE GARLIC BREAD

**1 (1-pound) French baguette, or
    2 (8-ounce) French baguettes
6 garlic cloves, minced
2 tablespoons sesame seeds
1/2 cup (1 stick) butter
1 1/2 cups sour cream
2 cups cubed Monterey Jack cheese
1/4 cup grated Parmesan cheese
2 tablespoons finely chopped parsley
2 teaspoons lemon pepper
1 (14-ounce) can artichoke hearts, drained, cut up
1 cup (4 ounces) shredded Cheddar cheese**

Cut the baguette into halves lengthwise. Tear out the soft part of each bread half with a fork to form a shell, reserving the torn bread. Sauté the garlic and sesame seeds in the butter in a skillet for 2 to 3 minutes or until tender. Do not brown. Add the torn bread. Sauté until the bread turns brown. Remove from the heat. Add the sour cream, Monterey Jack cheese, Parmesan cheese, parsley, lemon pepper and artichoke hearts and mix well. Arrange the bread shells on a baking sheet. Fill with the artichoke mixture. Sprinkle with the Cheddar cheese. Bake at 350 degrees for 30 minutes. Cool slightly. Cut into 1 1/2-inch slices.

Note: Do not use marinated artichoke hearts in this recipe.

YIELD: 8 TO 10 SERVINGS

GRILLED SOURDOUGH WITH CALIFORNIA ONION BUTTER

1/2 cup (1 stick) butter, softened
1/4 cup chopped scallion tops
1/2 teaspoon to 1 tablespoon
   minced garlic
1 (1-pound) loaf sourdough bread

Combine the butter, scallions and garlic in a bowl and mix well. Chill, covered, until set. Cut the bread into 1/2-inch slices. Arrange on a grill rack. Grill until the bread is toasted. Spread with the onion butter and serve immediately.

YIELD: 6 TO 10 SERVINGS

To complete your Santa Maria Barbecue, serve this crunchy French bread with Santa Maria Tri-Tip Barbecue on page 191.

SUPER GARLIC BREAD

1 loaf French bread
1 cup (2 sticks) butter, softened
3 garlic cloves, minced
1/2 cup shredded Romano cheese
1/2 cup shredded Parmesan cheese
1/2 cup mayonnaise
3 tablespoons chopped fresh
   parsley
1/2 teaspoon oregano

Cut the bread into halves lengthwise. Combine the butter, garlic, Romano cheese, Parmesan cheese, mayonnaise, parsley and oregano in a bowl and mix well. Spread on each bread half. Wrap each in foil. Bake at 350 degrees for 20 minutes. Remove the foil. Broil until light brown.

YIELD: 8 SERVINGS

Another good choice to go with your Santa Maria Tri-Tip Barbecue on page 191.

SAVOR THE EXTRAORDINARY

soups, sandwiches and condiments

WINE COUNTRY PICNIC SANDWICH

FANDANGO SANGRIA

DILLED ONIONS

GOLDEN STATE SOUP

(shown left to right)

Photograph © Michael Brown

El Paseo Courtyard   *Photograph © David Muench*

COLD AVOCADO SOUP

4 medium avocados

2 quarts chicken consommé

1 tablespoon chopped fresh
  cilantro

$^1/_2$ medium onion, chopped

Juice of 1 medium lemon

Salt and pepper to taste

Purée the avocados, 1 cup of the consommé, the cilantro, onion, lemon juice, salt and pepper in a blender until smooth. Pour into a large bowl. Add the remaining consommé and mix well. Chill, covered, in the refrigerator. Serve in a glass bowl with a dollop of sour cream and a sprinkling of chopped chives.

YIELD: 8 TO 10 SERVINGS

 A viognier is a perfect accompaniment to this chilled soup; a chardonnay would make a pleasant substitute.

GREEN GAZPACHO

2 cups seedless green grapes

2 avocados

$1^1/_4$ cups coarsely chopped peeled
  cucumber

1 cup coarsely chopped green bell
  pepper

1 cup coarsely chopped celery

1 cup coarsely chopped scallions

3 cups white grape juice

2 tablespoons fresh lime juice

$^1/_4$ cup chopped fresh mint leaves

Salt and white pepper to taste

Coarsely purée the grapes, avocados, cucumber, bell pepper, celery and scallions in a food processor or blender, adding white grape juice as necessary to keep the blade from clogging. The gazpacho should be chunky. Pour into a large bowl. Add the remaining grape juice, lime juice, mint, salt and white pepper. Chill, covered, for 4 to 12 hours. Ladle into soup bowls and garnish with sprigs of fresh mint.

YIELD: 12 SERVINGS

BAJA BLACK BEAN SOUP

2 pounds dried black beans, rinsed, drained
1 large white or yellow onion, chopped
2 carrots, finely chopped
2 ribs celery, finely chopped
1 garlic bulb, separated into cloves, peeled
8 ounces cooked ham, chopped
1 bay leaf
5 sprigs of parsley, trimmed, chopped
1 teaspoon thyme, or to taste
3 to 4 cups (or more) chicken or vegetable broth
¼ cup chili powder, or to taste
2 tablespoons cumin, or to taste
Salt to taste
Sour cream
Salsa

Combine the beans, onion, carrots, celery, garlic, ham, bay leaf and parsley in a 4- to 6-quart stockpot. Season with the thyme. Cover with the broth. Bring to a boil and reduce the heat. Simmer for 1½ to 2 hours or until the beans are tender, adding additional broth as necessary to keep the beans covered. Discard the bay leaf. Process the bean mixture in a food processor until puréed. The texture will be slightly gritty. Return to the stockpot. Add the chili powder, cumin and salt and mix well. Add enough additional broth to make of the desired consistency. Cook until heated through, stirring constantly. Ladle into soup bowls. Add a dollop of sour cream to each bowl and swirl through the soup. Top with a dollop of salsa.

Note: This soup freezes well. Thaw completely before heating, adding a little broth if needed.

YIELD: 8 TO 10 SERVINGS

CALIFORNIA GOLD SOUP

3 tablespoons butter	4 cups chicken stock
1 large yellow onion, finely chopped	1 cup fresh orange juice
	Salt and pepper to taste
12 large carrots, chopped	Freshly grated orange zest

Melt the butter in a stockpot. Add the onion. Cook, covered, over low heat for 15 minutes or until tender. Add the carrots and chicken stock. Bring to a boil and reduce the heat. Simmer for 30 minutes or until the carrots are tender. Strain the mixture, reserving the solids and liquid separately. Process the solids with 1 cup of the reserved liquid in a food processor fitted with a steel blade until puréed. Return to the stockpot. Add the orange juice and 2 to 3 cups of the remaining reserved liquid to make of the desired consistency. Season with salt and pepper. Stir in the orange zest. Simmer until heated through.

YIELD: 8 SERVINGS

GOLDEN STATE SOUP

Photograph for this recipe is shown on page 70.

$1/4$ cup ($1/2$ stick) butter	3 to 4 cups cubed peeled potatoes
2 cups finely chopped yellow onions	$1/4$ cup chopped fresh dill weed
	Salt and pepper to taste
2 cups chopped carrots	2 to 3 cups (8 to 12 ounces) shredded Cheddar cheese
6 sprigs of cilantro	
5 cups chicken stock	

Melt the butter in a stockpot. Add the onions and carrots. Cook, covered, over low heat for 25 minutes or until the vegetables are tender and light in color. Add the cilantro, chicken stock and potatoes. Bring to a boil and reduce the heat. Simmer, covered, for 30 minutes or until the potatoes are tender. Add the dill weed. Remove from the heat. Let stand, covered, for 5 minutes. Strain the mixture, reserving the solids and liquid separately. Process the solids with 1 cup of the reserved liquid in a blender until smooth. Return to the stockpot. Add the remaining reserved liquid. Season with salt and pepper. Stir in the cheese gradually. Cook over low heat until the cheese melts and the soup is heated through, stirring constantly. Serve immediately.

Note: For extra special flavor, substitute 1 cup chopped peeled parsnips for 1 cup of the carrots.

YIELD: 6 SERVINGS

LETTUCE SOUP

1 head butter lettuce, rinsed	1¼ cups whole or reduced-fat milk
1 cup chicken broth	Salt and pepper to taste
1 yellow onion, finely chopped	1 teaspoon sherry
2 tablespoons butter	1 lemon, thinly sliced
3 tablespoons all-purpose flour	

Bring the lettuce and chicken broth to a boil in a stockpot. Boil for 3 minutes. Process in a blender until puréed. Return to the stockpot. Sauté the onion in the butter in a skillet until translucent. Add the flour. Cook until golden brown. Add the milk. Cook until thickened, stirring constantly. Process in a blender until smooth. Add to the lettuce mixture in the stockpot. Season with salt and pepper. Cook until heated through. Stir in the sherry just before serving. Ladle into soup bowls. Top with lemon slices.

YIELD: 4 TO 6 SERVINGS

CALIFORNIA FRESH MINESTRONE

12 cups chicken broth	1 cup chopped fresh green beans
5 garlic cloves, minced	4 ounces pasta
2 cups chopped onions	1 (6-ounce) can tomato paste
2 cups chopped potatoes	1 tablespoon basil
2 cups chopped carrots	⅓ cup grated Parmesan cheese
1 (8-ounce) can kidney beans or red beans	2 to 4 tablespoons olive oil
2 cups chopped fresh zucchini	2 or 3 links turkey Italian sausage

Combine the broth, garlic, onions, potatoes and carrots in a stockpot and bring to a boil. Cook for 25 minutes or until the vegetables are tender. Add the kidney beans, zucchini, green beans and pasta. Cook for 7 minutes.

Mix the tomato paste, basil, olive oil and cheese in a bowl. Stir into the soup.

Cook the sausage in a skillet until brown and cooked through. Cut into slices. Add to the soup. Serve with corn bread or crusty French rolls.

YIELD: 8 SERVINGS

BUTTERNUT SQUASH SOUP

Eric Widmer, Chef, La Cumbre Country Club

2 tablespoons vegetable oil
6 ounces onion, coarsely chopped
6 ounces celery, coarsely chopped
6 ounces carrots, coarsely chopped
1 tablespoon minced garlic
2 pounds butternut squash, peeled, seeded, coarsely chopped
8 ounces Granny Smith apples, peeled, cored, coarsely chopped
3 quarts chicken stock
1 cup heavy cream
Oregano and nutmeg to taste
Salt, black pepper, cayenne pepper and white pepper to taste

Heat the oil in a stockpot. Add the onion, celery, carrots and garlic. Sauté until the vegetables are limp. Add the squash and apples. Stir in the chicken stock. Simmer for 1 hour or until the vegetables are tender. Process in batches in a food processor until puréed. Return to the stockpot, straining through a medium strainer if needed and discarding the solids. Stir in the cream. Return the soup to a simmer. Season with oregano, nutmeg, salt, black pepper, cayenne pepper and white pepper. Ladle into soup bowls. Garnish with thin slices of Gruyère cheese, pumpkin seeds and chopped fresh parsley.

YIELD: 1 GALLON

ESSENCE OF TOMATO SOUP

1 (1-quart) can tomatoes	1 teaspoon peppercorns
3/4 cup chopped celery	1 teaspoon salt
1/2 cup chopped carrots	Dash of cayenne pepper
1 small onion, chopped	Dash of mace
1 green bell pepper, chopped	3/4 cup whipping cream, whipped
3 whole cloves	Chopped fresh parsley

Combine the undrained tomatoes, celery, carrots, onion, bell pepper, cloves, peppercorns, salt, cayenne pepper and mace in a saucepan. Simmer for 1 hour or until the vegetables are tender. Strain into a saucepan, but do not force the vegetables through the sieve, as the soup should be clear. Cook until the soup is heated through. Ladle into bouillon cups. Dollop with the whipped cream. Sprinkle with chopped parsley.

YIELD: 4 TO 6 SERVINGS

VEGETABLE BARLEY SOUP

1 pound lean ground turkey or ground beef	Salt and pepper to taste
1 cup finely chopped onion	4 cups canned diced tomatoes
3 garlic cloves, minced	1 (10-ounce) can diced tomatoes with green chiles
1/4 cup olive oil	1 cup julienned whole baby carrots
1 1/2 quarts chicken broth	1 cup sliced zucchini
4 cups water	1/2 cup sliced celery
1 cup barley	1/4 cup chopped parsley and/or chives
1 teaspoon oregano, crumbled	
1/2 teaspoon thyme, crumbled	

Brown the ground turkey with the onion and garlic in the olive oil in a 4-quart stockpot, stirring until the ground turkey is crumbly. Add the broth, water, barley and seasonings. Bring to a boil and reduce the heat. Simmer, covered, for 30 minutes. Add the tomatoes, tomatoes with green chiles, carrots, zucchini and celery. Return to a boil and reduce the heat. Simmer for 20 minutes or until the barley is tender. Ladle into soup bowls. Sprinkle with the parsley.

YIELD: 8 TO 10 SERVINGS

MEXICAN VEGETARIAN SOUP WITH POSOLE

1 teaspoon olive oil

1 medium onion, chopped

2 medium garlic cloves, minced

1¹⁄₂ teaspoons cumin

1 teaspoon salt

1 (20-ounce) can hominy, drained

1 or 2 jalapeño chiles, finely chopped

1 pound tomatillos, chopped

1 bunch Swiss chard, chopped

4 cups vegetable broth

2 bay leaves

Thinly sliced radishes

Thinly sliced jalapeño chiles

Sliced avocados

Thinly sliced scallions

Sour cream

Sprigs of cilantro

Lime quarters

Heat the olive oil in a large stockpot. Add the onion and garlic. Cook, covered, for 5 minutes or until the onion is tender, stirring occasionally. Add the cumin and salt. Cook for 30 seconds or until fragrant. Add the hominy, chopped jalapeño chiles and tomatillos. Cook for 1 minute, stirring constantly. Add the Swiss chard, broth and bay leaves. Bring to a boil. Cook, covered, for 20 minutes or until the Swiss chard is wilted and the leaves are tender. Remove the bay leaves. Ladle into soup bowls. Top with radishes, sliced jalapeño chiles, avocados, scallions, sour cream, cilantro and a squeeze of lime.

YIELD: 6 SERVINGS

CILANTRO

Cilantro, also called Chinese parsley or coriander, is a bright green herb from the coriander plant. Its distinctive, pungent flavor lends itself to Caribbean, Latin American, and Asian cooking. To keep cilantro fresh for up to one week, place stems down in a glass container and fill with water. Cover the container with a plastic bag and refrigerate, changing the water every two to three days.

CHICKEN SOUP WITH CURRY AND WILD RICE

1 (6-ounce) package long grain and wild rice mix
2 cups chopped onions
1 cup chopped celery
1 cup chopped carrots
2 garlic cloves, minced
8 ounces fresh mushrooms, cut into halves
1 tablespoon vegetable or olive oil
$1/4$ cup all-purpose flour
$1/2$ teaspoon minced tarragon
$1/4$ teaspoon thyme
$1/2$ teaspoon curry powder, or to taste
2 cups water
3 tablespoons dry sherry
2 (15-ounce) cans chicken broth
1 (12-ounce) can evaporated milk
$3/4$ teaspoon salt, or to taste
$1/8$ teaspoon pepper, or to taste
1 tablespoon butter or margarine
3 cups chopped roasted chicken breasts

Cook the rice using the package directions. Sauté the onions, celery, carrots, garlic and mushrooms in the oil in a stockpot for 10 minutes or until tender. Add the flour, tarragon, thyme and curry powder. Cook for 1 minute or until slightly thickened, stirring frequently. Add the water, sherry, broth and evaporated milk. Season with the salt and pepper. Stir in the butter. Bring to a boil and reduce the heat. Simmer for 25 minutes or until slightly thickened, stirring occasionally. Stir in the cooked rice and chicken. Simmer for 20 to 30 minutes, stirring occasionally. Remove from the heat to cool slightly. Pour into a large container. Chill, covered, until ready to serve. To serve, pour into a stockpot. Heat for 20 minutes or until heated through.

YIELD: 6 TO 8 SERVINGS

CHILI BLANCO

4$\frac{1}{2}$ cups chopped chicken
    (about 2 pounds)
2 tablespoons vegetable oil
3 shallots, chopped
3 garlic cloves, minced
5 fresh tomatillos, peeled, chopped
1 (14-ounce) can tomatoes
1 (14-ounce) can chicken broth
1 (7-ounce) can chopped green
    chiles
$\frac{1}{2}$ teaspoon crumbled oregano

$\frac{1}{4}$ teaspoon cumin
2 (15-ounce) cans white kidney
    beans, drained
Juice of 1 lime
Salt and pepper to taste
Chopped red onion
Chopped fresh cilantro
Chopped Roma tomatoes
Chopped avocados
Shredded Monterey Jack cheese
Sour cream

Cook the chicken in the oil in a large skillet until cooked through. Add the shallots and garlic. Cook for 1 minute. Add the tomatillos, tomatoes, broth and green chiles. Simmer for 2 minutes. Add the oregano, cumin and kidney beans. Cook for 5 minutes. Add the lime juice, salt and pepper. At serving time, pass individual small bowls of red onion and remaining ingredients to top the chili.

YIELD: 4 TO 6 SERVINGS

PUMPKIN CHICKEN CHOWDER

1 tablespoon vegetable oil
8 ounces boneless skinless
    chicken breasts
1 cup chopped onion
1 cup chopped red bell pepper
1 garlic clove, minced
2 (14-ounce) cans fat-free chicken
    broth

1 (15-ounce) can pumpkin
$\frac{1}{2}$ cup frozen whole kernel corn
$\frac{1}{4}$ cup uncooked long grain white
    rice
$\frac{1}{2}$ teaspoon basil leaves, crushed,
    or to taste
$\frac{1}{4}$ teaspoon salt, or to taste
$\frac{1}{8}$ teaspoon pepper, or to taste

Heat the oil in a large heavy saucepan over medium heat. Cut the chicken into bite-size pieces. Add the chicken, onion, bell pepper and garlic. Sauté until the chicken is cooked through. Stir in the broth, pumpkin, corn, rice, basil, salt and pepper. Bring to a boil and reduce the heat. Simmer, covered, for 20 minutes or until the rice is tender, stirring occasionally.

YIELD: 6 SERVINGS

TOMATILLOS

(TOM-A-TEE-YOHS)

The tomatillo, a relative of the tomato, grows to maturity inside an inedible, papery husk. The husk can be easily removed after soaking the fruit in cold water. Tomatillos don't need to be peeled or seeded, but they should be rinsed after husking to remove the sticky substance. To cook, steam them whole or diced in a small amount of water in a covered saucepan for five to seven minutes.

ITALIAN SAUSAGE SOUP

1¹/₂ pounds medium-spiced Italian sausage, cut into ¹/₄-inch slices
2 garlic cloves, minced
2 onions, chopped
2 (16-ounce) cans stewed tomatoes
1¹/₂ cups dry red wine
5 cups beef stock
¹/₂ teaspoon basil
¹/₂ teaspoon oregano
1 medium green bell pepper, seeded, chopped
2 medium zucchini, cut into slices ¹/₄ inch thick
2 cups uncooked bow tie pasta
Salt and pepper to taste
¹/₂ cup grated Parmesan cheese

Cook the sausage in a 5-quart heavy saucepan over medium heat for 7 to 10 minutes or until light brown. Remove the sausage with a slotted spoon to a plate. Drain the saucepan, reserving 3 tablespoons of the drippings in the saucepan. Add the garlic and onions. Sauté for 2 to 3 minutes. Return the sausage to the saucepan. Add the tomatoes, wine, stock, basil and oregano. Simmer, uncovered, for 30 minutes. Add the bell pepper, zucchini and pasta. Simmer, covered, for 25 minutes or until the pasta is al dente. Ladle into deep soup bowls and sprinkle with the Parmesan cheese.

YIELD: 8 TO 10 SERVINGS

 Accompany this soup with a California pinot noir or merlot.

BOUILLABAISSE

¹/₂ cup (1 stick) butter
1 cup coarsely chopped onion
1 garlic clove, finely chopped
3 tablespoons all-purpose flour
1 cup coarsely chopped fresh tomato
2 cups fresh fish stock
¹/₂ lemon, sliced
2 teaspoons salt
¹/₈ teaspoon cayenne pepper
¹/₈ teaspoon thyme
3 whole allspice
1 small bay leaf
Pinch of saffron
2 pounds skinned red snapper fillets, cut into chunks
1 pound fresh shrimp, peeled
1 pint oysters with liquid

Melt the butter in a large stockpot. Add the onion and garlic. Sauté until tender. Stir in the flour. Add the tomato and stock and mix well. Add the lemon. Season with salt, cayenne pepper, thyme, allspice, bay leaf and saffron. Simmer for 30 minutes or until the flavors are blended. Add the fish, shrimp and undrained oysters. Simmer for 15 to 20 minutes or until the shrimp turn pink and the edges of the oysters begin to curl. Do not overcook. Remove the bay leaf and allspice before serving.

Note: You may substitute 1½ cups tomato juice and ½ cup water for the fish stock.

YIELD: 6 SERVINGS

 Either a rich chardonnay or a rich sauvignon blanc is perfect with this hearty soup.

FISH STEW

¹⁄₄ cup vegetable oil	¹⁄₂ cup sliced green Spanish olives
1¹⁄₂ pounds unpeeled red potatoes, chopped	2¹⁄₂ pounds cod or other firm fish, cut into pieces
1 red bell pepper, chopped	2 tablespoons fresh lime juice
1 medium onion, chopped	1 tablespoon fresh dill weed, or
³⁄₄ cup chopped celery with leaves	1 teaspoon dried dill weed
1 quart chicken broth	4 garlic cloves, minced
1 (14-ounce) can stewed tomatoes	

Heat the oil in a large saucepan. Add the potatoes, bell pepper, onion and celery. Cook for 15 minutes or until brown. Add the broth. Simmer for 15 minutes. Add the tomatoes, olives, fish, lime juice, dill weed and garlic. Simmer, covered, for 5 minutes.

YIELD: 6 SERVINGS

LA GOLETA CLAM CHOWDER

8 ounces bacon	4 (7-ounce) cans clams
1 large onion, minced	¹⁄₄ teaspoon salt
1 cup chopped celery	¹⁄₄ teaspoon pepper
1 cup chicken stock	¹⁄₂ teaspoon thyme
2 cups chopped peeled potatoes	¹⁄₄ cup chopped fresh cilantro
2 cups milk	12 saltine crackers, crumbled
1 cup cream	

Cook the bacon in a stockpot until crisp. Add the onion and celery. Cook until tender; drain. Add the stock and potatoes. Cook, covered, for 10 minutes or until the potatoes are fork tender. Add the milk, cream, undrained clams, salt, pepper, thyme, cilantro and crackers. Cook until the crackers are dissolved and the chowder is heated through.

Note: The crackers add flavor and are used as a thickening agent.

YIELD: 4 TO 6 SERVINGS

 Serve a sauvignon blanc or chardonnay with this rich creamy soup.

CRAB AND CURRIED SQUASH SOUP

1 onion, chopped
$1/2$ cup chopped celery
1 tablespoon butter or margarine
2 tablespoons tomato paste
2 to 3 teaspoons curry powder
1 (1-pound) butternut squash, peeled, cut into 1-inch chunks
1 large Granny Smith apple, peeled, coarsely chopped
3 cups chicken broth
2 cups water
1 teaspoon ginger
1 bay leaf
1 whole clove
$1/4$ teaspoon pepper
$1/4$ cup dry sherry
8 ounces shelled cooked crab meat
Thinly sliced red bell pepper
Salt to taste

Sauté the onion and celery in the butter in a 4-quart saucepan for 5 minutes or until the vegetables are tender. Add the tomato paste and curry powder. Cook for 1 minute or until blended, stirring constantly. Add the squash, apple, broth, water, ginger, bay leaf, clove and pepper. Bring to a boil and reduce the heat. Simmer, covered, for 45 minutes or until the squash softens, stirring occasionally. Discard the bay leaf and clove. Purée the soup in batches in a blender, returning to the saucepan. Add the sherry. Cook for 2 minutes over medium heat, stirring constantly. Ladle into wide soup bowls. Mound the crab meat in the center of each bowl. Top with bell pepper slices. Season with salt. Serve with crusty bread.

YIELD: 4 SERVINGS

SHRIMP AND CORN BISQUE

1/4 cup chopped onion	4 cups whole milk
1/4 cup chopped celery (optional)	1 cup half-and-half
1/3 cup butter	Salt and freshly ground black
1/2 teaspoon curry powder	pepper to taste
Dash of cayenne pepper	1 pound shrimp, cooked, peeled,
2 tablespoons all-purpose flour	cut up
4 cups fresh or frozen whole kernel	Crumbled crisp-cooked bacon
corn	

Sauté the onion and celery in the butter in a 4-quart saucepan until tender. Add the curry powder, cayenne pepper and flour. Cook for 2 minutes, stirring constantly. Process the corn in a food processor until chopped. Add to the onion mixture. Cook for 5 to 10 minutes. Add the milk, half-and-half, salt and black pepper. Bring to a boil. Stir in the shrimp. Ladle into soup bowls. Sprinkle with crumbled bacon.

YIELD: 4 SERVINGS

For a real crowd pleaser, substitute lobster for the shrimp.

SAND DOLLAR SANDWICHES

1 cup chopped black olives	1/2 cup mayonnaise
1/2 cup thinly sliced scallions	1/2 teaspoon curry powder
1 1/2 cups (6 ounces) shredded	6 English muffins, split
Cheddar cheese	

Combine the olives, scallions, cheese, mayonnaise and curry powder in a bowl and mix well. Arrange the split English muffins on a baking sheet. Bake at 350 degrees until toasted. Spread with the olive mixture. Broil 8 inches from the heat source until the cheese is melted and bubbly.

YIELD: 6 SERVINGS

WINE COUNTRY PICNIC SANDWICH

Photo for this recipe is shown on page 70 and below.

1 (14×16-inch) loaf unsliced sourdough bread
1/2 cup favorite vinaigrette or Italian salad dressing
1/2 cup finely chopped peeled cucumber
1/2 cup finely chopped tomato
2 tablespoons thinly sliced scallions

4 ounces thinly sliced Swiss cheese
9 ounces thinly sliced cooked turkey breast
12 thin slices salami or ham
3 thinly sliced red onion rings
12 thinly sliced green bell pepper rings

Cut 1 inch from the top of the bread using a serrated knife, reserving the bread top. Remove the soft center, leaving a ½-inch shell. Mix the vinaigrette, cucumber, tomato and scallions in a bowl. Spread ½ of the vegetable mixture in the bread shell. Layer the cheese, turkey, salami, red onion rings and bell pepper rings over the vegetable mixture. Top with the remaining vegetable mixture. Replace the bread top. Wrap tightly in plastic wrap and then wrap tightly in foil. Chill for 3 to 24 hours. Unwrap and cut into slices to serve.

YIELD: 4 TO 6 SERVINGS

 To complete the perfect Wine Country picnic, open a bottle of pinot grigio or merlot. A chenin blanc would also be a good choice.

Hot Horseradish Ham Sandwiches

1 cup (2 sticks) butter, softened	24 small soft dinner rolls
2 tablespoons horseradish mustard	1½ pounds thinly sliced ham
2 tablespoons poppy seeds	3 cups (12 ounces) shredded
1 teaspoon Worcestershire sauce	Swiss cheese
1 medium onion, minced	

Mix the butter, horseradish mustard, poppy seeds, Worcestershire sauce and onion in a bowl. Split the rolls horizontally. Spread the butter mixture on the cut sides of the rolls. Layer the ham and cheese on the bottom halves. Replace the tops. Arrange on a baking sheet and cover loosely with foil. Bake at 400 degrees for 10 to 15 minutes or until the cheese melts.

YIELD: 24 SERVINGS

Grilled Sausage Sandwiches with Caramelized Onions

2 pounds red onions, thinly sliced	4 large slices rye or pumpernickel
2 tablespoons olive oil	bread
1½ tablespoons red wine vinegar	4 teaspoons Dijon mustard
1 tablespoon packed dark brown	4 ounces Gruyère cheese,
sugar	thinly sliced
Salt and pepper to taste	3 tablespoons butter, softened
3 Italian sausage links, fully cooked	

Sauté the onions in the olive oil in a large heavy skillet over medium-high heat for 5 minutes or until slightly softened. Stir in the vinegar and brown sugar. Reduce the heat to medium-low. Cook for 20 minutes or until the onions are deep brown. Season with salt and pepper. The onions may be prepared up to 2 hours ahead. Let stand at room temperature. Reheat over low heat.

Arrange the sausage in a greased 7×11-inch metal baking pan. Broil for 6 minutes on each side or until brown and crisp. Cut the sausage into halves lengthwise. Arrange 3 sausage halves on each of 2 bread slices. Spread each with 2 teaspoons Dijon mustard. Top with the caramelized onions and cheese. Top with the remaining bread slices. Spread with ½ of the butter. Arrange on a baking sheet. Broil until golden brown. Remove from the oven and turn. Spread with the remaining butter. Broil until brown, watching carefully to prevent overbrowning.

YIELD: 2 SERVINGS

CARAMELIZING

Sugar develops a rich and complex flavor when caramelized. Two procedures will accomplish the desired results: sugar can be dissolved in water to form a syrup or sprinkled over food and then heated under a broiler. Sugar is considered caramelized when it melts and forms a sweet, crunchy crust. The flavor of some vegetables, such as onions or carrots, can be intensified by cooking over medium-high heat until the natural sugars are caramelized.

CRAB MELT

2 cups crab meat, flaked
1/2 cup finely chopped celery
5 tablespoons finely chopped
    scallions
1 cup (4 ounces) shredded sharp
    Cheddar cheese

1 cup mayonnaise
4 to 6 hamburger buns or French
    rolls, split

Combine the crab meat, celery, scallions, cheese and mayonnaise in a large bowl and mix well. Spread over the bottom halves of the buns. Replace the top halves. Place on a baking sheet and cover loosely with foil. Bake at 350 degrees for 20 to 30 minutes or until the cheese melts.

YIELD: 4 TO 6 SERVINGS

PEACH AND MANGO CHUTNEY

1 (29-ounce) can sliced peaches
2 cups packed brown sugar
2 cups white vinegar
1 garlic clove, minced
1/2 cup chopped candied ginger
2 tablespoons mustard seeds

1/2 teaspoon chili powder
1 teaspoon ground cloves
1 teaspoon salt
1 onion, finely chopped
2 ripe mangoes, peeled, chopped
1 cup raisins

Drain the peaches, reserving the syrup. Chop the peaches. Combine the reserved syrup, brown sugar, vinegar, garlic, ginger, mustard seeds, chili powder, ground cloves, salt and onion in a large heavy stockpot. Boil for 30 minutes. Watch carefully to prevent burning. Add the mangoes, peaches and raisins. Boil for 20 to 30 minutes, stirring frequently. Ladle into 6 to 8 sterilized 1/2-pint jars, leaving 1/2 inch headspace; seal with 2-piece lids. Process in a boiling water bath for 10 minutes.

YIELD: 6 TO 8 (1/2-PINT) JARS

MANGOES

Eating a ripe mango is a mouthwatering experience. Sweet and juicy, mangoes can be either peeled and eaten whole or sliced, cutting away from the large flat pit with a sharp knife. Mangoes are equally delicious as an uncooked or cooked ingredient in desserts, relishes, salads, and sauces.

CALIFORNIA PICO DE GALLO

PICO DE GALLO
(PEE-KOH DAY GI-YOH)

Spanish for "rooster's beak," pico de gallo got its unusual name from the practice of eating it with the thumb and finger, an action resembling a beak pecking at its food. Variations are as extensive as one's creativity. Corn, bell peppers, cilantro, lime juice, and cucumbers make interesting additions. Pico de gallo is a welcome accompaniment to fajitas, fish, or chicken dishes, or as an appetizer with chips.

5 oranges, coarsely chopped
1/2 red onion, finely chopped
1 medium tomato, finely chopped
1 jalapeño chile, finely chopped
1/2 red bell pepper, julienned

1 cup julienned jicama
1/2 cup unseasoned rice vinegar
1/4 cup vegetable oil
Salt and pepper to taste

Combine the oranges, onion, tomato, jalapeño chile, bell pepper, jicama, rice vinegar, oil, salt and pepper in a bowl and mix well.

YIELD: 8 CUPS

CRANBERRY APRICOT SAUCE AMANDINE

2 cups sugar
1 cup water
1 pound fresh cranberries
7 tablespoons apricot jam

Juice of 2 lemons
1 teaspoon almond extract
1 1/2 cups blanched slivered
   almonds

Combine the sugar and water in a heavy 3-quart saucepan. Bring to a boil. Do not stir. Cook for 5 minutes. Add the cranberries. Cook for 4 minutes. Remove from the heat. Add the apricot jam and mix well. Add the lemon juice and almond extract. Let stand until cool. Stir in the almonds.

YIELD: 8 SERVINGS

CARAMEL-GLAZED ORANGE SLICES

6 large navel oranges
2 tablespoons brandy
Grated zest of 1 small orange
1 cup sugar

Peel the navel oranges. Cut into ¼-inch slices. Arrange in a single layer on a large platter. Sprinkle with the brandy and orange zest. Heat the sugar in a 10-inch skillet until melted and deep amber in color, stirring to dissolve any lumps. Drizzle over the oranges. Chill, covered, for 2 hours.

YIELD: 8 TO 10 SERVINGS

DILLED ONIONS

Photograph for this recipe is shown on page 70.

2 or 3 yellow onions, thinly sliced
1 teaspoon dill weed
1½ teaspoons salt
½ cup vinegar
½ cup sugar
¼ cup water

Combine the onions, dill weed and salt in a large bowl. Boil the vinegar, sugar and water in a saucepan. Pour over the onion mixture. Marinate, covered, in the refrigerator until ready to serve.

YIELD: 6 TO 8 SERVINGS

JICAMA (HEE-KAH-MAH)

Jicama is that big brown-skinned, bulbous root you may have wondered about when you've seen it in the produce section. Give it a try! It boasts a sweet, white, crunchy flesh that you can enjoy uncooked or cooked. Jicama's season ranges from November through May, and if it's not in your supermarket, try a Mexican grocery store. Peeled and cut into sticks, jicama is an excellent addition to a raw vegetable platter.

HORSERADISH PICKLES

HORSERADISH

Prepared horseradish
is available preserved
either in vinegar (white)
or in beet juice (red).
After the jar has been
open for a month or
so, horseradish can
lose its peppery taste
and turn bitter unless it
is frozen. For convenient
serving-size portions,
freeze spoonfuls of
horseradish on a
baking sheet lined
with waxed paper, then
place in a sealable
plastic bag and return
to the freezer.

1 (46-ounce) jar baby dill pickles
6 tablespoons prepared
  horseradish (from the
  refrigerated section)

2 cups sugar
2/3 cup vinegar
1/3 cup water

Drain the pickles. Cut the pickles into slices lengthwise and return to the jar. Add the horseradish to the top of the pickles. Bring the sugar, vinegar and water to a boil in a saucepan. Pour over the pickles and horseradish. Replace the lid. Chill for several days before serving, turning the jar occasionally to mix.

YIELD: 8 SERVINGS

REFRIGERATOR PICKLES

8 cups sliced cucumbers
2 tablespoons salt
Ice cubes
1 cup white or cider vinegar
2 cups sugar
1 tablespoon celery seeds

1 tablespoon dill weed
Pepper to taste
2 cups sliced onions
1 green bell pepper, sliced
1 red bell pepper, sliced

Soak the cucumbers in salt and ice cubes in a large bowl for at least 2 hours; drain thoroughly. Heat the vinegar and sugar in a saucepan until the sugar is dissolved. Add the celery seeds, dill weed and pepper. Combine the cucumbers, onions and bell peppers in a large bowl. Cover with the vinegar mixture. Pack into sterilized jars and store in the refrigerator.

YIELD: 16 SERVINGS

SHAKE PICKLES

Cucumbers, thinly sliced
4 to 8 onions, thinly sliced
3¹/₂ cups sugar
3 cups cider vinegar
¹/₃ cup kosher salt

1 teaspoon alum
1 teaspoon celery seeds
1 teaspoon mustard seeds
1 teaspoon turmeric

Alternate layers of cucumbers and onions in a widemouthed 1-gallon jar until full. Combine the sugar, vinegar, kosher salt, alum, celery seeds, mustard seeds and turmeric in a saucepan. Cook for 20 minutes. Pour over the cucumbers and onions. Cover with the lid. Refrigerate for 1 week before serving, shaking the jar twice a day.

YIELD: 1 GALLON

CRANBERRY SALSA

1 (16-ounce) package fresh
   cranberries
1 orange, peeled, chopped
Grated zest of 1 orange

Juice of ¹/₂ lime
1 scallion, chopped
1 tablespoon chopped cilantro
¹/₂ jalapeño chile, finely chopped

Cook the cranberries using the package directions; drain. Combine the cranberries, orange, orange zest, lime juice, scallion, cilantro and jalapeño chile in a large bowl and mix well. Chill, covered, for 8 to 12 hours to blend the flavors.

YIELD: 12 SERVINGS

CRANBERRIES

Extremely tart when uncooked, cranberries are usually sweetened when made into juice, sauces, relishes, and desserts. When selecting cranberries, look for ones that are shiny, smooth, and firm. To clean, rinse the berries thoroughly, discarding any that are soft, shriveled, or discolored. Cook only until they pop, since overcooking will result in bitter, mushy berries.

PINEAPPLE AVOCADO SALSA

1 cup ($^1/_4$-inch pieces) chopped fresh pineapple
2 small tomatoes, cut into $^1/_4$-inch pieces
1 firm ripe avocado, cut into $^1/_4$-inch pieces
$1^1/_2$ teaspoons minced jalapeño chile
$^1/_2$ cup chopped fresh cilantro
$^1/_4$ cup chopped red onion
3 tablespoons fresh orange juice
3 tablespoons fresh lime juice
2 tablespoons extra-virgin olive oil
Salt and pepper to taste

Combine the pineapple, tomatoes, avocado, jalapeño chile, cilantro, onion, orange juice, lime juice, olive oil, salt and pepper in a container and mix well. Chill, covered, for at least 1 hour before serving.

Note: Use rubber gloves when mincing the jalapeño chile.

YIELD: 2½ CUPS

Kiwifruit, mango, or papaya may be substituted for the pineapple, or try a combination of several tropical fruits.

CHERIMOYA

Cherimoyas look like a cross between an avocado and a pinecone, light green, thin-skinned, and covered with scale-like indentations. They range in size from four to eight inches long and two to four inches wide and are conical or heart-shaped. Inside you'll find fragrant, sweet, white pulp with a custard-like texture. Cherimoyas are fragile and will begin to deteriorate soon after ripening, so handle gently and eat promptly.

STRAWBERRY SALSA

1 jalapeño chile
1 cup finely chopped strawberries
1/4 cup finely chopped white onion
2 tablespoons finely chopped cilantro
1/2 teaspoon fresh lime juice
1/2 teaspoon sugar
1/4 teaspoon salt

Remove the stems, seeds and veins from the jalapeño chile wearing rubber gloves. Chop the jalapeño chile finely. Combine with the strawberries, onion, cilantro, lime juice, sugar and salt in a bowl and mix well. Serve immediately or chill, covered, for several hours before serving.

YIELD: 1½ CUPS

JALAPEÑOS
(HAH-LAH-PEH-NYOH)

These fiery favorites are named after Jalapa, the capital of Veracruz, Mexico. Dark green, but red when ripe, the chiles are smooth-skinned with a rounded tip and measure about two inches in length. They range from hot to very hot, especially the seeds and veins. Jalapeños that are slow roasted over a fire are known as *chipotles,* which have a rich, smoky flavor.

THREE-MELON SALSA

¹/₂ cup (¹/₂-inch pieces) cantaloupe
¹/₂ cup (¹/₂-inch pieces) honeydew melon
¹/₂ cup (¹/₂-inch pieces) watermelon
¹/₂ cup unseasoned rice vinegar
¹/₂ cup (¹/₂-inch pieces) red bell pepper
1 jalapeño chile, deveined, seeded, minced
¹/₂ cup chopped fresh cilantro
¹/₄ cup vegetable oil
Salt and pepper to taste

Combine the cantaloupe, honeydew melon, watermelon, rice vinegar, bell pepper, jalapeño chile, cilantro, oil, salt and pepper in a bowl and toss to mix well.

YIELD: ABOUT 3 CUPS

RICE VINEGAR

Both Japanese and Chinese rice vinegars are made from fermented rice and are slightly milder than most Western vinegars. *White* rice vinegar is used mainly in sweet-and-sour dishes, while *red* is popular on shellfish, and *black* is used predominately as a table condiment.

OLÉ SALSA

4 or 5 yellow chiles
1 garlic clove, minced
1/2 yellow onion, finely chopped
3/4 cup chopped fresh cilantro

2 1/4 cups chopped peeled
  tomatoes
Salt and pepper to taste

Remove the ends of the chiles wearing rubber gloves. Remove the veins and seeds, reserving the seeds from 1 chile. Chop the chiles finely. Combine the chiles, reserved chile seeds, garlic, onion, cilantro, tomatoes, salt and pepper in a bowl and mix well. Chill, covered, for 4 to 6 hours to allow the flavors to blend.

Note: Peel tomatoes by placing in boiling water for about 10 to 15 seconds. The peels will come off easily.

YIELD: ABOUT 3 CUPS

SISSY SALSA

3 (14-ounce) cans diced
  unseasoned tomatoes, drained
4 or 5 scallions, thinly sliced
1/3 cup minced onion
2 tablespoons chopped fresh
  parsley

1 garlic clove, minced
1/2 teaspoon salt
3 tablespoons red wine vinegar
1 tablespoon fresh lime juice
1 tablespoon light olive oil

Combine the tomatoes, scallions, onion, parsley, garlic, salt, red wine vinegar, lime juice and olive oil in a bowl and mix well. Process 1/2 of the mixture in a food processor until of a sauce consistency. Return to the bowl and mix well.

Note: If the tomatoes are too chunky, you may want to process in a food processor lightly.

YIELD: ABOUT 3 CUPS

CHILES

There are hundreds of varieties of chile peppers, ranging from the mild Anaheim to the exceptionally hot habanero. Generally, the larger the chile the milder the taste, since smaller ones have a greater concentration of seeds and membranes containing the fiery compound, capsaicin. Capsaicin can seriously irritate skin and eyes, so it's advisable to wear rubber gloves while handling chiles, and be careful not to rub your eyes.

SAVOR THE FRESHNESS

salads and dressings

CANDIED WALNUT SALAD
WITH GOAT CHEESE

POPPY SEED FRUIT SALAD

CHICKEN ALMOND SALAD

AVOCADO FESTIVAL SALAD

SANTA YNEZ RICE SALAD

NEW POTATO AND
GREEN BEAN SALAD

(shown left to right)

Shoreline Bluffs, Goleta Beach   *Photograph © David Muench*

POPPY SEED FRUIT SALAD

Photograph for this recipe is shown on page 98.

1 (20-ounce) can pineapple chunks	2 bananas, sliced
1 orange, peeled, sectioned	1/4 teaspoon grated lime zest
1 kiwifruit, peeled, sliced	2 tablespoons lime juice
1 cup red or green seedless grapes	1 tablespoon honey
1 cup quartered strawberries	1 teaspoon poppy seeds

Drain the pineapple, reserving the juice. Combine the pineapple, orange, kiwifruit, grapes, strawberries and bananas in a large bowl and toss to mix well. Mix the reserved pineapple juice, lime zest, lime juice, honey and poppy seeds in a small bowl until blended. Pour over the fruit and toss to coat.

YIELD: 4 SERVINGS

WHITE CHOCOLATE AND FRUIT SALAD

1 cup whipping cream	5 ounces (about) dried apricots,
2 egg yolks	chopped
3 tablespoons sugar	1/2 cup chopped white chocolate
1 teaspoon vanilla extract	2/3 cup shelled pistachios or
1 pint raspberries	unsalted macadamia nuts
1 pint strawberries	
2 or 3 sliced peaches or other fruit	
such as plums, grapes,	
cherimoya, orange and kiwifruit	

Heat the cream in a saucepan until it comes to a boil. Beat the egg yolks and sugar in a bowl. Add the hot cream gradually, whisking constantly. Return to the saucepan. Cook over low heat until slightly thickened, stirring constantly. Stir in the vanilla. Remove from the heat to cool. Pour into a bowl. Chill, covered, in the refrigerator.

Layer the raspberries, strawberries and peaches in a large glass bowl. Sprinkle with the apricots, white chocolate and pistachios. Serve with the cream custard on the side, or toss with the fruit just before serving.

YIELD: 6 SERVINGS

Mandarin Orange and Bibb Lettuce Salad

1 or 2 heads Bibb lettuce, rinsed, drained
1 (10-ounce) can mandarin oranges, chilled, drained
1 avocado, chopped
1 red onion, sliced, separated into rings
1 cup bean sprouts
Vinaigrette (below)
1/2 cup coarsely chopped cashews

Tear the lettuce into pieces and place in a salad bowl. Add the mandarin oranges, avocado, red onion and bean sprouts. Add the Vinaigrette just before serving and toss to coat. Sprinkle with the cashews.

Note: You may add bay shrimp or chopped cooked chicken to make this a main dish salad.

YIELD: 6 TO 10 SERVINGS

Vinaigrette

6 tablespoons olive oil
2 tablespoons red wine vinegar
1 teaspoon Dijon mustard
Salt and freshly ground pepper to taste

Combine the olive oil, red wine vinegar, Dijon mustard, salt and pepper in a jar with a lid. Shake, covered, until blended.

RED, WHITE AND GINGERED GREENS

2 tablespoons sugar
12 ounces macadamia nuts
2 tablespoons water
3 egg yolks
1/3 cup finely chopped fresh gingerroot
2 tablespoons soy sauce
2 tablespoons rice vinegar
1 teaspoon sesame oil
3/4 cup honey
1 teaspoon salt
1 tablespoon Dijon mustard
2 jalapeño chiles, seeded, chopped
1 1/2 cups vegetable oil
2 tablespoons water
1/4 cup lemon juice
2 pounds mixed seasonal salad greens
1 cup dried cranberries

Heat the sugar in a skillet over medium-high heat until golden brown, stirring constantly. Add the macadamia nuts and 2 tablespoons water. Cook until the macadamia nuts are coated with sugar and the water evaporates. Remove from the heat. Cool to room temperature.

Blend the egg yolks, gingerroot and soy sauce in a blender or food processor for 10 seconds. Add the rice vinegar, sesame oil, honey, salt, Dijon mustard and jalapeño chiles. Add the vegetable oil gradually, processing constantly at low speed until the mixture begins to thicken. Add 2 tablespoons water and the lemon juice and blend well. Chill, covered, for at least 10 minutes.

Combine the salad greens, cranberries and sugar-coated macadamia nuts in a large salad bowl. Add the dressing just before serving and toss to coat.

YIELD: 8 SERVINGS

GINGER

To keep gingerroot fresh, cut the gingerroot into small pieces and place them in a glass jar with a little dry sherry. Cover the jar and refrigerate. To freeze gingerroot, slice, wrap in foil, and freeze for up to two weeks. For a delicate hint of flavor, squeeze thin slices of gingerroot through a garlic press.

STRAWBERRY SPINACH SALAD

1/2 cup sugar	1 tablespoon poppy seeds
1/2 cup vegetable oil	1 1/2 tablespoons minced red onion
1/4 cup cider vinegar	2 bunches spinach, trimmed
1/4 teaspoon Worcestershire sauce	2 cups sliced strawberries
2 tablespoons sesame seeds, toasted	1/2 cup roasted sunflower seeds

Dissolve the sugar in the oil, cider vinegar and Worcestershire sauce in a bowl. Add the sesame seeds, poppy seeds and red onion and mix well.

Rinse the spinach and pat dry. Tear into bite-size pieces. Combine the spinach, strawberries and sunflower seeds in a salad bowl. Add the dressing just before serving and toss to coat.

YIELD: 8 SERVINGS

CHUTNEY SPINACH SALAD

3/4 cup mango chutney	8 cups baby spinach
1/4 cup olive oil	3 red apples, thinly sliced
3 tablespoons white wine vinegar	1/2 cup crumbled feta cheese
1/8 teaspoon dry mustard	1/2 cup pecans, chopped
1/8 teaspoon salt	

Combine the chutney, olive oil, vinegar, dry mustard and salt in a small bowl and mix well. Combine the spinach and apples in a large salad bowl. Add the dressing and toss to coat. Sprinkle with the cheese and pecans.

YIELD: 6 SERVINGS

For that extra special flavor, use the recipe for Peach and Mango Chutney on page 89.

CANDIED WALNUT SALAD WITH GOAT CHEESE

Photograph for this recipe is shown on page 98.

5 cups baby lettuce greens
1¹/₂ cups torn arugula leaves
1 small red bell pepper, seeded, julienned
³/₄ cup Candied Walnuts (below)

Herb and Walnut Oil Salad Dressing (below)
1¹/₂ ounces soft goat cheese, crumbled

Rinse the lettuce and pat dry. Combine the lettuce, arugula, bell pepper and Candied Walnuts in a large salad bowl. Add just enough Herb and Walnut Oil Salad Dressing to lightly coat the lettuce. Add the goat cheese and toss to mix. Serve immediately.

YIELD: 4 TO 6 SERVINGS

CANDIED WALNUTS

4 cups walnut halves
¹/₄ cup honey

Grated zest of 1 orange

Combine the walnut halves, honey and orange zest in a bowl and toss well. Spread on a baking sheet. Bake at 375 degrees for 25 to 30 minutes or until golden brown. Remove from the oven. Let stand until cool, stirring frequently. Store in a sealable plastic freezer bag in the freezer.

HERB AND WALNUT OIL SALAD DRESSING

1 shallot, chopped
2 garlic cloves, chopped
2 tablespoons minced fresh gingerroot
2 tablespoons chopped fresh cilantro or basil

¹/₄ cup walnut oil
3 tablespoons balsamic vinegar
2 tablespoons soy sauce
2 tablespoons white wine
Salt and freshly ground pepper to taste

Process the shallot, garlic, gingerroot, cilantro, walnut oil, vinegar, soy sauce, wine, salt and pepper in a blender. Adjust the seasonings. Chill, covered, for up to 8 hours before serving.

SPINACH

Young, tender spinach will have slender, flexible stems and crisp, bright green leaves. Store fresh spinach in the refrigerator in dry plastic bags and keep away from apples, melons, and tomatoes, which accelerate yellowing. To clean spinach, gently wash in a basin of cold water and drain in a colander. Repeat if any of the leaves feel gritty.

HOLIDAY SPINACH SALAD

2 bunches fresh spinach leaves
1 ripe avocado, thinly sliced
1½ cups thinly sliced mushrooms
Seeds from 1 medium pomegranate
½ cup coarsely chopped cashews

3 slices bacon
¼ cup packed brown sugar
½ cup cider vinegar
⅓ cup olive oil
Freshly ground pepper to taste

Trim the spinach. Rinse and pat dry. Tear into bite-size pieces. Combine the spinach, avocado, mushrooms and pomegranate seeds in a large bowl and toss to mix. Toast the cashews in a large skillet over high heat for 1 to 1½ minutes, tossing and shaking constantly. Sprinkle over the salad. Add the bacon to the skillet. Fry until the bacon is crisp. Remove the bacon to paper towels to drain. Drain the skillet, reserving 1 tablespoon drippings. Add the brown sugar, vinegar, olive oil and pepper to the reserved drippings and mix well. Cook over medium heat until the sugar is dissolved, stirring occasionally. Crumble the bacon over the salad. Add the hot dressing and toss to coat. Serve immediately.

YIELD: 6 SERVINGS

SUMPTUOUS SALAD

Photograph for this recipe is shown on page 150 and facing page.

1½ heads romaine, torn
1 (10-ounce) can cashews
6 Braeburn apples, peeled, chopped
1 (6-ounce) package dried cranberries

1 red onion, finely chopped
1 (6-ounce) package seasoned croutons
Poppy Seed Dressing (page 123)
Freshly grated Parmesan cheese to taste

Combine the romaine, cashews, apples, dried cranberries and red onion in a large salad bowl and toss to mix well. Add the croutons and Poppy Seed Dressing and toss to coat just before serving. Sprinkle with the cheese.

YIELD: 8 SERVINGS

AVOCADO FESTIVAL SALAD

Photograph for this recipe is shown on page 98.

- **1/4 cup chili sauce**
- **1/4 cup water**
- **2 tablespoons cider vinegar**
- **1/4 cup (1/2 stick) butter**
- **1/4 cup packed brown sugar**
- **1 teaspoon Worcestershire sauce**
- **1/4 teaspoon Tabasco sauce**
- **2 ripe avocados**
- **Lemon juice**
- **Butter lettuce leaves**
- **6 slices bacon, crisp-cooked, crumbled**

Combine the chili sauce, water, vinegar, butter, brown sugar, Worcestershire sauce and Tabasco sauce in a double boiler. Heat over boiling water until the brown sugar is completely dissolved.

Peel the avocados. Cut into halves, discarding the pits. Sprinkle the avocado halves with lemon juice. Arrange on butter lettuce-lined salad plates. Spoon the warm dressing over the top. Sprinkle with the crumbled bacon.

YIELD: 4 SERVINGS

CALIFORNIA AVOCADO FESTIVAL

In the mood for avocado ice cream? It's just one of the many treats in store for you at the California Avocado Festival. Held every October since 1984 in Carpenteria, a city twelve miles southeast of Santa Barbara, the festival offers three days of fabulous food, lively music, original crafts, and family fun.

Since Santa Barbara County is the third largest avocado producer in North America, the festival is an appropriate way to celebrate.

SOUTHWESTERN CAESAR SALAD

David Michael Cane, Host of "A Matter of Taste," Talk America Radio Networks

1 egg
4 or 5 garlic cloves, crushed
1/2 cup extra-virgin olive oil
2 tablespoons capers, drained
1 jalapeño chile, pickled or roasted, finely chopped
1 teaspoon kosher salt
1 teaspoon Dijon mustard
1 tablespoon fresh lemon juice
1/2 teaspoon Worcestershire sauce
1 tablespoon red wine vinegar
2 tablespoons balsamic vinegar
2 heads romaine, trimmed, or 3 hearts of romaine
1/2 cup coarsely chopped cilantro
Freshly ground pepper to taste
1/2 cup grated Parmesan cheese
1 cup croutons
1/2 lime

Boil the egg in water to cover in a saucepan for 1 minute; drain. Season a salad bowl with the garlic and then discard. Add the olive oil, capers and jalapeño chile and mash against the side of the bowl. Separate the egg, discarding the egg white. Add the egg yolk, kosher salt and Dijon mustard to the bowl and mix well. Add the lemon juice, Worcestershire sauce, red wine vinegar and balsamic vinegar and mix well. Tear the romaine into bite-size pieces. Add the romaine and cilantro to the bowl and toss to coat. Sprinkle with pepper. Add the cheese and croutons. Squeeze the lime over the salad just before serving. Toss the salad and serve.

YIELD: 4 TO 6 SERVINGS

SUMMERTIME SALAD

¹/₄ cup finely chopped green bell pepper
¹/₄ cup finely chopped cucumber
2 teaspoons minced onion
1 cup sour cream
¹/₂ cup mayonnaise
1 tablespoon tarragon vinegar
1 tablespoon sugar
1 teaspoon salt
¹/₂ teaspoon pepper
1 garlic clove, minced
1 tablespoon butter
¹/₂ cup sesame seeds
¹/₃ cup grated Parmesan cheese
Assorted varieties of lettuce

Combine the bell pepper, cucumber, onion, sour cream, mayonnaise, vinegar, sugar, salt, pepper and garlic in a bowl and mix well. Chill, covered, in the refrigerator.

Melt the butter in a baking pan. Spread the sesame seeds and cheese in the butter. Bake at 350 degrees until brown, stirring frequently. Remove from the oven to cool.

Tear the lettuce into bite-size pieces and place in a salad bowl. Pour the dressing over the lettuce mixture and toss to coat. Sprinkle with the sesame seed mixture and toss to mix.

YIELD: 8 SERVINGS

BELGIAN ENDIVE

Belgian endive is grown in total darkness to prevent the creamy white leaves from turning green. There are two other types of endive—curly endive and escarole. Belgian endive is distinguished by a small, cigar-shaped head of tightly packed leaves, which are crunchy and slightly bitter. Although mainly used in salads or as edible scoops for dips, Belgian endive can also be an exotic side dish when baked or braised.

salads and dressings

WATERCRESS AND HEARTS OF PALM SALAD

HEARTS OF PALM

The inner portion of
the stem of the
cabbage palm tree is
where you'll find the
edible heart of the
palm. The tree grows
in tropical climates,
including Florida, where
it is the official state
tree. Hearts of palm
are slender, smooth-
textured, delicately
flavored stalks that
resemble white
asparagus. You'll find
fresh hearts only in
regions where they
are grown, so look for
canned ones packed
in water.

1 (14-ounce) can hearts of palm
3 bunches watercress, rinsed,
    trimmed
1¹/₂ pounds fresh mushrooms,
    sliced
5 ounces sliced almonds, toasted
²/₃ cup vegetable oil
¹/₃ cup cider vinegar

2 teaspoons sugar
1 teaspoon salt
1 tablespoon drained capers
2 tablespoons grated onion
1¹/₂ teaspoons parsley flakes
1 hard-cooked egg, finely chopped
Dash of red pepper

Drain the hearts of palm. Cut into slices ¼ inch thick. Combine the watercress, mushrooms, hearts of palm and almonds in a large salad bowl and toss to mix.

Combine the oil, vinegar, sugar, salt, capers, onion, parsley, egg and red pepper in a bowl and whisk to mix. Pour over the salad and toss to coat just before serving.

YIELD: 10 SERVINGS

RICE TACO SALAD

1 pound ground beef
¹/₂ onion, finely chopped
1 garlic clove, minced
¹/₂ teaspoon salt
¹/₄ teaspoon pepper
¹/₂ teaspoon cumin
2 cups cooked white rice

¹/₂ head lettuce, shredded
2 tomatoes, coarsely chopped
¹/₂ cup (2 ounces) shredded
    Cheddar cheese
1 large avocado, chopped
¹/₄ cup sour cream

Brown the ground beef in a large skillet over medium heat, stirring until crumbly. Add the onion and garlic. Cook until the onion is tender but not brown; drain. Add the salt, pepper, cumin and rice and mix well. Remove from the heat to cool.

Combine the lettuce, tomatoes, cheese, avocado and ground beef mixture in a large bowl. Add the sour cream and toss lightly to coat. Serve immediately with picante sauce and corn chips.

YIELD: 6 SERVINGS

BEEF SALAD WITH BLEU CHEESE AND ANCHOVY DRESSING

1/2 teaspoon minced garlic

4 anchovy fillets

1 tablespoon Dijon mustard

2 tablespoons red wine vinegar or balsamic vinegar

1 tablespoon chopped fresh oregano, or
    1 teaspoon dried oregano

1/2 teaspoon freshly ground pepper

1/3 cup extra-virgin olive oil

1 large head romaine, torn or chopped into small pieces

4 ounces bleu cheese, crumbled

8 to 16 ounces cooked steak or roast beef,
    cut into 1/4×1-inch pieces

Chopped scallions or chives

Process the garlic and anchovies in a food processor or blender to form a paste. Add the Dijon mustard, vinegar, oregano and pepper. Add the olive oil in a fine stream, processing constantly to form a creamy dressing. Combine the romaine and bleu cheese in a salad bowl and toss to mix. Add the dressing and toss to coat. Layer the beef over the top. Sprinkle with the scallions.

YIELD: 4 TO 6 SERVINGS

ANCHOVIES

Anchovy fillets too salty for your taste? Try soaking them in cool water or milk for ten to twenty minutes. Then drain and pat dry. Anchovy paste, found in the gourmet or canned fish section of the supermarket, is a convenient way to add flavor to your food. One-half teaspoon is the equivalent of one anchovy fillet. To store anchovies, add a little olive oil, cover, and refrigerate.

Warm Goat Cheese and Chicken Salad

4 boneless skinless chicken breasts
Kosher salt and freshly ground pepper to taste
2 tablespoons olive oil
4 garlic cloves
1/4 cup pinot blanc
Snipped fresh thyme to taste
8 ounces fresh goat cheese
2 packages mixed baby salad greens
1/4 cup slivered almonds, toasted
Dijon vinaigrette

Season the chicken with kosher salt and pepper. Heat the olive oil in a large sauté pan. Add the garlic cloves. Sauté until soft, watching carefully to prevent burning. Add the wine, chicken and thyme. Sauté over medium-low heat until the chicken is cooked through.

Arrange the chicken in a baking dish, discarding the garlic and thyme. Cut the goat cheese into four 2-ounce rounds. Arrange on top of each chicken breast. Bake at 325 degrees until the cheese melts.

Arrange the baby salad greens on individual serving plates. Top each with a cheese-smothered chicken breast. Sprinkle with the toasted almonds. Serve with your favorite Dijon vinaigrette. Garnish with sprigs of fresh thyme.

YIELD: 4 SERVINGS

 Enjoy with pinot blanc or pinot grigio.

CHICKEN ALMOND SALAD

Photograph for this recipe is shown on page 98.

1/4 cup dried currants or cranberries	**1 apple, chopped**
1/2 head leaf lettuce, torn into bite-size pieces	**1/2 cup crumbled bleu cheese**
1/2 head romaine, torn into bite-size pieces	**3 boneless skinless chicken breasts, cooked, shredded**
1 cup chopped celery	**1 avocado, cut into chunks (optional)**
4 scallions, thinly sliced	**Candied Almonds (below)**
1 (11-ounce) can mandarin oranges, drained	**Vinaigrette (below)**

Plump the currants in boiling water to cover in a bowl; drain. Combine the leaf lettuce, romaine, celery, scallions, mandarin oranges, apple, bleu cheese, chicken and avocado in a large salad bowl. Add the Candied Almonds and toss to mix. Pour the Vinaigrette over the salad mixture and toss to coat.

YIELD: 8 SERVINGS

 Pair this delicious luncheon salad with a sauvignon blanc or riesling.

CANDIED ALMONDS

1/2 cup slivered almonds	**3 tablespoons sugar**

Combine the almonds and sugar in a nonstick skillet. Cook over medium-low heat until the sugar is melted and the almonds are coated. Do not let the sugar burn. Spread on foil to cool.

VINAIGRETTE

1/4 cup vegetable oil	**1 tablespoon chopped fresh parsley**
3 tablespoons white wine vinegar	**1/2 teaspoon salt**
2 tablespoons sugar	**1/2 teaspoon pepper**

Combine the oil, vinegar, sugar, parsley, salt and pepper in a bowl and whisk to blend.

SCALLIONS

A scallion is an immature onion with a white base (not fully developed into a bulb) and long, straight green leaves. Scallions, or green onions as they are sometimes called, are cousins to leeks, shallots, and chives, and are somewhat milder than mature onions. Enjoy scallions uncooked or cooked year-round, although the peak seasons are spring and summer.

CUCUMBER AND CRAB MEAT SALAD

PEPPERCORNS

Peppercorns are the berries grown on a vine, and they are sold whole or ground into a spice. The most pungent are the *black peppercorns*, which are picked slightly underripe and dried. *White peppercorns* are fully ripened berries that have been soaked until the black shell comes off. Unripened peppercorns are *green* and have a somewhat sharp taste.

1 (6-ounce) can crab meat
2 medium cucumbers
1/4 cup canola oil
1/2 teaspoon sesame oil
1 tablespoon tarragon vinegar
1 tablespoon sugar
1/4 teaspoon salt
1/8 teaspoon pepper
1 scallion, cut into 1/2-inch lengths, julienned
1 tablespoon slivered almonds, toasted
1 teaspoon sesame seeds, toasted
Butter lettuce leaves

Drain the crab meat well to remove all of the liquid. Peel the cucumbers and cut into halves lengthwise. Remove the seeds. Cut diagonally into thin slices. Pat dry with a paper towel if necessary.

Combine the canola oil, sesame oil, vinegar, sugar, salt and pepper in a bowl and whisk to blend well.

Flake the crab meat into a large bowl. Add the cucumbers, scallion, almonds and sesame seeds. Pour a small amount of the dressing over the salad to moisten and mix gently. Chill, covered, for 1 hour.

Trim the butter lettuce leaves. Rinse and pat dry. Arrange on individual salad plates. Spoon the salad onto the lettuce leaves. Drizzle the remaining dressing over the edges of the lettuce leaves.

YIELD: 4 TO 6 SERVINGS

WARM SCALLOP SALAD AND CHAMPAGNE BEURRE BLANC

Eric Widmer, Chef, La Cumbre Country Club

2 tablespoons minced shallots

³/₄ cup Champagne

1 cup (2 sticks) butter, cut into small pieces

12 (10- to 20-count) scallops

Salt to taste

2 tablespoons olive oil

4 ounces button mushrooms, cut into quarters

White portion of ¹/₂ leek, sliced

1 tomato, peeled, seeded, chopped

1 garlic clove, minced

2 tablespoons rice vinegar

White pepper to taste

6 tablespoons olive oil

6 cups mixed salad greens

Combine the shallots and Champagne in a saucepan. Cook until reduced to *sec* (French for dry). Whisk in the butter 1 piece at a time.

Season the scallops with salt. Sauté in 2 tablespoons olive oil in a skillet until brown. Remove the scallops from the skillet. Add the mushrooms to the skillet. Sauté until golden brown. Add the leek and tomato. Drain any excess liquid. Add the butter sauce and scallops. Simmer for 2 to 3 minutes or until the scallops are tender.

Combine the garlic, vinegar, salt and white pepper in a bowl. Whisk in 6 tablespoons olive oil. Pour over the mixed salad greens in a salad bowl and toss to mix gently.

Arrange the scallops on individual salad plates. Pour the sauce over the scallops. Distribute the salad greens evenly on the plates. Serve immediately.

YIELD: 4 SERVINGS

GREEK PALAKA SALAD

FETA CHEESE (FEHT-UH)

Feta, a classic Greek cheese, is traditionally made from goat's or sheep's milk, but is often produced from cow's milk. Feta is cured and stored in its own salty brine and is distinguished by its strong, tangy flavor. The white, crumbly, rindless cheese is usually pressed into square blocks, but is also marketed loose in small plastic containers.

1 envelope Italian salad dressing mix
15 kalamata olives, drained, juice reserved
Grapeseed oil or garlic-flavored olive oil
1 (15-ounce) can artichokes, drained, cut into quarters
2 cucumbers, peeled
6 Roma tomatoes
1 medium red onion, coarsely chopped
1 (8-ounce) can red beans, drained
6 to 8 fresh basil leaves, finely chopped
8 ounces feta cheese with basil and tomato, crumbled

Prepare the salad dressing mix using the package directions, substituting juice from the olives for the water and grapeseed oil for the vegetable oil. Pour over the artichokes in a bowl. Marinate, covered, for 8 to 12 hours.

Cut the cucumbers and tomatoes into ¼- to ½-inch pieces. Combine the cucumbers, tomatoes, onion, red beans, olives, basil and feta cheese in a large salad bowl and toss to mix. Add the marinated artichokes and toss to mix.

YIELD: 6 TO 8 SERVINGS

Pita bread stuffed with this salad makes great and healthy sandwiches.

ALMOND BROCCOLI SALAD

4 cups finely chopped fresh
 broccoli
1 cup chopped celery
1 cup red seedless grapes
1 cup green seedless grapes
8 slices bacon, crisp-cooked,
 crumbled

$^1/_2$ cup sliced scallions
1 cup mayonnaise
$^1/_4$ cup sugar
2 tablespoons cider vinegar
$^1/_2$ teaspoon pepper
$^1/_2$ teaspoon curry powder
$^2/_3$ cup slivered almonds, toasted

Combine the broccoli, celery, red grapes, green grapes, bacon and scallions in a large salad bowl and toss to mix. Mix the mayonnaise, sugar, vinegar, pepper and curry powder in a small bowl. Add to the broccoli mixture and toss to coat. Sprinkle with the almonds just before serving.

YIELD: 8 SERVINGS

Substitute dried cranberries or raisins for the grapes and sunflower seeds for the toasted almonds.

ASIAN SALAD WITH ALMONDS AND TOFU

1 head bok choy or napa cabbage,
 coarsely chopped
1 cup snow peas, trimmed
1 bunch scallions, chopped
2 ribs celery, chopped
1 red bell pepper, chopped
1 jalapeño chile, seeded, chopped
1 (8-ounce) can sliced water
 chestnuts, drained
$^1/_4$ cup chopped almonds, toasted

2 tablespoons sesame seeds,
 toasted
8 ounces smoked or firm tofu,
 drained, chopped
$^1/_4$ cup chopped fresh cilantro
2 tablespoons rice wine vinegar
$1^1/_2$ teaspoons toasted sesame oil
$1^1/_2$ teaspoons tamari or soy sauce
1 tablespoon canola oil

Combine the bok choy, snow peas, scallions, celery, bell pepper and jalapeño chile in a steamer. Steam for 3 to 5 minutes; drain. Plunge immediately into cold water; drain. Combine the steamed vegetables, water chestnuts, almonds, sesame seeds, tofu and cilantro in a large salad bowl and toss to mix. Blend the vinegar, sesame oil, tamari and canola oil in a small bowl. Pour over the salad and toss to coat.

YIELD: 6 SERVINGS

BROCCOLI

Broccoli is a hardy member of the mustard family and the top crop of Santa Barbara County. The quicker you cook the vegetable, the greener it will remain. To blanch broccoli, parboil for a few minutes and immediately plunge into ice water to stop the cooking process and retain the rich color.

PICNIC COLESLAW

10 cups shredded green cabbage (about 1 head)	1 teaspoon dry mustard
	2 teaspoons sugar
1 large green bell pepper, thinly sliced	1 teaspoon celery seeds
	1 tablespoon salt
2 medium Spanish onions, thinly sliced	1 cup white vinegar
	$3/4$ cup vegetable oil
1 cup sugar	

Layer the cabbage, bell pepper and onions in a large salad bowl. Sprinkle with 1 cup sugar. Combine the dry mustard, 2 teaspoons sugar, celery seeds, salt, vinegar and oil in a saucepan and mix well. Bring to a boil, stirring constantly. Pour over the vegetable layers. Chill, covered, for 4 to 12 hours. Toss the coleslaw to mix just before serving.

YIELD: 12 SERVINGS

NEW POTATO AND GREEN BEAN SALAD

Photograph for this recipe is shown on page 98.

$1/4$ cup balsamic vinegar	Salt and pepper to taste
2 tablespoons Dijon mustard	$1 1/2$ pounds small red potatoes
2 tablespoons fresh lemon juice	12 ounces green beans, trimmed
1 garlic clove, minced	1 small red onion, coarsely chopped
Dash of Worcestershire sauce	
$1/2$ cup extra-virgin olive oil	$1/4$ cup chopped fresh basil

Whisk the vinegar, Dijon mustard, lemon juice, garlic and Worcestershire sauce in a medium bowl. Add the olive oil gradually, whisking constantly. Season with salt and pepper. The dressing may be prepared 1 day ahead. Cover and refrigerate. Bring to room temperature and whisk before using.

Steam the potatoes in a steamer until tender. Cool and cut into quarters. Cook the green beans in boiling salted water in a large saucepan for 5 minutes or until tender; drain. Plunge immediately into a bowl of ice water to cool; drain. Cut the green beans into halves. Combine the green beans, potatoes, onion and basil in a large bowl. Add the dressing and toss to coat. Season with salt and pepper. Serve immediately, or cover and let stand at room temperature for up to 4 hours before serving.

YIELD: 6 SERVINGS

BLEU CHEESE POTATO SALAD

5 pounds red potatoes	**2¹/₂ tablespoons Dijon mustard**
¹/₂ cup dry white wine	**2¹/₂ tablespoons cider vinegar**
Salt and pepper to taste	**8 ounces bleu cheese, crumbled**
1¹/₄ cups mayonnaise	**5 scallions, chopped**
1¹/₄ cups sour cream	**1¹/₂ cups chopped celery**

Boil the potatoes in water to cover in a saucepan until tender; drain. Cool until easy to handle. Peel the potatoes. Cut into 1-inch pieces. Combine the potatoes, wine, salt and pepper in a large bowl and toss to coat. Let stand until cool.

Combine the mayonnaise, sour cream, Dijon mustard, vinegar and bleu cheese in a small bowl and blend well. Stir in the scallions and celery. Add to the potato mixture and mix well. Adjust the seasonings to taste. Chill, covered, in the refrigerator. Bring to room temperature before serving.

YIELD: 10 TO 12 SERVINGS

VALLEY CUCUMBERS

Photograph for this recipe is shown on page 150.

2 large English cucumbers, or 4	**2 tablespoons snipped fresh**
cucumbers	**dill weed**
¹/₂ large white onion	**2 or 3 tablespoons sour cream, or**
1 tablespoon salt	**to taste**
¹/₂ cup apple cider vinegar	**1 tablespoon snipped fresh**
¹/₂ cup cold water	**dill weed**

Peel the cucumbers. Cut into very thin slices. Cut the onion into thin slices and separate into rings. Cut the rings into halves. Combine the cucumbers and onion in a deep bowl. Add the salt and toss to coat. Add the vinegar, water and 2 tablespoons dill weed and mix well. Place a plate over the top to keep the cucumbers weighted under the vinegar mixture. Chill, covered, for at least 3 hours.

Pour the cucumbers into a colander to drain. Squeeze out as much liquid from the cucumber mixture as possible. This is very important. The cucumbers will be wilted. Place the cucumber mixture in a serving bowl. Add the sour cream and mix well. Sprinkle with 1 tablespoon dill weed. Chill, covered, until ready to serve.

YIELD: 4 TO 6 SERVINGS

CUCUMBERS

The cucumber, a member of the gourd family, has been cultivated for thousands of years. The thin, green skin does not need to be peeled, unless it has been waxed. *English cucumbers* can grow up to two feet long and are usually sold wrapped in plastic. Since they are virtually seedless (seeds are the cause of indigestion), English cucumbers are also known as *Burpless*.

Pasta Salad Vinaigrette

8 ounces uncooked linguini	**1 cup sliced fresh mushrooms**
Vinaigrette (below)	**1/2 cup diagonally cut snow peas**
2 carrots, grated	**1/2 cup (or more) grated fresh**
1/2 cup finely chopped fresh parsley	**Parmesan cheese**

Break the linguini into thirds. Cook using the package directions; rinse and drain. Add the Vinaigrette and toss to coat. Let stand until cool. Add the carrots, parsley, mushrooms and snow peas. Add the cheese and toss to mix. Chill, covered, until ready to serve.

YIELD: 6 TO 8 SERVINGS

Vinaigrette

1/2 cup vegetable oil	**2 teaspoons salt**
5 tablespoons tarragon vinegar	**1 teaspoon white pepper**
Juice of 1/2 lemon	**1/2 teaspoon freshly ground black**
2 garlic cloves, minced	**pepper**
1 egg, lightly beaten	**1/2 teaspoon dry mustard**
1/2 cup light cream	**1/4 teaspoon sugar**

Combine the oil, vinegar, lemon juice, garlic, egg and cream in a bowl and beat well. Add the salt, white pepper, black pepper, dry mustard and sugar and mix well.

A dry chardonnay or a sauvignon blanc will pair nicely with this pasta salad.

SUMMER VEGETABLE SALAD

4 to 6 English cucumbers, sliced
3 tablespoons salt
1 medium bunch celery, sliced
4 medium carrots, sliced

1 yellow onion, thinly sliced
1/4 cup sugar
1 cup vinegar
1 pint cherry tomatoes

Arrange the cucumbers in a shallow pan. Sprinkle with the salt. Chill, covered, for 2 hours. Rinse the cucumbers. Drain and pat dry. Combine the cucumbers, celery, carrots and onion in a large salad bowl. Dissolve the sugar in the vinegar in a bowl. Add to the vegetable mixture and toss to coat. Chill, covered, until ready to serve. Add the cherry tomatoes and toss to mix just before serving. The salad may be stored in the refrigerator for 4 to 6 days.

YIELD: 6 SERVINGS

SHRIMP AND VEGETABLE PASTA SALAD

1¹/2 pounds large shrimp, cooked, peeled
8 ounces tri-color rotelle, cooked, drained
8 ounces fresh green beans, cooked
4 tomatoes, peeled, chopped
1 (2-ounce) can sliced black olives, drained

2 tablespoons thinly sliced scallions
1/2 cup slivered fresh basil
2 teaspoons minced garlic
Salt and freshly ground pepper to taste
3 tablespoons balsamic vinegar
1/4 cup extra-virgin olive oil
5 to 6 cups mixed salad greens

Combine the shrimp, pasta, green beans, tomatoes, black olives, scallions, basil and garlic in a large bowl and mix gently. Sprinkle with salt and pepper. Blend the vinegar and olive oil in a bowl. Pour over the shrimp mixture and toss to coat. Adjust the seasonings. Serve over the salad greens.

YIELD: 4 TO 6 SERVINGS

FARMERS MARKET

The Santa Barbara Farmers Market was listed as one of the "top ten" in California by *Sunset Magazine*. You'll find a wide selection of fresh vegetables, salad greens, fruits, nuts, honey, flowers, and even fresh eggs at any of the six area markets. You will also enjoy the soft sounds of live music as you stroll among the stalls.

WATERFRONT PASTA SALAD

32 ounces rigatoni
1 red onion, thinly sliced
1 green bell pepper, chopped
1 red bell pepper, chopped
1/2 cup chopped fresh cilantro or parsley
2 pounds cooked crab meat, flaked

1 (8-ounce) bottle Italian salad dressing
1 1/2 to 2 cups mayonnaise or mayonnaise-type salad dressing
Salt and freshly ground pepper to taste

Cook the pasta using the package directions; rinse and drain. Let stand until cool. Combine the onion, bell peppers, cilantro and crab meat in a large bowl and toss to mix. Add the salad dressing and mayonnaise and mix well. Add the pasta and toss to coat. Season with salt and pepper. Chill, covered, until ready to serve.

YIELD: 12 SERVINGS

 Serve either a chardonnay or fumé blanc to compliment this crab pasta salad.

SANTA YNEZ RICE SALAD

Photograph for this recipe is shown on page 98.

1 1/3 cups wild rice
3 cups water
1/4 teaspoon salt
1 tart apple, cut into 1-inch chunks
1/2 cup chopped red bell pepper
1/2 cup dried cranberries or currants

1/2 cup pecans, chopped
1/4 cup chopped red onion
2 tablespoons balsamic vinegar
2 tablespoons olive oil
1/2 teaspoon salt
1/4 teaspoon pepper

Rinse the rice. Place in a large saucepan with the water and 1/4 teaspoon salt. Bring to a boil and reduce the heat. Simmer, covered, for 35 minutes or until the rice is tender. Drain the rice and place in a large bowl. Add the apple, bell pepper, dried cranberries, pecans and onion.

Whisk the vinegar, olive oil, 1/2 teaspoon salt and pepper in a small bowl. Pour over the rice mixture and stir to mix well. Serve immediately or chill, covered, for up to 4 hours.

YIELD: 6 SERVINGS

RICE

For dry, fluffy rice, try this easy trick. After the rice cooks, place two paper towels under the lid and let stand for thirty minutes before serving. The paper towels will absorb the excess moisture and leave the rice light and fluffy. To keep the grains of rice bright white and separated, add a teaspoon of lemon juice to the water before cooking.

WILD RICE AND ORANGE SALAD

1 cup uncooked wild rice
2³/₄ cups chicken broth
2³/₄ cups water
1 cup pecan halves
Grated zest of 1 orange
1 (10-ounce) package frozen tiny
   peas, thawed

¹/₄ cup vegetable oil
¹/₃ cup fresh orange juice
1 teaspoon salt
Freshly ground pepper to taste

Rinse the rice in a strainer under cold running water. Combine the rice, broth and water in a saucepan. Bring to a boil and reduce the heat. Simmer for 35 to 45 minutes. The rice should not be too soft.

Combine the rice, pecans, orange zest, peas, oil, orange juice, salt and pepper in a bowl and toss to mix well. Let stand for 2 hours. Serve at room temperature.

YIELD: 6 SERVINGS

POPPY SEED DRESSING

¹/₃ cup honey
1 teaspoon salt
2 tablespoons white vinegar
1 tablespoon prepared mustard

³/₄ cup vegetable oil
1 tablespoon chopped scallions
2 or 3 teaspoons poppy seeds

Process the honey, salt, vinegar and prepared mustard in a blender. Add the oil gradually, processing constantly. Add the scallions and poppy seeds.

YIELD: 4 TO 6 SERVINGS

POPPY SEEDS

Tiny, round, and ranging from beige to bluish-black, poppy seeds add a satisfying crunch and slightly nutty taste to foods. They were cultivated by Egyptians as early as 1500 B.C. as a source of cooking oil. Yes, they come from the opium poppy, and no, they don't have narcotic properties. Try toasting the seeds for an enhanced flavor.

SAVOR
THE DISTINCTION

vegetables and side dishes

GARDEN VEGETABLE ROAST

APRICOT AND PINE NUT PILAF

FARFALLE WITH PROSCIUTTO,
SNOW PEAS AND ASPARAGUS

ROQUEFORT SCALLOPED POTATOES

SESAME ASPARAGUS

(shown left to right)

Photograph © Michael Brown

Old Mission *Photograph © David Muench*

SESAME ASPARAGUS

Photograph for this recipe is shown on page 124.

8 ounces fresh asparagus, trimmed
4 teaspoons sesame oil
4 teaspoons sugar
2 teaspoons vinegar

2 teaspoons soy sauce
2 teaspoons sesame seeds,
    toasted

Steam the asparagus in a steamer until tender-crisp. Arrange in a glass dish. Combine the sesame oil, sugar, vinegar, soy sauce and sesame seeds in a bowl and mix well. Pour over the asparagus. Marinate, covered, in the refrigerator for 8 hours, turning the asparagus occasionally.

YIELD: 6 SERVINGS

ORIENTAL ASPARAGUS WITH PORK

1 pound fresh asparagus
4 ounces pork cutlet
1½ teaspoons canola oil
¼ cup chicken broth
¼ cup white wine

1 teaspoon soy sauce
1 teaspoon oyster sauce
1 tablespoon cornstarch
2 tablespoons cold water

Trim the asparagus. Rinse and pat dry. Cut the asparagus into diagonal slices. Remove the fat from the pork. Cut into thin slices. Cut into small pieces no larger than a nickel.

Heat a wok or skillet over high heat. Add the oil and pork. Add a small amount of the broth if the pork begins to stick. Add the wine, soy sauce and asparagus. Add the remaining broth and oyster sauce. Stir-fry until the asparagus is tender. Dissolve the cornstarch in the water in a small bowl. Add to the asparagus mixture. Cook until the sauce is thickened, stirring constantly.

Note: The mixture of cornstarch and water used as a thickener is known as a slurry.

YIELD: 6 TO 8 SERVINGS

SANTA MARIA BEANS

SANTA MARIA-STYLE BARBECUE

The California city of Santa Maria has kept alive a tradition started in the early 1800s by the *vaqueros*, America's first cowboys. The cowboys held large barbecues following cattle roundups where they served thick cuts of beef (tri-tip) cooked over red oak coals, salsa, beans, macaroni and cheese, green salad, grilled French bread, and ice cream or sherbet.

1 pound dried small pink beans (pinkitas or pintos)	3/4 cup tomato purée
1 slice bacon, chopped	1/4 cup canned red chile sauce
1/4 cup chopped ham	1 tablespoon sugar
1 small garlic clove, minced	1 teaspoon dry mustard
	1 teaspoon salt

Sort and rinse the beans. Cover the beans with water in a large bowl. Soak for 8 to 12 hours. Rinse and drain the beans. Place in a large ovenproof saucepan. Cover with water. Bring to a boil and reduce the heat. Simmer for 2 hours or until tender.

Sauté the bacon and ham in a skillet until light brown. Add the garlic. Sauté for 1 to 2 minutes. Add the tomato purée, chile sauce, sugar, dry mustard and salt.

Drain most of the liquid from the beans. Stir in the sauce mixture. Keep warm over low heat or in a warm oven until ready to serve.

YIELD: 6 TO 8 SERVINGS

For an authentic Santa Maria Barbecue, pair this with Santa Maria Tri-Tip Marinade and Barbecue on page 191, Super Garlic Bread on page 69, and a tossed green salad.

MEXICAN REFRIED BEANS

2 to 3 tablespoons bacon drippings, lard or shortening	1/2 cup (2 ounces) Cheddar, mozzarella or Monterey Jack cheese, shredded
2 cups cooked Mexican Pinto Beans (page 129)	

Melt the bacon drippings in a skillet. Add Mexican Pinto Beans and mash well. Cook until a thick paste forms, stirring occasionally to prevent burning. Sprinkle with the cheese and serve.

YIELD: 4 SERVINGS

In the Hispanic community, refried beans are served with most meals. Consider replacing the cheese with queso blanco, a delicious white cheese available in Hispanic markets.

MEXICAN PINTO BEANS

1 pound dried pinto beans
7 to 9 cups water
3 tablespoons salt

$^1/_4$ teaspoon cumin (optional)
2 garlic cloves, minced (optional)

Sort and rinse the beans, removing any loose skins or beans not fully developed. Combine the beans with enough of the water to cover in a saucepan. Cook, covered, for 2 to 3 hours or until tender, adding the salt, cumin and garlic when the beans begin to turn brown and adding the remaining water as needed to keep the beans covered, stirring occasionally.

YIELD: 4 TO 5 CUPS

CAULIFLOWER AND TOMATOES EN CASSEROLE

1 large head cauliflower, cut into
    florets
1 pound firm ripe tomatoes, cut
    into quarters
$^1/_2$ teaspoon salt

Dash of pepper
$^1/_2$ cup (1 stick) butter, melted
$^1/_4$ cup dry bread crumbs
$^1/_4$ cup shredded Swiss cheese
$^1/_4$ cup grated Parmesan cheese

Cook the cauliflower in a small amount of water in a saucepan until al dente. Rinse in cold water and drain. Arrange in a buttered shallow 10-inch baking dish. Arrange the tomatoes around the edge. Season with salt and pepper. Pour $^1/_2$ of the butter over the vegetables. Mix the bread crumbs, Swiss cheese and Parmesan cheese in a bowl. Sprinkle over the vegetables. Drizzle the remaining butter over the top. Bake at 375 degrees for 30 minutes or until light brown.

YIELD: 4 TO 6 SERVINGS

Al dente literally means "to the tooth." Pasta or other foods cooked al dente will be tender but chewy, adding an interesting texture.

CAULIFLOWER

A fresh, healthy head of cauliflower will be firm, heavy, and snowy white without yellow or brownish mottling on the surface. To prepare cauliflower, remove the core in a cone shape with a sharp knife. The green leaves will come away with the core. Refrigerated whole and unwashed in a sealable plastic bag, cauliflower should last up to four days.

ROASTED CAULIFLOWER WITH ROSEMARY

**3 pounds cauliflower, cut into
  1-inch florets**
2 tablespoons olive oil
**2 tablespoons chopped fresh
  rosemary**

Salt and pepper to taste
Paprika to taste

Toss the cauliflower with the olive oil, rosemary, salt and pepper in a bowl to coat well. Arrange in a shallow baking dish. Bake at 500 degrees for 12 to 15 minutes or until tender and brown in spots. Sprinkle with paprika just before serving.

YIELD: 8 SERVINGS

BAKED FENNEL WITH GORGONZOLA CHEESE

**4 (3½-inch-wide) heads fennel
  with leaves**
1¾ cups chicken broth
4 ounces Gorgonzola cheese

**2 tablespoons fine dry bread
  crumbs**
Salt to taste

Trim the stems from the fennel, reserving 1 cup fennel leaves. Cut the fennel heads into halves lengthwise. Combine the broth and fennel halves in a 10- to 12-inch skillet. Cover and bring to a boil. Reduce the heat and simmer until tender. Drain the fennel, reserving the broth in the skillet. Arrange the fennel cup side up in a shallow 9×13-inch baking dish. Boil the broth in the skillet until reduced to ⅓ cup. Stir in ½ of the reserved fennel leaves. Spoon over the fennel in the baking dish.

Mix the Gorgonzola cheese and bread crumbs in a bowl. Sprinkle over the top. You may make ahead up to this point and chill, covered, for up to 1 day.

Bake, uncovered, at 375 degrees for 20 to 25 minutes or until the fennel is hot and the Gorgonzola cheese begins to brown. Arrange the remaining reserved fennel leaves around the fennel halves. Season with salt.

YIELD: 8 SERVINGS

**GORGONZOLA CHEESE
(GOHR-GUHN-ZOH-LAH)**

To liven up a meal, consider serving one of Italy's oldest bleu cheeses. Named for the town of Gorgonzola, near Milan, this variety has light, golden curd streaked with bluish-green veins, and a rich, pungent taste. Molds are injected during the curing process to create the veins and enhance the flavor. Gorgonzola is the perfect partner to fruits, vegetables, and salads, and is best served with aged port or a fruity beaujolais.

EGGPLANT TIMBALE

Chef Alberto Morello, Olio e Limone Ristorante

1/2 cup olive oil	1 cup bread crumbs
1 yellow onion, peeled, julienned	2 eggs
1 potato, peeled, julienned	1/2 cup grated Parmesan cheese
3 eggplant, peeled, diagonally	Salt and pepper to taste
sliced	1/4 cup (1/2 stick) butter, softened
3 ripe tomatoes, peeled, chopped	1 red bell pepper, chopped
1 bunch fresh basil, coarsely	1 yellow bell pepper, chopped
chopped	3 ounces goat cheese
1 pinch oregano	Tomato Basil Sauce (below)

Heat 1/2 cup olive oil in a saucepan over medium heat. Add the onion, potato and eggplant. Cook until the potato is tender, stirring frequently. Add the tomatoes, basil and oregano and stir until the tomatoes are incorporated into the mixture. Remove from the heat to cool. Purée in a food processor. Spoon into a large bowl. Add the bread crumbs, eggs, Parmesan cheese, salt and pepper and mix well.

Spread the butter into 6 ramekins. Mix the bell peppers together. Sprinkle into the prepared ramekins. Add the eggplant mixture. Press 1 teaspoon goat cheese into the center of each ramekin with your finger, making sure the goat cheese is covered with the eggplant mixture. Arrange the ramekins in a roasting pan. Pour enough hot water into the roasting pan to come halfway up the sides of the ramekins. Bake at 350 degrees for 30 minutes.

To serve, spoon the warm Tomato Basil Sauce onto each serving plate. Unmold the eggplant mixture into the center of each plate. Garnish with basil tips.

YIELD: 6 SERVINGS

TOMATO BASIL SAUCE

6 tablespoons extra-virgin olive oil	1 1/2 ounces fresh basil, coarsely
1 yellow onion, peeled, julienned	chopped
3 garlic cloves, minced	Pinch of red pepper flakes
4 pounds ripe tomatoes, peeled,	(optional)
seeded, diced	

Heat the olive oil in a skillet. Add the onion and garlic. Sauté until golden brown. Add the tomatoes, basil and red pepper flakes. Simmer for 20 to 30 minutes or until thickened, stirring frequently. Purée in batches in a blender until smooth.

BAKED MUSHROOMS

VERMOUTH

Vermouth is offered
in three varieties: dry,
sweet, and half-sweet.
Dry vermouth is white,
usually eighteen
percent alcohol.
Without a splash of
dry vermouth, a dry
martini would simply
be a jigger of gin or
vodka. Sweet vermouth
is white or red and
contains fifteen to
sixteen percent alcohol
and up to fifteen
percent sugar. It's a
popular choice for
slightly sweet cocktails,
such as the Manhattan.

2 pounds fresh mushrooms, sliced
1/4 cup (1/2 stick) butter
2/3 cup sour cream
2 tablespoons all-purpose flour

Salt and pepper to taste
**1 cup (4 ounces) shredded Swiss
  cheese**
1/2 cup finely chopped fresh parsley

Sauté the mushrooms in the butter in a skillet. Cook, covered, for 2 minutes. Combine the sour cream, flour, salt and pepper in a bowl and blend well. Stir into the mushrooms. Cook until heated through. Spread in a shallow glass baking dish. Sprinkle with the Swiss cheese and parsley. Bake at 425 degrees for 10 minutes.

YIELD: 8 TO 10 SERVINGS

ONION CHEESE BAKE

4 medium onions, sliced
3 tablespoons butter
2 tablespoons all-purpose flour
Salt to taste
Dash of pepper
3/4 cup beef bouillon
1/4 cup vermouth (optional)

1 1/2 cups plain croutons
2 tablespoons butter, melted
**1 cup (4 ounces) shredded Swiss
  cheese**
**3 tablespoons grated Parmesan
  cheese**

Sauté the onions in 3 tablespoons butter in a skillet until tender and golden brown. Blend in the flour, salt and pepper. Add the bouillon and vermouth. Cook until thickened and bubbly, stirring constantly. Spoon into a 1-quart baking dish. Toss the croutons with 2 tablespoons butter in a bowl. Spread over the onion mixture. Sprinkle with the Swiss cheese and Parmesan cheese. Broil for 1 minute or until the cheeses melt. Serve immediately.

Note: Increase the beef bouillon to 1 cup if the vermouth is omitted. You can also bake at 375 degrees for 20 minutes instead of broiling.

YIELD: 5 TO 6 SERVINGS

Like eating French onion soup with a fork.

PANCETTA ROSEMARY POTATOES

6 pounds new potatoes, peeled
1/2 cup (1 stick) unsalted butter,
   softened
6 ounces pancetta, thinly sliced
   and chopped

1/4 cup light olive oil
1 teaspoon salt
1/8 teaspoon freshly ground pepper
8 sprigs of fresh rosemary

Place the potatoes in a stockpot and cover with cold water. Bring to a boil over high heat. Cook for 15 to 20 minutes or until the potatoes are still a bit firm. Do not overcook. Drain the potatoes and cool for several minutes. Coat the bottom and sides of a broiler pan or large shallow baking pan with the butter. Cut the cooled potatoes into large chunks. Arrange in the prepared broiler pan. Sprinkle with the pancetta, olive oil, salt, pepper and rosemary. Bake at 450 degrees for 1 to 1¼ hours or until the butter and oil are absorbed and the potatoes are very crisp, turning frequently.

YIELD: 8 SERVINGS

ROQUEFORT SCALLOPED POTATOES

Photograph for this recipe is shown on page 124.

5½ pounds russet potatoes
Salt and pepper to taste
2 cups heavy cream
6 ounces Roquefort cheese,
   crumbled

1 cup dry bread crumbs
1½ teaspoons rosemary
1/2 cup (1 stick) butter, cut into
   small pieces

Peel the potatoes and cut into ⅛-inch slices. Layer the potatoes in a buttered 10×15-inch glass baking dish, sprinkling salt and pepper between each layer. Bring the cream to a boil in a medium saucepan over high heat, stirring constantly. Add the Roquefort cheese. Reduce the heat to medium. Cook until the Roquefort cheese melts, whisking constantly. Pour over the potatoes. Cover with foil. Bake at 425 degrees for 1 hour or until the potatoes are tender.

Mix the bread crumbs and rosemary in a small bowl. Sprinkle over the potatoes. Dot with the butter. Broil for 3 to 4 minutes or until the butter melts and the bread crumbs are light brown. Let stand for 10 minutes before serving.

YIELD: 12 SERVINGS

POTATOES

Potatoes will have a longer shelf life if the storage area is dark, dry, and cool. If they become too cold, the potato starch will turn to sugar, and the potatoes will become brown when cooked. If they're too warm, they may sprout and shrivel. Marvelously versatile, potatoes are also waistline-friendly (120 calories in a six-ounce potato), nutritionally rich, low in sodium, and a good source of complex carbohydrates.

TOMATOES STUFFED WITH PESTO AND GOAT CHEESE

2 tablespoons olive oil
2 cups loosely packed fresh bread crumbs
4 ounces soft creamy goat cheese

$1/4$ cup Pesto (below)
4 large ripe tomatoes
Salt and pepper to taste

Heat the olive oil in a large heavy skillet over medium-high heat. Add the bread crumbs. Cook until the crumbs are a rich golden brown, stirring constantly. Combine the bread crumbs, goat cheese and Pesto in a bowl and mix well.

Remove the stems from the tomatoes. Cut the tomatoes horizontally into halves. Scoop out the seeds and membranes. Season the cavities with salt and pepper. Turn upside down on paper towels. Drain for 5 to 10 minutes.

Line a baking sheet with foil. Spray with nonstick cooking spray. Mound the pesto mixture into the tomato shells. Arrange on the prepared baking sheet. Bake at 400 degrees for 10 minutes. Do not overbake. Garnish with sprigs of fresh parsley.

YIELD: 8 SERVINGS

PESTO

2 cups fresh basil leaves, rinsed, patted dry
4 garlic cloves, chopped
1 cup pine nuts
1 cup olive oil
1 cup freshly grated Parmesan cheese

$1/4$ cup freshly grated Romano cheese
Salt and freshly ground pepper to taste

Process the basil, garlic and pine nuts in a food processor. Add the olive oil gradually, processing constantly. Add the Parmesan cheese, Romano cheese, salt and pepper and process briefly to combine.

YAMS WITH PRALINE TOPPING

2 (40-ounce) cans yams, drained
²/₃ cup orange juice
5 tablespoons brandy
¹/₄ cup (¹/₂ stick) butter, melted
¹/₃ cup packed brown sugar
3 egg yolks
1 teaspoon ginger
2 teaspoons salt
Freshly ground pepper to taste
1 cup packed brown sugar
9 tablespoons butter, melted
1 cup chopped pecans
1 teaspoon cinnamon

Beat the yams in a mixing bowl until smooth. Add the orange juice, brandy, ¼ cup butter, ⅓ cup brown sugar, egg yolks, ginger, salt and pepper and beat until light and fluffy. Pour into a 2-quart baking dish, smoothing the top evenly.

Mix 1 cup brown sugar, 9 tablespoons butter, the pecans and cinnamon in a bowl. Spread evenly over the yam mixture. Bake at 350 degrees for 45 to 50 minutes or until bubbly. Remove from the oven and let stand for 10 minutes before serving.

YIELD: 10 TO 12 SERVINGS

YAMS

The terms "yam" and "sweet potato" are often interchangeable in the United States, but a true yam rarely finds its way to an American supermarket. Yams range in color from cream and yellow to pink or purple and can be found in Latin American countries where they are sold in chunks by weight. Although available year-round, you'll find the freshest and moistest sweet potatoes from August to October.

Zucchini Casserole Supreme

2 eggs
1 cup mayonnaise
1 small onion, finely chopped
1/2 cup grated Parmesan cheese
Salt and pepper to taste

4 cups (1/4-inch) zucchini slices
2 tablespoons seasoned bread
 crumbs
2 tablespoons butter or margarine,
 melted

Beat the eggs in a large bowl for 1 minute. Stir in the mayonnaise, onion, cheese, salt and pepper. Add the zucchini and mix well. Spoon into a 1½-quart baking dish buttered or sprayed with nonstick cooking spray. Sprinkle with the bread crumbs. Pour 2 tablespoons butter evenly over the top. Bake, covered, at 350 degrees for 30 minutes. Bake, uncovered, for 5 to 10 minutes or until light brown.

YIELD: 6 SERVINGS

Garden Vegetable Roast

Photograph for this recipe is shown on page 124.

5 zucchini
4 cups fresh corn from the cob
2 cups quartered small tomatoes
 or whole cherry tomatoes

2 medium onions, thinly sliced
2 garlic cloves, minced
Salt and pepper to taste
1/2 cup (1 stick) butter

Cut the zucchini into quarters lengthwise. Cut each quarter into halves. Combine the zucchini, corn, tomatoes, onions, garlic, salt and pepper in a bowl and mix well. Spoon into a baking dish. Dot with the butter. Bake, covered, at 325 degrees for 45 minutes.

YIELD: 6 SERVINGS

FENNEL

Fennel resembles celery, except that the stalks have a bulbous knot at the bottom and the leaves are soft and feathery, similar to dill. The upper portion of the stalk should be discarded, while the bulbous end, which has a mild licorice flavor, can be cut into small cubes and served fresh in a salad. It can also be cooked in a variety of ways or used as a garnish.

HERB-ROASTED VEGETABLES

4 carrots, cut diagonally into
   1/2-inch slices
4 parsnips, cut diagonally into
   1/2-inch slices
1 pound boiling onions, peeled
8 Yukon Gold potatoes, cut into
   quarters

1/4 cup olive oil
2 tablespoons minced fresh thyme
Salt and freshly ground pepper
   to taste
1/4 cup (1/2 stick) butter, softened
1/2 cup chopped fresh parsley

Toss the vegetables with the olive oil, thyme, salt and pepper in a large bowl until coated. Arrange in a single layer on a large baking sheet. Bake at 425 degrees for 30 to 35 minutes or until tender and golden brown, turning occasionally. Spoon into a large serving dish. Add the butter and parsley and toss to coat.

Note: Serve with Fillet of Beef Extraordinaire (page 187).

YIELD: 8 SERVINGS

VERY VEGGIE ENCHILADAS

4 onions, chopped
4 pickled chiles, chopped
1 bunch radishes, chopped
2 (14-ounce) cans sliced black
   olives, drained
1 (14-ounce) can tomatoes,
   drained, mashed

2 tablespoons vinegar
1 teaspoon salt
24 corn tortillas
Vegetable oil for frying
1 (28-ounce) can enchilada sauce
2 pounds Cheddar cheese,
   shredded (8 cups)

Cook the onions in boiling water in a saucepan for 2 minutes; drain. Combine the onions, pickled chiles, radishes, black olives and tomatoes in a bowl and mix well. Stir in the vinegar and salt.

Fry the tortillas 1 at a time in hot oil in a skillet for 2 seconds. Dip 1 tortilla at a time into the enchilada sauce in a bowl. Fill each with the onion mixture and sprinkle with cheese; roll up. Arrange seam side down in two 9×13-inch baking dishes. Sprinkle with the remaining cheese. Top with the remaining enchilada sauce. Bake at 375 degrees for 15 minutes or until the cheese melts.

Note: You may find pickled chiles in your local Mexican market. This recipe freezes well. After thawing, add salsa or additional enchilada sauce around the edges of the dish to add moisture before heating.

YIELD: 24 SERVINGS

ENCHILADAS VERDE

ENCHILADA SAUCE

Arrange 3 fresh green chiles on a baking sheet. Bake at 350 degrees until lightly toasted. Cut the chiles open and remove the seeds and veins. Place the chiles in boiling water to cover in a bowl. Let stand for 30 minutes. Remove the chiles from the bowl, reserving the liquid. Scrape the pulp from the chiles into the reserved liquid, discarding the skins. Sauté 1 chopped onion and 2 crushed garlic cloves in 1/4 cup (1/2 stick) butter in a skillet over medium heat until tender. Add 1/4 cup all-purpose flour and mix well. Add 3 cups chicken stock. Cook until thickened, stirring constantly. Add the chile pulp mixture, 3/4 teaspoon oregano and 3/4 teaspoon cumin. Purée in a food processor until smooth. Season with salt and pepper to taste.

1 (7-ounce) can whole green chiles, drained
1 cup sour cream
1¹/₂ cups cottage cheese
1 onion, chopped
1 teaspoon cumin
¹/₂ teaspoon salt
¹/₄ teaspoon pepper
10 corn tortillas
¹/₄ cup (¹/₂ stick) butter
1 pound Monterey Jack cheese, shredded (4 cups)
2 (7-ounce) cans green chile salsa, or Enchilada Sauce
    (at left)

Remove the seeds from the green chiles and cut into strips. Combine the sour cream, cottage cheese, onion, cumin, salt and pepper in a bowl and mix well. Sauté the tortillas in the butter in a skillet for a few seconds on each side to soften; drain on paper towels. Spread each tortilla with 2 to 3 tablespoons of the cottage cheese mixture, reserving the excess for topping. Reserve ¹/₃ of the cheese and chile strips. Divide the remaining cheese and chile strips among the tortillas and roll up.

Spread ¹/₂ of the salsa in a 9×13-inch baking dish. Arrange the enchiladas seam side down in the prepared dish. Pour the remaining salsa over the enchiladas. Bake, covered, at 350 degrees for 30 minutes or until heated through. Spoon the reserved cottage cheese mixture over the top just before serving. Sprinkle with the reserved chile strips and cheese. Broil until the cheese is bubbly.

YIELD: 5 SERVINGS

VEGETARIAN MEAT LOAF

1¹/₂ cups chopped celery
2 large onions, chopped
1 cup sliced mushrooms
¹/₄ cup green bell pepper, chopped
¹/₃ cup butter
3 cups shredded carrots
³/₄ cup chopped walnuts
¹/₂ cup sunflower seeds
5 eggs, lightly beaten

3 cups soft bread crumbs
1 teaspoon basil
1 teaspoon oregano
Salt and pepper to taste
1 (10-ounce) can cream of
    mushroom soup
³/₄ cup water
¹/₄ to ¹/₂ cup sherry

Sauté the celery, onions, mushrooms and bell pepper in the butter in a skillet for 5 minutes. Add the carrots, walnuts, sunflower seeds, eggs, bread crumbs, basil, oregano, salt and pepper and mix well. Spoon into a greased 5×8-inch loaf pan. Bake at 325 degrees for 1 hour.

Combine the mushroom soup, water and sherry in a small saucepan and mix well. Cook until heated through, stirring frequently. Unmold the vegetable loaf on a serving platter. Spoon some of the mushroom sauce over the loaf. Serve with the remaining mushroom sauce.

YIELD: 8 SERVINGS

HARVEST TORTA

10 slices white bread, toasted
8 ounces shredded Swiss cheese (2 cups)
8 ounces shredded fontinella cheese (2 cups)
8 ounces shredded Cheddar cheese (2 cups)
4 carrots, sliced
2 onions, chopped
2 tomatoes, chopped
2 yellow zucchini, sliced
2 green zucchini, sliced
1 small eggplant, sliced, sautéed (optional)
2 tablespoons olive oil

Crumble the toasted bread. Mix the Swiss cheese, fontinella cheese and Cheddar cheese in a bowl. Layer ⅓ of the bread crumbs, carrots, ½ of the onions, tomatoes, ½ of the cheese mixture, ½ of the remaining bread crumbs, remaining onions, yellow zucchini, green zucchini, remaining cheese mixture, eggplant and remaining bread crumbs in a 9×13-inch baking dish. Drizzle with the olive oil. Bake at 350 degrees for 45 minutes.

YIELD: 10 TO 12 SERVINGS

GNOCCHI VERDI (SMALL SPINACH DUMPLINGS)

GNOCCHI (NYOH-KEE)

Gnocchi is simply the Italian word for "dumplings." These little round or pillow-shaped morsels are made of flour, potatoes, or farina. Cheese, spinach, and mushrooms are popular additions to the dough. When preparing gnocchi, place a little "dough boy" dimple into it so it will hold more sauce. For a creative use of old potatoes, do as the Romans do, make gnocchi!

1/4 cup (1/2 stick) butter
11/2 pounds fresh spinach, cooked, squeezed dry, finely chopped
3/4 cup ricotta cheese
2 eggs, lightly beaten
6 tablespoons all-purpose flour
1/4 cup freshly grated imported Parmesan cheese

1/2 teaspoon salt
1/2 teaspoon freshly ground pepper
Pinch of nutmeg
6 to 8 quarts water
1 tablespoon salt
1/4 cup (1/2 stick) butter, melted
1/2 cup freshly grated imported Parmesan cheese

Melt ¼ cup butter in an 8- or 10-inch skillet. Add the spinach. Cook for 2 to 3 minutes or until almost all of the moisture evaporates and the spinach begins to lightly stick to the skillet, stirring constantly. Add the ricotta cheese. Cook for 3 to 4 minutes, stirring constantly. Combine the spinach mixture, eggs, flour, ¼ cup Parmesan cheese, ½ teaspoon salt, pepper and nutmeg in a large bowl and mix well. Chill, covered, for up to 1 hour or until the mixture is quite firm.

Bring the water and 1 tablespoon salt to a simmer in a large saucepan. Shape 1 tablespoon of the spinach mixture at a time into 1½-inch balls with lightly floured hands. Drop the balls gently into the simmering water. Cook, uncovered, for 5 to 8 minutes or until puffed slightly and firm to the touch. Remove with a slotted spoon to paper towels to drain.

Pour 2 tablespoons of the remaining ¼ cup butter in an 8×12-inch baking dish. Arrange the gnocchi in layers in the prepared dish. Drizzle with the remaining 2 tablespoons butter. Sprinkle with ½ cup Parmesan cheese. Place on the middle oven rack. Bake at 400 degrees for 5 minutes or until the Parmesan cheese melts. Serve immediately.

Note: You may use two 10-ounce packages frozen chopped spinach, thawed and squeezed dry, instead of the fresh spinach.

YIELD: 4 TO 6 SERVINGS

FARFALLE WITH PROSCIUTTO, SNOW PEAS AND ASPARAGUS

Photograph for this recipe is shown on page 124.

Photograph for this recipe is shown on page 124.

PASTA

Pasta is available in a multitude of sizes, colors, shapes, and names. It's also available fresh or dried. The dried is a better value for the price and can hold up to robust sauces, while the fresh requires a delicate touch. Plain pasta that has been cooked and drained can be stored, covered, in the refrigerator for several days. A little olive oil will keep it from sticking together.

1 pound asparagus	³/₄ cup chicken or vegetable broth
4 quarts water	1 cup white wine
1 tablespoon salt	1 cup half-and-half
10 to 12 ounces uncooked farfalle or penne	³/₄ cup grated Parmigiano-Reggiano
3 garlic cloves, minced	Grated zest of 1 lemon
1 large shallot, chopped	5 ounces snow peas
1 tablespoon olive oil	Salt and pepper to taste
1 tablespoon butter	¹/₄ cup grated Parmigiano-Reggiano
5¹/₃ ounces thinly sliced prosciutto, chopped into small pieces	

Trim the asparagus, removing and discarding the bottom half of each stalk. Cut the asparagus into 1-inch pieces. Place in a small amount of water in a microwave-safe dish. Microwave on High until tender.

Bring 4 quarts water and 1 tablespoon salt to a boil in a large saucepan. Add the pasta. Cook until al dente. Remove from the heat.

Sauté the garlic and shallot in the olive oil and butter in a large skillet for 2 minutes. Add the prosciutto. Cook for 7 to 8 minutes, stirring constantly. Stir in the broth, wine and half-and-half. Add ³/₄ cup Parmigiano-Reggiano and stir to mix well. Stir in the lemon zest and snow peas. Cook until tender. Season with salt and pepper to taste.

Drain the pasta and place in a warm serving bowl. Add the sauce and toss to coat. Sprinkle with ¹/₄ cup Parmigiano-Reggiano.

YIELD: 4 TO 6 SERVINGS

You may substitute large sea scallops (four per person) for the prosciutto. Do not substitute the lemon zest or Parmigiano-Reggiano; these are necessary ingredients in this spectacular pasta dish.

BAKED BROCCOLI MOSTACCIOLI

1/3 cup butter
1/3 cup all-purpose flour
3 cups milk
1 cup (4 ounces) shredded
    Parmesan cheese
1 garlic clove, minced
1 teaspoon salt
1/4 teaspoon nutmeg

1/8 teaspoon thyme leaves
1 (1-pound) package frozen
    broccoli cuts, thawed, drained
8 ounces mostaccioli, cooked,
    rinsed, drained
2 cups (8 ounces) shredded
    mozzarella cheese

Melt the butter in a saucepan over medium heat. Stir in the flour with a whisk. Add the milk gradually, whisking constantly. Add the Parmesan cheese, garlic, salt, nutmeg and thyme. Cook until thickened, stirring constantly. Remove from the heat.

Combine the broccoli and cooked pasta in a large bowl. Add the cheese sauce and stir until the sauce is evenly distributed throughout. Spoon into a lightly greased 9×13-inch baking dish. Sprinkle the mozzarella cheese over the top. Bake at 375 degrees for 20 minutes or until bubbly.

YIELD: 6 TO 8 SERVINGS

PENNE WITH FETA, EGGPLANT AND OLIVES

1 onion, chopped
3 tablespoons olive oil
1 eggplant, cut into 1/2-inch cubes
2 cups coarsely chopped seeded
    peeled Roma tomatoes
5 garlic cloves, finely chopped
1 tablespoon red wine vinegar
1 teaspoon thyme

1/3 cup drained capers
16 ounces uncooked penne
Salt to taste
2 tablespoons olive oil
1 1/2 cups crumbled feta cheese
1/2 cup pitted kalamata olives
1/2 cup chopped fresh parsley

Sauté the onion in 3 tablespoons olive oil in a 12-inch sauté pan for 1 minute. Add the eggplant. Sauté for 15 minutes. Add the tomatoes, garlic, vinegar and thyme. Cook for 3 minutes. Remove from the heat. Stir in the capers.

Cook the pasta in salted boiling water in a large saucepan until al dente; drain. Combine the pasta, 2 tablespoons olive oil, the eggplant mixture, cheese, kalamata olives and parsley in a large serving bowl and toss to mix well.

YIELD: 8 SERVINGS

PORTOBELLO AND GOAT CHEESE PASTA

MUSHROOMS

Mushrooms are like little round sponges that readily absorb liquids. Therefore, they shouldn't be soaked in water to clean. Simply wipe them with a moist paper towel, taking care not to remove the skin while doing so. Dry, unwashed mushrooms stored in a paper bag and refrigerated will stay fresh longer. To slice, place the mushroom upside down in an egg slicer and you'll have clean, uniform slices.

1 tablespoon butter
2 tablespoons olive oil
6 medium onions, chopped
1 teaspoon salt
1 teaspoon sugar
2 pounds portobello mushrooms
1 tablespoon butter
1 tablespoon olive oil
1/2 teaspoon salt
6 tablespoons chopped fresh
    Italian parsley

Salt and pepper to taste
24 ounces uncooked short tube
    pasta
8 ounces crumbled herbed soft
    goat cheese
3 tablespoons freshly grated
    Parmesan cheese
1 tablespoon olive oil

Melt 1 tablespoon butter in 2 tablespoons olive oil in a large skillet. Add the onions, 1 teaspoon salt and the sugar. Cook over medium heat for 20 to 30 minutes or until the onions are brown, stirring frequently. Remove to a bowl.

Remove the gills and stems from the mushrooms. Cut the caps into halves. Cut the halves horizontally 1/4 inch thick. Melt 1 tablespoon butter in 1 tablespoon olive oil in the skillet. Add the mushrooms and 1/2 teaspoon salt. Cook over medium heat for 8 to 10 minutes or until tender and brown, stirring occasionally. Add the cooked onions and parsley. Season with salt and pepper to taste.

Cook the pasta in boiling salted water in a large saucepan until al dente. Drain the pasta, reserving 2 cups of the water. Place the pasta in a large serving bowl. Add 1 cup of the reserved water, mushroom mixture, goat cheese, Parmesan cheese and 1 tablespoon olive oil and toss to mix well. Add the remaining reserved water 1/4 cup at a time until the pasta is the desired consistency. Serve immediately with additional Parmesan cheese.

Note: If the herbed goat cheese is unavailable, use plain goat cheese mixed with 1 garlic clove, minced, and 1 teaspoon basil.

YIELD: 10 SERVINGS

CLASSIC ITALIAN MANICOTTI

2 pounds ricotta cheese, at room
   temperature
8 ounces (2 cups) mozzarella
   cheese, shredded
2 eggs
3/4 cup grated Parmesan cheese
3 tablespoons finely chopped fresh
   parsley

1/8 teaspoon nutmeg
Salt and pepper to taste
3 onions, chopped
3 garlic cloves, chopped
Olive oil or butter for sautéing
4 (8-ounce) cans tomato sauce
1/4 cup finely chopped fresh parsley
8 ounces uncooked manicotti

Combine the ricotta cheese, mozzarella cheese, eggs, Parmesan cheese, 3 tablespoons parsley, nutmeg, salt and pepper in a large bowl and mix well. Sauté the onions and garlic in a small amount of olive oil in a skillet until the onions are transparent. Add the tomato sauce and 1/4 cup parsley and mix well.

    Cook the pasta using the package directions; drain. Stuff the pasta with the ricotta cheese mixture. Arrange in a greased 9×13-inch baking dish. Pour the sauce over the top. Cover with foil. Bake at 350 degrees for 20 to 30 minutes or until hot and bubbly.

YIELD: 8 SERVINGS

PASTA WITH FRESH SPINACH

2 garlic cloves, pressed
1 teaspoon olive oil
1 pound fresh spinach, coarsely
   chopped
1 teaspoon vegetable bouillon
   granules

3 plum tomatoes, seeded, chopped
8 ounces pasta, cooked, drained
1/4 cup freshly grated asiago
   cheese
2 tablespoons sliced almonds,
   toasted

Sauté the garlic in the olive oil in a 12-inch skillet until golden brown. Add the spinach and bouillon. Cook over medium-high heat until the spinach wilts. Add the tomatoes. Cook until heated through. Add the hot cooked pasta and toss to mix. Sprinkle with asiago cheese and almonds. Serve immediately.

YIELD: 4 SERVINGS

ASIAGO CHEESE

Asiago is a semifirm, pleasantly sharp, Italian cow's milk cheese. It comes in wheels that are covered with a glossy, inedible rind. The straw-colored cheese, dotted with small holes, is available young or aged. Asiago adds a strong, nutty taste when baked into bread (or even bagels) or grated over fresh pasta.

Santa Barbara Primavera

1 cup julienned carrots
1 cup broccoli florets
1 cup pistachio nuts, toasted
1 cup chopped red bell pepper
1/2 cup chopped fresh parsley
1/3 cup chopped scallions
2 medium garlic cloves, minced
1/4 teaspoon salt
1 teaspoon pepper
8 ounces Brie or Camembert cheese
8 ounces bleu cheese
3/4 cup olive oil
16 ounces uncooked bow tie pasta

Blanch the carrots and broccoli in boiling water in a medium saucepan for 2 minutes; drain. Rinse under cold running water. Drain on paper towels. Blot the broccoli to remove as much water as possible. Combine the carrots, broccoli, pistachio nuts, bell pepper, parsley, scallions, garlic, salt and pepper in a large bowl. Remove the rind from the Brie cheese. Cut into large pieces and add to the bowl. Crumble the bleu cheese over the top. Add the olive oil and toss to mix gently. Marinate, covered, at room temperature for 2 to 4 hours.

Cook the pasta using the package directions; drain well. Add to the vegetable mixture and toss gently to mix. Do not overmix or the cheese will melt too much. The dish is best if there are chunks of Brie cheese throughout. Serve warm or at room temperature.

YIELD: 8 SERVINGS

SPINACH LASAGNA

8 ounces uncooked lasagna noodles
2 pounds cottage cheese
3 garlic cloves, minced
1 tablespoon parsley
2 eggs
1/2 cup (1 stick) butter or margarine, softened
Salt and pepper to taste
1 1/2 pounds fresh spinach, cooked, squeezed dry
1 pound Monterey Jack cheese, shredded (4 cups)
1 cup grated Parmesan cheese

Cook the noodles using the package directions; drain. Combine the cottage cheese, garlic, parsley, eggs, butter, salt and pepper in a bowl and mix well. Layer the noodles, cottage cheese mixture, spinach, Monterey Jack cheese and Parmesan cheese 1/2 at a time in a greased 9×13-inch baking dish. Bake at 350 degrees for 30 minutes. Let stand for 10 minutes before serving.

Note: You may use two (10-ounce) packages frozen spinach, thawed and squeezed dry instead of the fresh spinach.

YIELD: 6 TO 8 SERVINGS

LASAGNA

It is rumored that on Christmas Eve the grandmother in an Italian household would measure the children's mouths to determine the width of the noodles.

CHILLY DILLY PASTA

1/2 cup vegetable oil	12 ounces bow tie pasta, cooked,
1 cup sour cream	drained
2 tablespoons lemon juice	6 cherry tomatoes, cut into halves
1/3 cup chopped fresh dill weed	5 ounces smoked salmon, cut into
2 teaspoons minced onion	small pieces
1/4 teaspoon salt	1/4 cup chopped fresh chives
1/4 teaspoon pepper	1/4 cup drained capers

Combine the oil, sour cream, lemon juice, dill weed, onion, salt and pepper in a large bowl and whisk well. Add the hot pasta, tomatoes, salmon, chives and capers and toss to mix. Chill, covered, until ready to serve.

YIELD: 4 SERVINGS

FIESTA RICE CASSEROLE

1 cup chopped onion	1 (4-ounce) can chopped black
1/4 cup (1/2 stick) butter	olives, drained (optional)
4 cups cooked white rice	1/2 teaspoon salt
1 cup sour cream	1/8 teaspoon pepper
1 cup cottage cheese	2 cups (8 ounces) shredded
2 (7-ounce) can diced green chiles,	Monterey Jack or Cheddar
drained	cheese

Sauté the onion in the butter in a skillet until translucent. Add the cooked rice, sour cream, cottage cheese, green chiles, black olives, salt and pepper and mix well. Layer the rice mixture and the Monterey Jack cheese 1/2 at a time in a 9×13-inch baking dish. Bake at 375 degrees for 30 minutes.

YIELD: 8 SERVINGS

TORTELLINI

Tortellini is a ravioli-like delicacy that's made from fresh, flattened pasta cut into small rounds, filled, folded, and sealed. They are usually filled with meat, cheese, or seafood plus a variety of herbs and spices. These little hat-shaped bundles of flavor should be handled gently and never overcooked, since they can come apart easily. For a pleasant variation, add chilled leftover tortellini to salads.

APRICOT AND PINE NUT PILAF

Photograph for this recipe is shown on page 124 and below.

1/3 cup pine nuts
1/4 cup (1/2 stick) butter
1 medium onion, chopped
1 cup long grain white rice
1/2 cup crushed vermicelli
1 3/4 cups chicken broth
1/2 cup chopped dried apricots
2 tablespoons butter
Chopped fresh parsley

Brown the pine nuts in 1/4 cup butter in a large heavy saucepan over medium heat. Remove the pine nuts with a slotted spoon to paper towels to drain.

Add the onion to the skillet. Sauté until the onion is transparent. Add the rice and vermicelli. Sauté for 3 to 5 minutes or until brown. Add the broth. Bring to a boil and reduce the heat. Simmer, covered, for 20 minutes or until most of the broth is absorbed. Add the apricots and pine nuts. Cook for 10 minutes. Add 2 tablespoons butter and toss to coat. Sprinkle with parsley.

YIELD: 4 TO 6 SERVINGS

PINE NUTS

Pine nuts are the seeds of pine trees and are harvested from the cones. They are also called Indian nuts, piñons, pignolis, and pignolias. The nut is small, beige, and sweet and grows in a thin, brown shell tucked within the segments of the cone. Pine nuts have a high fat content and can turn rancid quickly, so keep refrigerated or frozen in an airtight container.

Savor the Sensational

seafood and poultry

Moroccan Vegetable
and Chicken Stew

Lake Cachuma Baked Trout

Valley Cucumbers

Sumptuous Salad

(shown left to right)

Santa Ynez Mountains *Photograph © Marc Muench*

GRILLED HALIBUT WITH EAST BEACH TARTAR SAUCE

6 (6- to 8-ounce) fresh halibut
  fillets
Extra-virgin olive oil
Old Bay seasoning to taste
1 tablespoon chopped fresh parsley
2 cups mayonnaise
4 scallions, minced
1 teaspoon minced black olives

1/2 teaspoon dill pickle relish
1/2 teaspoon minced fresh dill
  weed
1/4 teaspoon dry mustard
1/4 teaspoon minced capers
Pinch of cayenne pepper
Dash of lemon juice

Coat the fish in olive oil. Sprinkle with Old Bay seasoning. Arrange on a grill rack. Grill over medium-low heat for 10 minutes or until the fish flakes easily. Grill longer for a crispy texture. Sprinkle with the parsley. Combine the mayonnaise, scallions, black olives, pickle relish, dill weed, dry mustard, capers, cayenne pepper and lemon juice in a small bowl and mix well. Chill, covered, for 1 hour. Serve with the halibut.

YIELD: 6 SERVINGS

HALLELUJAH HALIBUT

2 pounds halibut steaks
1/2 cup mayonnaise
1/2 cup sour cream
2 teaspoons all-purpose flour
1 1/2 teaspoons lemon juice

1 tablespoon minced onion
1/8 teaspoon cayenne pepper
1/2 cup (2 ounces) shredded
  Cheddar cheese
Chopped fresh parsley to taste

Arrange the fish in a 7×11-inch baking dish. Combine the mayonnaise, sour cream, flour, lemon juice, onion and cayenne pepper in a small bowl and mix well. Brush over the fish. Bake at 425 degrees for 20 to 25 minutes or until the fish flakes easily. Sprinkle the cheese and parsley over the fish. Bake for 2 minutes longer or until the cheese melts.

YIELD: 4 TO 6 SERVINGS

Halibut is best accompanied by a light-bodied white wine such as pinot blanc, sauvignon blanc, or a dry riesling.

153

Coconut Red Snapper with Chutney Sauce

3 tablespoons olive oil or vegetable oil
¹/₂ cup (1 stick) butter, melted
2 tablespoons fresh lemon juice
¹/₄ cup fresh orange juice
2¹/₂ teaspoons garlic powder, or 5 teaspoons minced fresh garlic
2 teaspoons ginger
2 teaspoons crushed red pepper flakes
¹/₂ teaspoon salt
¹/₂ teaspoon pepper
1¹/₂ cups plain bread crumbs
1³/₄ cups flaked coconut
8 (6-ounce) red snapper fillets
Chutney Sauce (below)

Coat a 10×15-inch baking pan with the olive oil. Combine the butter, lemon juice, orange juice, garlic powder, ginger, red pepper flakes, salt and pepper in a small bowl and blend well. Mix the bread crumbs and coconut in a bowl. Dip the fish into the butter mixture. Coat with the coconut mixture. Arrange in the prepared baking pan. Bake at 425 degrees for 6 minutes. Turn and pat with any remaining coconut mixture. Bake for 12 to 15 minutes or until the fish flakes easily. Arrange on a serving platter. Pour ¹/₂ of the Chutney Sauce over the top. Garnish with lemon wedges and chopped fresh parsley. Serve with the remaining Chutney Sauce.

Note: Bass or turbot may be substituted for the red snapper.

YIELD: 8 SERVINGS

Chutney Sauce

²/₃ cup mango chutney, finely chopped
1 cup mayonnaise
2 tablespoons fresh lemon juice
2 teaspoons curry powder

Combine the mango chutney, mayonnaise, lemon juice and curry powder in a small bowl and mix well. Chill, covered, until ready to serve.

SALMON WITH BALSAMIC MAPLE GLAZE

1/4 cup orange juice
1/4 cup maple syrup
3 tablespoons balsamic vinegar
2 garlic cloves, minced

1 tablespoon olive oil
4 (5- to 6-ounce) salmon fillets
Salt and pepper to taste

Boil the orange juice, maple syrup, vinegar and garlic in a small saucepan until of a glaze consistency, stirring constantly. Add the olive oil and remove from the heat.

Season the fish with salt and pepper. Brush with the glaze. Arrange on a grill rack. Grill until the fish flakes easily, basting frequently with the remaining glaze.

YIELD: 4 SERVINGS

GRILLED SALMON

3/4 cup (1 1/2 sticks) butter
2 garlic cloves, crushed
1 1/2 tablespoons soy sauce
1 1/2 tablespoons dry mustard
1/3 cup cream sherry

3 tablespoons ketchup
4 (8-ounce) salmon steaks
1/4 cup olive oil
Salt and pepper to taste

Melt the butter in a medium saucepan. Add the garlic, soy sauce, dry mustard, sherry and ketchup and whisk gently to break up any lumps. Heat just to the boiling point. Remove from the heat. You may make the sauce a few hours ahead of time and chill in the refrigerator. Reheat until the sauce is warm just before serving.

Rub the fish with the olive oil. Season with salt and pepper. Arrange on a grill rack. Grill over low heat until the fish flakes easily, turning once. Spoon some of the warm sauce over the fish just before serving. Serve with the remaining sauce.

YIELD: 4 SERVINGS

 Salmon is best accompanied by a full-bodied white wine such as chardonnay or try a pinot noir.

SALMON WITH GINGER SOY BUTTER

4 (6-ounce) salmon fillets
Salt and pepper to taste
1/2 cup grated fresh gingerroot
2 tablespoons grated orange zest
2 tablespoons grated lemon zest
3 tablespoons finely chopped
   cilantro

1/2 cup bread crumbs
2 tablespoons olive oil
Ginger Soy Butter Sauce (below)
1 tablespoon chopped chives

Season the fish with salt and pepper. Combine the gingerroot, orange zest, lemon zest and cilantro in a small bowl. Stir in enough of the bread crumbs to bind. Season with salt and pepper. Heat the olive oil in an ovenproof sauté pan. Add the fish. Sear for 1 to 2 minutes on each side. Remove from the heat. Cover with the crumb mixture. Bake at 400 degrees for 6 to 8 minutes for medium-rare or until the crust is golden brown. Remove from the oven and keep warm until ready to serve.

To serve, spoon Ginger Soy Butter Sauce in the center of each individual serving plate. Arrange the fish in the sauce. Sprinkle with the chives.

YIELD: 4 SERVINGS

GINGER SOY BUTTER SAUCE

1/4 cup soy sauce
1/4 cup honey
1 1/2 teaspoons brown sugar
1 ounce fresh gingerroot, minced
1 1/2 teaspoons minced garlic

1 tablespoon minced shallots
1/2 cup (1 stick) butter
Juice of 1 orange
Salt and pepper to taste

Combine the soy sauce, honey, brown sugar, gingerroot, garlic and shallots in a saucepan. Bring to a boil and reduce the heat. Simmer for 5 to 6 minutes or until the sauce is dark in color and reduced by 1/2. Remove from the heat. Add the butter. Stir in the orange juice. Strain through a sieve, discarding the solids. Season with salt and pepper.

Micro-Poached Salmon

2 tablespoons butter or margarine
2 large salmon steaks, or 1 (1-pound) salmon fillet
2 to 3 tablespoons lemon juice
Seasoned salt or seafood seasoning to taste
Freshly ground pepper to taste
Chopped fresh dill weed to taste
Chopped fresh parsley to taste
Drained capers to taste
2 to 3 tablespoons white wine
Fresh dill weed

Microwave the butter on High in a microwave-safe dish. Add the fish and turn to coat. Arrange the fish with the thickest portion to the outside of the dish. Sprinkle with the lemon juice. Season with seasoned salt, pepper and chopped dill weed. Sprinkle with parsley and capers. Add the wine. Cover with plastic wrap. Cut a vent in the top. Microwave on High for 5 minutes per pound or until the fish flakes easily. Arrange the fish on a bed of fresh dill weed on a serving platter. Garnish with lemon wedges and fresh parsley.

Note: To prepare in the oven, cut foil or parchment paper into desired shape large enough to enclose each steak or fillet. Arrange the salmon on each piece of foil and top each with ½ of the ingredients as above. Seal the packets. Arrange on a baking sheet. Bake at 400 degrees for 8 to 10 minutes per inch of thickness or until the fish flakes easily.

YIELD: 2 SERVINGS

EN PAPILLOTTE
(EN PAH-PEE-YOHT)

Originally, this term meant "baked in paper," since cooks used to bake certain dishes in oiled paper sacks to retain the moisture. Today, however, it can also mean "baked in foil." As food bakes and releases steam, the paper puffs up. At the table, the paper (or foil) is cut and peeled back.

FISH FILLETS CANTONESE

4 (5- to 6-ounce) sea bass or salmon fillets
¹/₈ teaspoon salt
¹/₈ teaspoon lemon pepper
1 tablespoon soy sauce
1 tablespoon dry wine or dry sherry
1¹/₂ teaspoons black bean garlic sauce
1 teaspoon canola oil
¹/₄ teaspoon sesame oil
2 teaspoons minced fresh gingerroot
2 teaspoons minced garlic
3 scallions, cut into 2-inch lengths, thinly sliced
¹/₂ cup sliced fresh mushrooms

Rinse the fish with cold water and pat dry with paper towels. Sprinkle salt and lemon pepper on each side of the fish. Arrange in a shallow 8×11-inch pan lined with a double thickness of foil. Mix the soy sauce, wine and black bean garlic sauce in a small bowl. Pour over the fish. Marinate until ready to bake.

Heat the canola oil and sesame oil in a skillet. Add the gingerroot and garlic. Sauté for 1 minute. Add ½ of the scallions and ½ of the mushrooms. Sauté for 1 to 2 minutes. Spread evenly over the fish. Sprinkle with the remaining scallions and mushrooms. Bake at 425 degrees for 15 to 18 minutes or until the fish flakes easily. Garnish with sprigs of fresh cilantro.

YIELD: 4 SERVINGS

OIL

Oils can be divided into two main groups: the neutrally flavored vegetable oils derived from corn, peanuts, soybeans, cottonseeds, sunflower seeds, or safflower seeds, and the flavorful oils pressed from olives, sesame seeds, or various nuts such as almonds, walnuts, or hazelnuts. Freshness deteriorates quickly after opening, so oil should be kept in the refrigerator to avoid rancidity.

LAKE CACHUMA BAKED TROUT

Photograph for this recipe is shown on page 150.

1 medium fresh trout, cleaned
1 tablespoon Italian Salad Dressing (below)
2 tablespoons butter, melted
1/2 teaspoon dill weed
1 tablespoon lemon juice

Arrange the fish on a baking pan sprayed with nonstick cooking spray. Pour the Italian Salad Dressing inside and outside the fish. Bake at 400 degrees for 10 to 15 minutes or until the fish flakes easily. Remove from the oven. Remove the bones by opening the fish and pulling out the center bone. Sprinkle with butter, dill weed and lemon juice. Broil for 5 minutes and serve.

YIELD: 2 SERVINGS

ITALIAN SALAD DRESSING

3/4 cup vegetable oil
1/4 cup vinegar
1 teaspoon minced garlic
1 teaspoon salt
1/2 teaspoon basil

Combine the oil, vinegar, garlic, salt and basil in a jar with a lid. Secure the lid and shake to mix well.

TESTING FISH FOR DONENESS

The general rule for making sure fish is cooked thoroughly is to allow eight to ten minutes of cooking time per inch of thickness. To test for doneness, pierce the fish at its thickest point with a sharp knife. It should be opaque with milky-white juices. Overdone fish will be dry and flaky, while underdone fish will appear translucent.

RIVIERA LINGUINI IN CLAM SAUCE

1 pound lean bacon
1 garlic clove, minced
3 (7-ounce) cans chopped clams
1/2 cup (1 stick) butter
1/2 cup white dry vermouth
1 tablespoon chopped fresh basil, or 1 teaspoon dried basil
1/4 cup chopped fresh parsley or cilantro
12 ounces uncooked fresh linguini
Freshly grated Parmesan cheese
Salt and pepper to taste

Cut the bacon into 1/2-inch strips. Cook in a skillet over low heat until crisp. Drain the bacon, reserving 1/4 cup bacon drippings in the skillet. Add the garlic, undrained clams, butter, vermouth, basil and parsley. Simmer for 5 minutes. You may make ahead up to this point and reheat when ready to serve.

Cook the linguini using the package directions; drain. Pour into a hot pasta bowl. Add the clam mixture, cheese, salt and pepper and toss to coat. Serve with sliced olives, lemon wedges and additional cheese.

YIELD: 6 SERVINGS

 A dry chardonnay or pinot blanc pairs nicely with this seafood pasta.

Santa Barbara Crab Cakes with Tomatillo and Lime Vinaigrette

Chef Charles Fredericks, Bouchon Santa Barbara

2 ears fresh corn, shucked
1 bunch scallions, trimmed
1 fennel bulb, chopped
4 garlic cloves, sliced
1 red bell pepper, chopped
8 ounces fresh lump crab meat
1 tablespoon whole-grain mustard
2 tablespoons cumin seeds, toasted
1 bunch fresh thyme, trimmed

2 tablespoons minced lime zest
1 egg, lightly beaten
1/4 cup all-purpose flour
8 ounces fresh bread crumbs
Salt and pepper to taste
Grapeseed oil
Mixed salad greens
Tomatillo and Lime Vinaigrette (below)

Remove the silks from the corn. Cut the corn from the cob into a bowl using a sharp knife, scraping the cob to extract the juices. Cut the bulbs from the scallions and chop. Chop the scallion tops finely. Sauté the fennel, garlic, chopped scallion bulbs, bell pepper and corn in a skillet until the fennel is soft. Combine the crab meat, mustard, cumin seeds, scallion tops, thyme, lime zest, egg, flour and bread crumbs in a bowl and mix well. Add the fennel mixture, salt and pepper and mix well. Add additional bread crumbs if needed for the desired consistency. Shape the mixture into 2-inch circles 1/2 inch thick. Cook in a small amount of grapeseed oil in a skillet until cooked through and brown on both sides. Arrange over mixed salad greens. Drizzle with Tomatillo and Lime Vinaigrette.

YIELD: 4 SERVINGS

 Chef Charles recommends a crisp, acidic chardonnay.

Tomatillo and Lime Vinaigrette

12 tomatillos, husks removed
6 garlic cloves, peeled
1 white onion, coarsely chopped
1 bunch cilantro, coarsely chopped
Tops of 1 bunch scallions, coarsely chopped

1/2 cup Champagne vinegar
1/2 cup lime juice
2 tablespoons sugar
2 cups olive oil
Salt and pepper to taste

Simmer the tomatillos, garlic and onion in water to cover in a saucepan for 35 minutes; drain. Process with the cilantro and scallions in a food processor. Add the vinegar, lime juice and sugar. Add the olive oil in a fine stream, processing until blended. Season with salt and pepper.

SANTA BARBARA
CRAB CAKES

According to Chef Charles Fredericks of the elegant restaurant, Bouchon Santa Barbara, "We call this dish 'Santa Barbara Crab Cakes' for the following reasons: We have excellent stone crab locally, and use it for this recipe, and the Tomatillo and Lime Vinaigrette shows the local Hispanic influence on our cuisine."

SHRIMP AND SCALLOP CAKES WITH DILL SAUCE

Executive Chef Tim Neenan, El Rancho Marketplace

12 ounces scallops	1^1/$_2$ cups mayonnaise
12 ounces shrimp, peeled, deveined	1 teaspoon dry mustard
	Dash of cayenne pepper
1^1/$_2$ cups cooked whole kernel corn	Salt and black pepper to taste
	2 eggs, lightly beaten
^{3}/$_4$ cup finely chopped onion	2 cups saltine cracker crumbs
^{3}/$_4$ cup finely chopped red bell pepper	3 tablespoons vegetable oil
	3 tablespoons butter
^{3}/$_4$ cup finely chopped celery	Dill Sauce (below)

Chop the scallops and shrimp and place in a large bowl. Add the corn, onion, bell pepper, celery, mayonnaise, dry mustard, cayenne pepper, salt and black pepper and mix well. Fold in the eggs and ½ cup of the cracker crumbs. Shape into 12 patties. Coat with the remaining cracker crumbs. Chill, covered, for at least 1 hour.

Heat 1 tablespoon of the oil and 1 tablespoon of the butter in a large skillet over medium-high heat. Brown the patties in batches, adding the remaining oil and butter as needed. Arrange on a baking sheet. Bake at 350 degrees for 15 minutes. Serve immediately with Dill Sauce.

YIELD: 6 SERVINGS

With all seafood, freshness is the most essential quality. Look for scallops that are cream-colored or slightly pink, and shrimp that are firm and translucent.

DILL SAUCE

^{1}/$_2$ cup mayonnaise	^{1}/$_2$ bunch dill weed, finely chopped
^{1}/$_2$ cup sour cream	Salt and pepper to taste
2 tablespoons red wine vinegar	
^{1}/$_2$ medium cucumber, peeled, seeded, grated	

Combine the mayonnaise, sour cream, vinegar, cucumber, dill weed, salt and pepper in a small bowl and mix well. Chill, covered, until ready to serve.

Cajun Shrimp Tacos

Kate C. Firestone

1 tablespoon (or more) safflower oil	1½ tablespoons olive oil
24 corn tortillas	1½ teaspoons minced garlic
1½ teaspoons paprika	Spicy Sour Cream (below)
1½ teaspoons chili powder	Chopped iceberg lettuce
2 pounds cooked medium shrimp, peeled, deveined	Chopped fresh cilantro
	2 or 3 avocados, chopped
	Green salsa

Heat 1 tablespoon safflower oil in a skillet. Fry the tortillas 1 at a time until crispy, shaping into tacos and adding additional safflower oil as needed. Drain upside down on paper towels. Keep warm in the oven.

Mix the paprika and chili powder in a large bowl. Add the shrimp and toss to coat. Let stand for 5 minutes. Heat the olive oil in a skillet over medium heat. Add the garlic. Sauté for 1 minute. Add the shrimp. Sauté until heated through. Spoon into a serving bowl.

To serve, place the Spicy Sour Cream, lettuce, cilantro, avocados and green salsa in separate bowls and create a taco bar for guests to serve themselves.

YIELD: 8 SERVINGS

Spicy Sour Cream

1½ cups sour cream
1½ teaspoons chili powder
½ teaspoon cayenne pepper, or to taste

Combine the sour cream, chili powder and cayenne pepper in a bowl and mix well.

SHRIMP

Shrimp are classified by the average number per pound. *Jumbo* are eleven to fifteen per pound; *extra-large* are sixteen to twenty; *large* are twenty-one to thirty per pound; *medium* are thirty-one to thirty-five; and *small* are thirty-six to forty-five. To peel shrimp, tear open the shell on the inside of the curve and peel off. The tails can be pulled off or cut.

Stir-Fried Shrimp and Snow Pea Pods

Snow Peas

Also known as Chinese peas or mange-touts, snow peas are an exotic substitute for ordinary peas. Sometimes called sugar peas, these dull green, flat gems should always be purchased at the peak of freshness. To prepare, snip off the ends and remove the central string. Steam or stir-fry for no longer than a minute or so, since overcooking will destroy their crispness.

1 pound fresh large shrimp
1/2 teaspoon vegetable oil
8 ounces snow pea pods, trimmed
1/2 cup sliced shiitake mushrooms
2 teaspoons cornstarch
1 egg white
2 teaspoons dry sherry
1/2 teaspoon salt
Pinch of lemon pepper

1/2 teaspoon vegetable oil
2 scallions, cut into 2-inch lengths
1 teaspoon minced garlic
1 teaspoon minced fresh
   gingerroot
5 teaspoons vegetable oil
1/2 teaspoon black bean garlic
   sauce
1 teaspoon soy sauce

Peel the shrimp and devein. Rinse under cold running water and pat dry with paper towels.

Heat 1/2 teaspoon oil in a 10- or 12-inch wok or skillet. Add the pea pods and mushrooms. Sauté for 2 minutes. Remove to a bowl.

Combine the shrimp and cornstarch in a bowl and toss to coat lightly. Add the egg white, sherry, salt and lemon pepper and stir to mix.

Heat the wok or skillet for 30 seconds or until hot. Add 1/2 teaspoon oil. Reduce the heat slightly. Add the scallions, garlic and gingerroot. Stir-fry for 30 seconds. Remove the scallion mixture to a bowl.

Pour 5 teaspoons oil into the wok or skillet. Stir in the black bean garlic sauce. Add the shrimp mixture and soy sauce. Stir-fry for 2 minutes. Add the scallion mixture and pea pod mixture and mix gently. Spoon onto a warm platter. Garnish with a few sprigs of fresh cilantro. Serve immediately.

Note: You may find black bean garlic sauce in your local Asian markets.

YIELD: 2 TO 4 SERVINGS

SHRIMP IN CHAMPAGNE SAUCE WITH PASTA

2 cups sliced mushrooms
2 tablespoons olive oil
2 pounds fresh medium shrimp, peeled
3 cups Champagne
1/2 teaspoon salt
1/4 cup minced shallots or scallions
4 small tomatoes, peeled, chopped
1 1/2 cups heavy cream
Salt and pepper to taste
32 ounces uncooked angel hair pasta or cheese ravioli
1/2 cup heavy cream
2 tablespoons chopped parsley

Sauté the mushrooms in the olive oil in a medium saucepan over medium-high heat. Cook just long enough for the mushrooms to release their juices and for the liquid to evaporate. Remove from the saucepan.

Add the shrimp, Champagne and 1/2 teaspoon salt to the saucepan. Simmer over high heat until the shrimp turn pink. Remove the shrimp to a warm bowl using a slotted spoon.

Add the shallots and tomatoes to the saucepan. Boil over high heat until the liquid is reduced by 1/2. Add 1 1/2 cups cream. Boil for 1 to 2 minutes or until slightly thickened and reduced. Return the shrimp and mushrooms to the saucepan. Cook until heated through. Season with salt and pepper.

Cook the pasta in a saucepan using the package directions. Drain and return to the saucepan. Add the 1/2 cup cream and the parsley and toss to coat. Divide the pasta among 8 serving plates. Spoon the shrimp sauce over the pasta.

YIELD: 8 SERVINGS

CHAMPAGNE

Only wine which is made in the Champagne district of France can be called Champagne. Sparkling wines made in other areas are just that "sparkling wines." Fine Champagne, which is made from a blend of black and white grapes, goes through several processes before the final bottling. The bubbles are a result of escaping carbonic acid gas created during the fermentation stage. Champagne is at its best when it is seven to ten years old.

SEAFOOD MEDLEY CASSEROLE

BELL PEPPERS

Peppers stored in the
refrigerator in a
sealable plastic bag
should stay fresh for
about a week, but
seeded and chopped
peppers may be frozen
for up to six months.
An easy way to seed
a pepper is to hit the
stem end hard on the
counter or cutting
board. This will loosen
the core so it can be
pulled out easily.

1 cup peeled fresh small shrimp	**1 teaspoon Worcestershire sauce**
1 cup flaked crab meat	**1/2 teaspoon salt**
1 cup chopped celery	**1/4 teaspoon pepper**
1 cup chopped bell pepper	**1/4 cup (1/2 stick) butter**
1/4 cup grated onion	**1/2 cup dry bread crumbs**
1 cup mayonnaise	**1/3 cup sliced almonds**
3 hard-cooked eggs, chopped	

Combine the shrimp and crab meat in a large bowl and toss to mix. Add the celery, bell pepper, onion, mayonnaise, eggs, Worcestershire sauce, salt and pepper and mix carefully so as not to break up the shrimp. Spoon into a 2-quart baking dish.

Melt the butter in a small skillet. Add the bread crumbs and stir until the mixture is combined. Sprinkle over the seafood mixture. Top with the sliced almonds. Bake, uncovered, at 350 degrees for 40 minutes or until bubbly.

YIELD: 4 SERVINGS

SPICY SHRIMP ÉTOUFFÉE

1/4 teaspoon white pepper	**1/2 cup chopped onion**
1/4 teaspoon cayenne pepper	**1 green bell pepper, chopped**
1/8 teaspoon black pepper	**2 ribs celery, chopped**
1/2 teaspoon basil	**2 garlic cloves, minced**
1/4 teaspoon thyme	**1 (10-ounce) can chicken broth**
1/4 cup water	**1 tablespoon tomato paste**
1/4 cup all-purpose flour	**1 to 11/4 pounds shrimp, cooked**
1 tablespoon olive oil	**1/4 cup chopped scallions**

Mix the white pepper, cayenne pepper, black pepper, basil and thyme together. Add the water to the flour in a bowl gradually, stirring constantly to form a paste.

Heat the olive oil in a wok or large skillet until hot. Add the onion, bell pepper, celery and garlic. Sauté until soft. Add the spice mixture and mix well. Stir in the broth and tomato paste. Add the flour mixture. Cook until the sauce is thickened, stirring constantly. Add the shrimp and scallions. Cook until heated through. Serve over hot cooked rice.

YIELD: 6 SERVINGS

SEAFOOD RISOTTO

Juice of 1 orange
12 ounces bay scallops
Juice of 1 lemon
1 pound shrimp, peeled, deveined
2 shallots, chopped
Butter for sautéing
2 cups arborio rice
4 cups vegetable broth, heated to
    boiling
Large pinch of saffron threads

Olive oil for sautéing
3 or 4 (6-inch) squid, cut into rings
2 large portobello mushrooms,
    sliced
1/2 cup freshly grated Parmesan
    cheese
Chopped fresh flat-leaf Italian
    parsley to taste
Salt and freshly ground pepper
    to taste

Pour the orange juice over the scallops in a bowl. Pour the lemon juice over the shrimp in a separate bowl. Marinate at room temperature while preparing the risotto.

Sauté the shallots in butter in a large saucepan until tender. Add the rice. Sauté until the rice is opaque. Add a ladle full of the boiling broth and the saffron. Cook over medium heat until all of the liquid is absorbed, stirring constantly. Add a ladle full of the boiling broth. Cook over medium heat until all of the liquid is absorbed. Repeat the process until all of the broth is used and the rice is tender but still a little firm. Total cooking time should take about 20 minutes.

Sauté the scallops in the olive oil in a skillet for 2 to 3 minutes or until tender. Remove the scallops to a warm bowl. Add a little more olive oil to the skillet. Add the shrimp. Sauté for 3 minutes or until the shrimp turn pink. Remove the shrimp to a warm bowl. Add a little more olive oil to the skillet. Add the squid. Sauté the squid for 2 to 3 minutes or until tender. Remove the squid to a warm bowl. Add a little more olive oil to the skillet. Add the mushrooms. Sauté for 5 to 6 minutes or until the mushrooms are softened.

Combine the risotto, scallops, shrimp, squid, mushrooms, cheese and parsley in a large bowl and toss to mix. Season with salt and pepper. Serve immediately.

YIELD: 8 SERVINGS

RISOTTO

Arborio rice, short grained and plump, is the popular choice for Italian risotto, but other varieties of white rice can be used with success. There are two main types of risotto, *Milanese* and *Venetian*. The *Milanese* version is more compact and sticky, since liquid not absorbed evaporates. The *Venetian* style has a small quantity of liquid added at the end, making it moist and slightly runny.

SAUTÉED CHICKEN WITH ARTICHOKE HEARTS

CHANNEL ISLANDS

There are four islands
in the Santa Barbara
Channel Islands group:
Anacapa, Santa Cruz,
Santa Rosa, and San
Miguel, which lie
twenty-five miles
offshore. There are few
signs of civilization on
the islands, since they
have been designated
a National Marine
Sanctuary. You may not
find hotels, but you will
find pristine beaches,
lush grasslands, rocky
reefs, sea caves, and
crystal clear water.

8 boneless skinless chicken breasts
$1/2$ cup all-purpose flour
Salt and pepper to taste
$1/2$ cup (1 stick) butter
Juice of 1 lemon
2 pounds mushrooms, sliced
1 (14-ounce) can artichoke hearts, drained
3 cups whipping cream
2 cups freshly grated Parmesan cheese
Minced fresh parsley to taste

Pound each chicken breast between 2 sheets of waxed paper until flattened. Mix the flour, salt and pepper in a sealable plastic bag. Add the chicken 1 piece at a time. Shake until the chicken is coated with the flour mixture, shaking off the excess.

Melt the butter in a sauté pan. Add the chicken in batches and sprinkle with lemon juice. Sauté for 1 to 2 minutes on each side until golden brown. Arrange the chicken in a 9×12-inch baking dish.

Add the mushrooms to the drippings in the skillet. Sauté until the mushrooms are softened. Stir in the artichoke hearts. Spoon over the chicken. You may prepare up to this point and refrigerate until ready to bake.

Pour the cream over the layers. Sprinkle with the cheese. Bake at 350 degrees for 25 minutes or until the chicken is cooked through. Sprinkle with parsley just before serving.

Note: Add 5 to 10 minutes to the baking time if the chicken has been refrigerated.

YIELD: 8 SERVINGS

BAKED CHICKEN ALFREDO

6 boneless chicken breasts	$1/2$ teaspoon salt
$1/2$ cup all-purpose flour	$3/4$ cup fine bread crumbs
3 eggs, beaten	3 tablespoons butter
3 tablespoons water	3 tablespoons vegetable oil
$1/2$ cup grated asiago or Parmesan cheese	Cheese Sauce (below)
	6 slices mozzarella cheese
$1/4$ cup minced fresh parsley	

Coat the chicken with the flour. Beat the eggs, water, asiago cheese, parsley and salt in a bowl. Dip the chicken into the egg mixture. Coat with the bread crumbs. Heat the butter and oil in a large skillet. Add the chicken. Cook over medium heat for 15 minutes or until brown. Arrange the chicken in a 7×11-inch baking dish. Pour Cheese Sauce over the chicken. Top each chicken breast with a slice of mozzarella cheese. Bake at 425 degrees for 10 to 15 minutes or until the chicken is cooked through.

YIELD: 6 SERVINGS

CHEESE SAUCE

1 cup whipping cream
$1/4$ cup ($1/2$ stick) butter
1 cup grated asiago or Romano cheese
$1/2$ cup minced fresh parsley

Heat the cream and butter in a small saucepan until the butter is melted. Add the asiago cheese. Cook for 5 minutes, stirring constantly. Stir in the parsley.

CHICKEN BREASTS WITH RED WINE SAUCE

2 cups chicken broth
1 cup dry red wine
2 tablespoons chopped fresh rosemary, or
    2 teaspoons dried rosemary
2 tablespoons olive oil
8 boneless chicken breasts
6 tablespoons butter, cut into 1/4-inch pieces
1/4 cup pitted niçoise olives

Combine the broth and wine in a saucepan and blend well. Cook over medium-low heat until the mixture is reduced to ¾ cup. Add the rosemary. Cover and remove from the heat.

Heat 1 tablespoon of the olive oil in a large skillet. Add ½ of the chicken. Cook for 8 to 10 minutes and turn. Cook for 3 to 5 minutes longer or until cooked through. Remove the chicken to a platter and cover. Repeat with the remaining chicken, adding the remaining olive oil if necessary. Return the sauce to a boil. Remove from the heat. Add the butter a small amount at a time, whisking constantly. Stir in the olives.

Cut the chicken diagonally into ½-inch slices. Serve with the sauce. The texture and flavor are best when the sauce is served just above room temperature.

YIELD: 8 SERVINGS

When making a red wine reduction sauce, it is ideal to use the same wine being served. It balances the acids.

 A California syrah or pinot noir is perfect both in preparation and as an accompaniment to this dish.

HAWAIIAN LUAU CHICKEN

1 (8-ounce) can juice-pack pineapple chunks
2 tablespoons all-purpose flour
8 chicken thighs
Salt and pepper to taste
1 tablespoon vegetable oil
2 garlic cloves, minced
1 tablespoon minced fresh gingerroot
1/2 onion, sliced
1/2 cup chicken broth
2 tablespoons soy sauce
2 tablespoons dry sherry
2 tablespoons honey
1/2 teaspoon cinnamon

Drain the pineapple, reserving the juice. Spread the flour on waxed paper. Roll the chicken in the flour. Season with salt and pepper.

Heat the oil in a 10- or 12-inch skillet. Add the chicken. Cook until the chicken is brown. Add the garlic, gingerroot and onion. Mix the reserved pineapple juice, broth, soy sauce, sherry, honey and cinnamon in a bowl. Pour over the chicken mixture. Simmer, covered, for 15 to 20 minutes. Turn the chicken. Cook for 15 to 20 minutes longer or until the chicken is cooked through, adding a small amount of water if needed. Add the pineapple. Cook until heated through.

YIELD: 4 TO 6 SERVINGS

CITRUS AND PINEAPPLE CHICKEN

1 medium pineapple, peeled, cored, coarsely chopped
1 medium jalapeño chile, seeded, finely chopped
1 teaspoon minced garlic
1 cup fresh orange juice
1/2 cup fresh lime juice
3 tablespoons soy sauce
2 tablespoons chopped fresh cilantro

2 tablespoons chopped fresh basil
1 tablespoon pepper
1 tablespoon grated orange zest
1 tablespoon grated lime zest
8 large boneless skinless chicken breasts
2 tablespoons honey
3 tablespoons butter
Salt and pepper to taste

Purée the pineapple, jalapeño chile and garlic in a blender until smooth. Pour into a 9×13-inch glass dish. Add the orange juice, lime juice, soy sauce, cilantro, basil, 1 tablespoon pepper, orange zest and lime zest and stir to mix well. Add the chicken and turn to coat. Cover with plastic wrap. Marinate in the refrigerator for at least 4 hours or up to 24 hours, turning frequently.

Drain the chicken, reserving the marinade and scraping the excess marinade from the chicken using a wooden spoon. Strain the reserved marinade into a measuring cup, discarding the solids. Pour 1/3 cup of the reserved marinade into a small saucepan. Add the honey and whisk until blended. Bring to a boil. Boil for 2 to 3 minutes, stirring frequently.

Pour the remaining marinade into a heavy saucepan. Bring to a boil. Cook for 15 minutes or until the sauce is reduced to 1½ cups. Add the butter and whisk to mix well. Season with salt and pepper.

Arrange the chicken on an oiled grill rack. Grill over medium heat for 10 minutes or until cooked through, basting with the cooked honey mixture. Arrange on a serving platter. Garnish with sprigs of fresh cilantro and basil. Serve with the sauce.

YIELD: 8 SERVINGS

BACON-WRAPPED TERIYAKI CHICKEN

1 cup soy sauce	1¹⁄₂ teaspoons grated fresh
¹⁄₄ cup bourbon	gingerroot
2 tablespoons sugar	6 boneless chicken breasts
1¹⁄₂ tablespoons sesame oil	6 slices bacon
1 large garlic clove, minced	

Combine the soy sauce, bourbon, sugar, sesame oil, garlic and gingerroot in a bowl and mix well. Add the chicken, turning to coat. Marinate, covered, in the refrigerator for 6 to 8 hours. Drain the chicken, reserving the marinade. Boil the reserved marinade in a saucepan for 2 to 3 minutes, stirring constantly. Wrap 1 bacon slice around each chicken breast and secure with wooden picks. Arrange on a grill rack or broiler pan. Grill or broil for 10 minutes on each side or until cooked through, basting frequently with the cooked marinade.

YIELD: 6 SERVINGS

CHICKEN CACCIATORE

1 large onion, finely chopped	1 teaspoon thyme
Olive oil for sautéing	¹⁄₂ teaspoon basil
4 or 5 large garlic cloves, crushed	1 bay leaf
2 (15-ounce) cans tomato sauce	2 teaspoons salt, or to taste
1 (6-ounce) can tomato paste	¹⁄₂ teaspoon freshly ground pepper
1¹⁄₂ cups water	4 chicken thighs and legs, skinned
1 cup dry white wine	16 ounces fusilli or penne pasta,
1 tablespoon sugar	cooked, drained
1 tablespoon oregano	Freshly grated Parmesan cheese

Sauté the onion in a small amount of olive oil in a skillet until tender. Add the garlic, tomato sauce, tomato paste, water, wine, sugar, oregano, thyme, basil, bay leaf, salt and pepper and mix well. Bring to a boil and reduce the heat. Simmer for 20 minutes, stirring occasionally. Adjust the seasonings to taste. Add the chicken. Simmer for 45 minutes or until the chicken is cooked through. Discard the bay leaf. Spoon over the pasta. Sprinkle with the cheese.

YIELD: 4 SERVINGS

 A perfect accompaniment is a hearty zinfandel or chianti.

CURRY CHICKEN WITH YOGURT SAUCE

2 cups yogurt
3/4 cup shredded coconut
1 tomato, chopped
1/2 cucumber, chopped
2 large onions, chopped
2 jalapeño chiles, chopped
2 teaspoons grated fresh
   gingerroot
3 garlic cloves, minced
2 teaspoons grated fresh
   gingerroot
1 or 2 teaspoons curry powder
1 1/2 teaspoons chili powder

1/4 teaspoon ground cloves
1/4 teaspoon cardamom
1/4 teaspoon turmeric
3 tablespoons vegetable oil
2 to 2 1/2 pounds chicken breasts,
   cut into cubes
1/2 cup water
3/4 cup coconut milk
1/3 cup golden raisins
1 1/2 tablespoons lemon juice
Salt to taste
Hot cooked rice

Combine the yogurt, coconut, tomato, cucumber, 1/2 cup of the onions, jalapeño chiles and 2 teaspoons gingerroot in a bowl and mix well. Let stand at room temperature for several hours before serving.

Sauté the remaining onions, garlic, 2 teaspoons gingerroot, curry powder, chili powder, cloves, cardamom and turmeric in the oil in a 12-inch heavy skillet until the onions are tender. Add the chicken. Sauté until the chicken is light brown. Add the water. Simmer for 7 to 10 minutes or until the chicken is cooked through, stirring frequently. Remove from the heat. Add the coconut milk, raisins, lemon juice and salt. Spoon over hot cooked rice. Garnish with lengthwise slices of bananas and sprigs of fresh cilantro. Serve with the yogurt sauce and Peach and Mango Chutney (page 89).

YIELD: 6 SERVINGS

You may purchase canned or frozen coconut milk, or you may purée 1/4 cup dried shredded coconut with 1 cup hot milk in a blender and strain.

CHICKEN CURRY

1¹⁄₂ cups (3 sticks) butter
4 cups chopped onions
4 tart apples, peeled, chopped
4 pounds chicken, cooked, shredded
5 garlic cloves, chopped
¹⁄₂ cup curry powder
4 teaspoons celery salt
1 teaspoon thyme leaves
2 cups chicken broth
1 cup dry vermouth or dry white wine
¹⁄₂ cup sherry
¹⁄₂ cup chutney
3 cups heavy cream
2 tablespoons cornstarch
Hot cooked rice

Melt the butter in a large skillet. Add the onions and apples. Cook until the onions are tender. Add the chicken, garlic, curry powder, celery salt, thyme, broth, vermouth, sherry and chutney and mix well. Simmer for 15 minutes. Stir in the cream. The curry may be frozen at this point.

To serve, thaw and reheat the curry. Add a mixture of the cornstarch dissolved in a small amount of water. Cook until thickened, stirring constantly. Spoon over hot cooked rice. Serve with condiments such as peanuts, shredded coconut, shredded hard-cooked eggs, chutney and chopped scallions.

YIELD: 8 SERVINGS

ENCHILADAS BLANCAS

1¹/₃ cups sour cream	6 boneless skinless chicken
1 (4-ounce) can sliced black	breasts, cooked, chopped
olives, drained	¹/₂ cup minced onion
1¹/₂ cups sliced scallions	¹/₄ cup (¹/₂ stick) butter
1¹/₂ pounds Monterey Jack	¹/₄ cup all-purpose flour
cheese, shredded (6 cups)	4 cups chicken broth
1 (7-ounce) can chopped green	¹/₂ cup half-and-half
chiles, drained	18 (6-inch) flour tortillas
1 cup slivered almonds	

Mix the sour cream, black olives, scallions, ¾ of the cheese, green chiles and almonds in a bowl. Add the chicken and mix well.

Sauté the onion in the butter in a skillet until translucent. Stir in the flour, broth and half-and-half. Cook until slightly thickened, stirring constantly. Remove from the heat to cool.

To assemble, spoon the chicken filling onto each tortilla and roll up. Pour a little of the sauce into two 9×13-inch baking pans. Arrange 9 tortillas in each prepared pan. Pour the remaining sauce over the top. Sprinkle with the remaining cheese. Bake, uncovered, for 35 to 45 minutes or until brown and bubbly.

Note: This recipe freezes well. Thaw and bring to room temperature before baking.

YIELD: 12 SERVINGS

CHICKEN WITH RED PEPPERS AND CASHEWS
(GONG-BAO JI-DING)

1 pound boneless skinless chicken breasts
4 teaspoons cornstarch
4 teaspoons soy sauce
2 tablespoons rice wine or dry sherry
1/2 teaspoon salt
1 egg white
4 teaspoons cornstarch
4 teaspoons rice wine or dry sherry
2 to 4 tablepoons soy sauce

2 teaspoons vinegar
1/2 teaspoon salt
2 to 3 teaspoons sugar
1/2 cup vegetable oil
2 to 5 dried red peppers, seeds removed
4 teaspoons finely chopped fresh gingerroot
4 scallions, cut into 3/4-inch pieces
1 cup cashews

Cut the chicken into 1-inch pieces. Combine 4 teaspoons cornstarch, 4 teaspoons soy sauce, 2 tablespoons rice wine, 1/2 teaspoon salt and egg white in a bowl and mix well. Add the chicken and stir to coat. Marinate, covered, in the refrigerator for at least 15 minutes or up to 12 hours.

Combine 4 teaspoons cornstarch, 4 teaspoons rice wine and 2 to 4 tablespoons soy sauce in a bowl and mix well. Add the vinegar, 1/2 teaspoon salt and sugar and mix well.

Heat the oil in a wok or large skillet. Add the red peppers. Cook over a medium flame until the red peppers begin to char. Increase the heat to high. Cook until the red peppers are black. Add the chicken mixture. Reduce the heat to medium. Stir-fry until the chicken is cooked through. Add the gingerroot and scallions. Stir-fry for a few more seconds. Add the cashews and soy sauce mixture. Cook until slightly thickened, stirring constantly. Remove to a serving dish and serve hot.

Note: Do not breathe the vapors from cooking the red peppers as the oil in them is volatile. Use a stove fan and/or open windows while charring the red peppers.

YIELD: 4 SERVINGS

 Gewürztraminer is the wine of choice for this spicy dish.

GONG-BAO JI-DING

When Ting Kung-Pao of Kweichow received an appointment as Imperial official to Szechwan, he prepared dinner for his friends that included this dish. It is one of the best known and most often prepared Szechwanese dishes. Whole dried peppers are purposely cooked until burned, flavoring the oil in which the chicken is cooked. The final result should be slightly sweet and spicy, but also hot.

Mustard Chicken in Phyllo Pastry

**6 or 7 boneless skinless chicken
    breasts, cut into cubes**
Salt and white pepper to taste
1/4 cup (1/2 stick) unsalted butter
1/4 cup Dijon mustard
**2 tablespoons chopped fresh
    tarragon, or 1 tablespoon dried
    tarragon**
11/2 cups heavy cream
3/4 cup fresh mushrooms, sliced
Butter for sautéing
10 sheets phyllo dough
3/4 cup (11/2 sticks) butter, melted

Sprinkle the chicken with salt and white pepper. Melt 1/4 cup butter in a skillet over medium heat. Add the chicken. Sauté for 7 minutes or until the chicken is cooked through. Do not overcook. Remove the chicken to a large bowl to keep warm.

Whisk the Dijon mustard into the drippings in the skillet. Add the tarragon. Cook until slightly reduced. Whisk in the cream. Reduce the heat to low. Simmer until slightly thickened and reduced by about 1/4, stirring constantly. Sauté the mushrooms in a small amount of butter in a small skillet. Add to the sauce and stir to mix well. Pour over the chicken and stir to coat. Fit 5 phyllo sheets into a buttered 9×13-inch baking dish, brushing each sheet with melted butter. Add the chicken mixture. Layer the remaining phyllo sheets over the top, brushing each sheet with melted butter. Trim the edges or tuck the edges under neatly. Brush with the remaining melted butter. Bake at 425 degrees for 15 minutes or until heated through and crisp and golden brown on top.

YIELD: 6 TO 8 SERVINGS

Mustards

Mustards come in a variety of colors, textures, and flavors, and from a variety of places. You'll find American, Chinese, Dijon, English, and German mustards, each with its own distinct flavor and texture. Yellow and white seeds of the mustard plant produce a mild mustard, while brown seeds create a spicier taste. For ultra-hot, try mustard oil, which is pressed from the seed and is sometimes used in Asian dishes.

PHYLLO PACKETS WITH SUN-DRIED TOMATOES AND PROSCIUTTO

³/₄ cup mayonnaise

3 tablespoons finely chopped drained oil-pack sun-dried tomatoes

2 tablespoons minced fresh basil, or 2 teaspoons dried basil

2 ounces prosciutto, finely chopped

3 garlic cloves, minced

¹/₂ cup freshly grated Parmesan cheese

12 sheets phyllo dough

6 tablespoons butter or margarine, melted

¹/₄ teaspoon pepper

6 boneless skinless chicken breasts

Mix the mayonnaise, sun-dried tomatoes, basil, prosciutto, garlic and cheese in a small bowl. For the packets, lay 1 phyllo sheet on a flat surface and brush lightly with melted butter, keeping the remaining phyllo sheets covered with plastic wrap to prevent drying. Top with another phyllo sheet and brush lightly with butter. Sprinkle pepper on 1 side of 1 chicken breast; spread the other side with about 1½ tablespoons of the mayonnaise mixture. Lay coated side down on 1 corner of the phyllo sheets. Spread the top with 1½ tablespoons of the mayonnaise mixture. Lift the corner of the phyllo over the chicken; roll chicken with phyllo over once. Fold 1 side of phyllo over chicken and roll again. Fold opposite side of phyllo over chicken and roll to the end. Repeat with the remaining phyllo dough, chicken and mayonnaise mixture. Brush with melted butter. At this point you may arrange the packets in a single layer in a container with a tight-fitting lid and freeze for up to 1 month. Thaw, covered, before baking.

Arrange the packets seam side down 2 inches apart in a 12×17-inch baking pan. Bake, uncovered, at 375 degrees for 30 minutes or until golden brown.

YIELD: 6 SERVINGS

Phyllo has a tendency to stick or tear when handled, so make sure your work surface is clean and dry, the filling is cool and the pastry sheets are fully thawed.

PROSCIUTTO (PROH-SHOO-TOH)

Italian for "ham," prosciutto is seasoned, salt-cured, and air-dried (but not smoked). It is then pressed and sold thinly sliced. Prosciutto is often referred to as Parma ham, as the Italian regions of Parma and San Daniele are the largest producers. Prosciutto, since it is cured, needs no cooking.

CHICKEN STROGANOFF

1 tablespoon butter
2 cups sliced mushrooms
1 garlic clove, crushed
1/4 cup vermouth or dry sherry
3 tablespoons butter
4 boneless skinless chicken
    breasts, cut into cubes
1 cup chicken broth
2 tablespoons chopped fresh
    chives, or 2 teaspoons dried
    chives

2 tablespoons chopped fresh
    parsley
1 teaspoon chopped fresh dill
    weed, or 1/2 teaspoon dried
    dill weed
1 teaspoon all-purpose flour
1 cup sour cream
Salt and pepper to taste
1 package fresh egg noodles or
    fettuccini
Chopped fresh parsley to taste

Melt 1 tablespoon butter in a large sauté pan. Add the mushrooms. Sauté until the mushrooms are tender. Add the garlic and vermouth. Simmer for 2 to 4 minutes. Remove the mushrooms to a warm bowl. Melt 3 tablespoons butter in the skillet. Add the chicken. Sauté until the chicken is brown. Remove the chicken to a warm bowl.

Add the broth, mushrooms, chives, 2 tablespoons parsley and dill weed to the skillet and mix well. Bring to a slow boil. Return the chicken to the skillet. Simmer for 10 minutes or until cooked through. Mix the flour into the sour cream in a small bowl. Stir into the chicken mixture. Simmer for 4 minutes. Season with salt and pepper to taste.

Cook the noodles using the package directions; drain. Divide the noodles among 6 pasta bowls. Ladle the chicken mixture over the top. Sprinkle with chopped fresh parsley to taste. Serve with warm French bread.

YIELD: 6 SERVINGS

AUTUMN CHICKEN RAGOUT WITH LINGUINI

Chef Eric Widmer, La Cumbre Country Club

6 chicken thighs	3 sprigs of fresh thyme
2 teaspoons curry powder	1 bay leaf
Salt and pepper to taste	1/2 cup (1 stick) butter
Vegetable oil for sautéing	1 basket pearl onions, blanched,
2 ounces onion, chopped	peeled
2 ounces carrots, chopped	Olive oil for sautéing
2 ounces celery, chopped	1/2 cup finely chopped carrots
1 pear, chopped	1/2 cup green peas
1 cup white wine	1/2 cup finely chopped pears
3 cups chicken stock	Hot cooked linguini

Season the chicken with curry powder, salt and pepper. Heat vegetable oil in a medium ovenproof sauté pan to the smoking point. Add the chicken. Cook until brown. Remove the chicken to a warm platter.

Add 2 ounces onion, 2 ounces carrots, celery and 1 pear to the sauté pan. Sauté until the vegetables are brown. Add the wine, stirring to deglaze the pan. Cook until the wine is reduced by 1/2. Return the chicken to the pan. Add the stock, thyme and bay leaf. Bake, covered with foil, at 320 degrees until the chicken is cooked through. Remove the chicken from the pan to a platter. Remove the thigh bones carefully. Cut each thigh into 4 pieces. Reduce the sauce over medium heat until of the desired consistency. Stir in the butter. Discard the bay leaf.

Sauté the pearl onions in a small amount of olive oil in a large sauté pan until golden brown. Add 1/2 cup carrots, the green peas and 1/2 cup pears. Sauté for 2 minutes. Add the sauce and chicken and stir to mix well. Spoon over hot cooked linguini. Garnish with pomegranate, pumpkin seeds and a sprig of thyme or rosemary.

YIELD: 4 SERVINGS

Moroccan Vegetable and Chicken Stew

Photograph for this recipe is shown on page 150 and below.

Photograph for this recipe is shown on page 150 and below.

1 tablespoon olive oil	2 cups chopped peeled parsnips
6 boneless skinless chicken breasts, cut into 1-inch pieces	2 cups chopped peeled turnips
	1 cup chopped peeled rutabaga
1½ cups chopped onions	1 cup chopped peeled carrots
2 garlic cloves, minced	2 cups chicken broth
1 tablespoon cumin	¼ cup dried currants
1 tablespoon curry powder	1 cup canned diced tomatoes
1 cinnamon stick	Chopped fresh cilantro to taste
2 cups chopped peeled yams	Hot cooked couscous

Heat the olive oil in a large heavy saucepan over medium-high heat. Add the chicken. Sauté until the chicken is light brown. Remove the chicken to a warm bowl. Add the onions. Sauté until golden brown. Add the garlic, cumin, curry powder, cinnamon stick, yams, parsnips, turnips, rutabaga, carrots, broth and currants. Bring to a boil and reduce the heat. Simmer, covered, for 20 minutes or until the vegetables are tender. Add the tomatoes and chicken. Simmer for 5 minutes or until the chicken is cooked through. Discard the cinnamon stick. Sprinkle with cilantro. Spoon over hot cooked couscous.

YIELD: 6 SERVINGS

TURNIPS

The ordinary white globe turnip and the larger reddish brown-skinned rutabaga are the two turnip varieties found in supermarkets. They are perfectly good substitutes for a starchy side dish and have only half the calories of potatoes and a quarter of the calories of noodles. Buy turnips that are rock-hard, avoiding soft, pithy, or woody ones. Their peak season is late summer through early winter.

BRANDIED CORNISH GAME HENS

3 Cornish game hens
3 cups white wine
Butter
Favorite stuffing
1 cup pineapple juice
1 cup orange juice
3/4 cup packed brown sugar
4 whole cloves
1 teaspoon grated orange zest
1 to 2 tablespoons cornstarch
1/2 cup brandy

Place the hens in a large bowl. Pour the wine over the hens. Marinate, covered, in the refrigerator for 8 to 12 hours, turning occasionally. Drain the hens, discarding the marinade. Rub the cavities with butter. Stuff with your favorite stuffing. Rub butter over the outside of the hens.

Combine the pineapple juice, orange juice, brown sugar, cloves and orange zest in a saucepan. Bring to a boil. Thicken with the cornstarch as needed for the desired glaze consistency. Remove from the heat. Add the brandy.

Place the hens on a rack in a roasting pan. Bake at 350 degrees for 30 minutes. Spoon the glaze over the hens. Bake for 30 minutes longer or until the hens are cooked through. Cool the hens for 20 minutes before cutting into halves to serve.

YIELD: 6 SERVINGS

STUFFING TIPS

Some call it stuffing and some call it dressing. But whatever you call it, don't stuff your bird before you're ready to cook it. Bacteria starts growing immediately so, if you make it in advance, keep it refrigerated until ready to stuff. Spoon the stuffing loosely into the cavity so it has room to expand. You'll need about a half cup of stuffing per pound of poultry.

SAVOR THE TRADITION

meat entrées

LAMB SHANKS WITH WINE AND HERBS

STIR-FRIED BEEF AND BROCCOLINI

ORANGE DIJON PORK MEDALLIONS

(shown left to right)

Photograph © Michael Brown

Poppies in Vineyard, Santa Ynez Valley *Photograph © Kirk Irwin*

Thomas and Barbara Brashears, LeRoy and Sherry Hunt, Cap and Diane Price, John M. and Lorraine Rasmussen, Marcia G. Vaile

Fillet of Beef Extraordinaire

1 (3-pound) fillet of beef, trimmed
Kosher salt and freshly ground
   pepper to taste
2 to 3 tablespoons olive oil
8 slices bacon, chopped
3 garlic cloves, minced
2 cups dry red wine
2 cups beef stock
2 tablespoons tomato paste

1 sprig of fresh thyme
2 tablespoons unsalted butter,
   softened
2 tablespoons all-purpose flour
12 ounces mushrooms, sliced
   1/4 inch thick
1 tablespoon butter
1 tablespoon olive oil

Cut the beef horizontally into 1¼-inch slices. Season both sides of the slices with kosher salt and pepper to taste. Sauté the beef in batches in 2 to 3 tablespoons olive oil in a skillet for 2 to 3 minutes on each side until brown on the outside and rare on the inside. Remove the beef to a warm platter.

Sauté the bacon in a skillet over medium-low heat for 5 minutes or until brown and crisp. Remove the bacon to paper towels to drain. Drain the the skillet, reserving 2 tablespoons bacon drippings. Sauté the garlic in the reserved bacon drippings in the skillet for 1 minute. Add the wine. Cook over high heat for 1 minute, stirring to deglaze the skillet. Add the stock, tomato paste and thyme. Bring to a boil. Cook, uncovered, over medium-high heat for 20 minutes. Strain the sauce, discarding the solids. Return the strained sauce to the skillet. Mash 2 tablespoons butter with the flour in a bowl to form a paste. Add to the sauce and whisk gently to incorporate. Simmer for 2 minutes or until thickened.

Sauté the mushrooms in 1 tablespoon butter and 1 tablespoon olive oil in a skillet until brown and tender. Add the mushrooms, beef and bacon to the sauce. Cook, covered, for 5 to 10 minutes or until heated through. Do not overcook. Season with kosher salt and pepper to taste. Garnish with a sprig of fresh thyme. Serve with Herbed Roasted Vegetables on page 137.

Note: This dish tastes even better the second day. Make it ahead and reheat it before dinner.

YIELD: 6 TO 8 SERVINGS

 Cabernet franc pairs perfectly with this extraordinary entrée or try a cabernet sauvignon.

BEEF TENDERLOIN IN RED WINE SAUCE

Kate C. Firestone

MEAT TENDERNESS

The most tender parts of an animal are those that have had the least exercise. Fillet, the round-shaped section of a T-bone, is the most tender cut of beef or pork. It is sold either in individual portions, such as filet mignon, or cut from the whole rack of meat and sold as the tenderloin.

2 tablespoons chopped fresh thyme
2 tablespoons chopped fresh rosemary
2 garlic cloves
2 bay leaves
1 large shallot, chopped
1 tablespoon grated orange zest
1 tablespoon salt
1 teaspoon pepper
1/2 teaspoon nutmeg
1/4 teaspoon ground cloves
2 tablespoons olive oil
2 (2-pound) beef tenderloins, trimmed
Red Wine Sauce (page 189)
Salt and pepper to taste

Process the thyme, rosemary, garlic, bay leaves, shallot, orange zest, 1 tablespoon salt, 1 teaspoon pepper, nutmeg and cloves in a food processor. Add the olive oil in a fine stream, processing constantly until blended. Spread over the beef in a shallow dish. Marinate, covered, in the refrigerator for 6 to 12 hours.

Place the beef on a rack in a roasting pan. Bake at 400 degrees for 35 minutes or until a meat thermometer registers 125 degrees for rare. Remove from the oven and cover with foil. Let stand for 10 minutes.

Bring the Red Wine Sauce to a boil in a saucepan. Season with salt and pepper to taste. Remove from the heat. Cut the beef into slices and arrange on a serving platter. Drizzle with some of the Red Wine Sauce. Garnish with sprigs of fresh thyme. Serve with the remaining Red Wine Sauce.

YIELD: 8 SERVINGS

RED WINE SAUCE

2 tablespoons olive oil
1½ cups sliced shallots
1 tablespoon minced garlic
1 teaspoon sugar
1 tablespoon all-purpose flour
1 tablespoon minced fresh thyme
2 teaspoons minced fresh
   rosemary

1 bay leaf
1 teaspoon grated orange zest
Pinch of nutmeg
Pinch of ground cloves
3¼ cups beef broth
1½ cups red wine
¼ cup brandy

Heat the olive oil in a large skillet over low heat. Add the shallots and garlic. Sauté until tender. Stir in the sugar. Sauté until golden brown. Add the flour, thyme, rosemary, bay leaf, orange zest, nutmeg and cloves. Sauté for 1 minute. Add the broth, wine and brandy. Boil for 20 minutes or until the sauce is reduced to 1¾ cups. Discard the bay leaf. Chill until ready to serve. The sauce may be made up to 2 days ahead.

YIELD: 1¾ CUPS

 Serve with a syrah or cabernet sauvignon.

BEEF BRISKET

1 (4- to 5-pound) fresh beef brisket
1 cup ketchup or chili sauce
¼ cup chopped onion
1 tablespoon prepared mustard
¼ teaspoon freshly ground pepper

2 tablespoons apple cider vinegar
1 tablespoon prepared horseradish
2 teaspoons salt
1 tablespoon cornstarch
2 tablespoons cold water

Trim the excess fat from the brisket. Place in a shallow baking pan. Mix the ketchup, onion, prepared mustard, pepper, vinegar and horseradish in a bowl. Pour over the brisket. Marinate, covered, in the refrigerator for 3 to 12 hours. Sprinkle with the salt. Cover tightly with foil. Bake at 300 degrees for 4 to 5 hours (1 hour per pound) or until tender. Remove the brisket to a serving platter. Cut into thin slices. Skim the fat from the pan drippings. Thicken the drippings slightly with a mixture of the cornstarch and water if needed. Serve with the brisket.

YIELD: 6 TO 8 SERVINGS

THICKENING SAUCES

To thicken a sauce, mix together equal amounts of butter and flour and drop small amounts into the hot sauce, stirring with a wire whisk. In French cooking, flour is the traditional thickening agent, but cornstarch will create a clearer, shinier sauce. Dissolve 1 tablespoon cornstarch into 2 tablespoons cold water in a bowl and add gradually to the sauce while whisking.

TIPSY TENDERLOIN OF BEEF

1 (750-milliliter) bottle tawny port
2 (750-milliliter) bottles dry red wine
4 cups beef broth
$1/4$ cup ($1/2$ stick) butter
$1^2/3$ pounds onions, chopped
6 tablespoons chopped fresh thyme
2 tablespoons butter
2 pounds mushrooms, sliced
2 tablespoons all-purpose flour
2 tablespoons olive oil
2 (2- to $2^1/4$-pound) beef tenderloins, trimmed
Salt and pepper to taste

Boil the port, wine and broth in a large stockpot for 35 to 40 minutes or until reduced to 6 cups.

Melt $1/4$ cup butter in a large skillet over medium-high heat. Add the onions. Sauté for 15 to 20 minutes or until tender. Add the thyme. Sauté for 10 minutes or until the onions are brown. Remove to a bowl. Melt 2 tablespoons butter in the skillet. Add the mushrooms. Sauté for 15 to 20 minutes or until tender. Return the onions to the skillet. Add the flour. Cook for 3 minutes, stirring constantly. Add to the wine mixture. Simmer over medium heat for 1 hour or until thickened and reduced to 6 cups. You may prepare up to this point and store, covered, in the refrigerator for 24 hours.

Rub the olive oil over the beef. Season with salt and pepper to taste. Arrange on a rack in a roasting pan. Insert a meat thermometer into the thickest portion. Bake at 400 degrees until the meat thermometer registers 125 degrees. Remove from the oven. Let stand for 10 minutes.

Drain the juices from the roast and add to the sauce. Cook until heated through. Cut the beef cross grain into $1/2$-inch slices. Arrange the beef in overlapping slices on a serving platter. Spoon some of the sauce down the center. Serve with the remaining sauce.

YIELD: 10 TO 12 SERVINGS

This is a versatile dish. It can be served hot for a formal occasion or be prepared well in advance and served at room temperature for a summer buffet.

MARINATED FILLET OF BEEF

4 pounds fillet of beef or other lean beef
1 cup soy sauce
1/2 cup medium-dry sherry
1/3 cup olive oil
3 garlic cloves, minced
2 teaspoons ginger

Place the beef in a shallow dish. Mix the soy sauce, sherry, olive oil, garlic and ginger in a large nonaluminum bowl. Rub into the beef. Marinate, covered, in the refrigerator for 8 to 12 hours. Let stand at room temperature for at least 1 hour before baking. Place the beef on a rack in a roasting pan. Insert a meat thermometer into the thickest portion of the beef. Bake at 350 degrees until the meat thermometer registers 140 degrees. Do not overcook. Remove from the oven. Let stand at room temperature for 30 minutes before serving.

YIELD: 8 SERVINGS

SANTA MARIA TRI-TIP MARINADE AND BARBECUE

1 (6- to 8-pound) beef tri-tip
1/2 cup red wine
1/2 cup vegetable oil
2 tablespoons Worcestershire sauce
1 tablespoon soy sauce
Juice of 1 lemon
3 garlic cloves, chopped
1/4 teaspoon dry mustard

Place the beef in a large sealable plastic bag. Mix the wine, oil, Worcestershire sauce, soy sauce, lemon juice, garlic and dry mustard in a bowl. Pour over the beef and seal the bag. Marinate in the refrigerator for 24 hours, turning frequently. Remove from the refrigerator. Let stand for 2 hours. Drain the beef, reserving the marinade. Pour the reserved marinade into a saucepan. Bring to a boil. Boil for 2 to 3 minutes, stirring constantly.

Place the beef on a grill rack. Grill for 20 to 30 minutes on each side, brushing frequently with the cooked reserved marinade. Let stand for 15 minutes. Cut into slices. Serve with beans, green salad and garlic bread.

YIELD: 10 TO 12 SERVINGS

TRI-TIP

The term "tri-tip" is relatively unknown east of California, but asking your butcher for a bottom sirloin butt will get you the same triangular cut of beef. The cut comes from the middle of the back in front of the hindquarters, and each animal has two. The city of Santa Maria, California, claims to have originated tri-tip in the 1800s where it was served as the main course at barbecues.

SAUERBRATEN

POTATO PANCAKES

Combine 4 grated
peeled potatoes,
1 chopped small onion,
1 beaten egg and
1/2 cup milk in a bowl
and mix well. Add
2 tablespoons
all-purpose flour or
bread crumbs, salt
and pepper to taste
and mix well. Heat
vegetable oil in a
skillet. Drop the batter
by tablespoonfuls into
the skillet. Cook for 4
minutes on each side
until brown and crisp.
Drain on paper towels.
Serve immediately.
These pancakes
are an excellent
accompaniment to
the Bavarian favorite
at right.

1 cup water
1 cup cider vinegar
2 teaspoons salt
1/2 teaspoon pepper
1/4 cup packed brown sugar
1 onion, thinly sliced
3 bay leaves
1 teaspoon peppercorns
1 (4-pound) rump roast
1 tablespoon butter
1/4 cup packed brown sugar
6 gingersnaps, broken
1 cup sour cream

Combine the water, vinegar, salt, pepper, 1/4 cup brown sugar, onion, bay leaves and peppercorns in a medium saucepan. Bring to a boil. Place the beef in a large bowl. Pour the hot mixture over the beef. Let stand until cool. Marinate, covered, in the refrigerator for 24 to 48 hours, turning occasionally.

Drain the beef, reserving the marinade. Brown the beef in the butter in a Dutch oven. Add the reserved marinade. Bring to a boil and reduce the heat. Simmer, covered, for 1½ hours or until tender. Remove the beef to a warm platter. Strain the liquid, discarding the solids. Return the liquid to the Dutch oven. Add 1/4 cup brown sugar. Cook until the brown sugar dissolves, stirring constantly. Add the gingersnaps. Cook for 5 minutes or until smooth and thickened, stirring constantly. Stir in the sour cream.

Cut the beef thinly cross grain. Pour the sauce over the beef. Serve with buttered noodles.

YIELD: 8 TO 10 SERVINGS

STIR-FRIED BEEF AND BROCCOLINI

Photograph for this recipe is shown on page 184 and below.

1 bunch broccolini, or 2 or 3 small broccoli crowns	1 tablespoon oyster sauce
12 ounces boneless rib-eye steak or filet mignon	¹/₂ teaspoon cornstarch
	1 teaspoon canola oil
¹/₄ teaspoon salt	¹/₄ teaspoon salt
Dash of pepper	Dash of pepper
1 teaspoon minced fresh gingerroot	1 tablespoon oyster sauce
	¹/₄ to ¹/₂ cup water
1 teaspoon cooking sherry	1 teaspoon canola oil
1 teaspoon soy sauce	¹/₄ cup sliced onions
	¹/₂ cup sliced mushrooms

Trim the outer stems of the broccolini. Cut into large bite-size pieces. Rinse and pat dry. Trim all fat from the steak. Cut the steak into very thin slices 1 inch long. Season with ¼ teaspoon salt and dash of pepper. Combine the steak, gingerroot, sherry, soy sauce and 1 tablespoon oyster sauce in a bowl and toss to coat. Add the cornstarch and mix well.

Heat a wok or skillet over high heat for 30 seconds. Add 1 teaspoon canola oil. Heat for 30 seconds. Add the broccolini, ¼ teaspoon salt and dash of pepper. Stir-fry for 1 minute. Stir in 1 tablespoon oyster sauce. Add the water. Cook, covered, for 3 minutes or until the broccolini is tender-crisp. Remove to a platter and place in a preheated 180-degree oven.

Return the wok to the heat. Add 1 teaspoon canola oil. Heat for 30 seconds or until very hot. Add the onions and mushrooms. Stir-fry for 30 seconds. Add the steak mixture. Stir-fry over high heat for 2 minutes or until the steak is cooked through. Add to the broccolini mixture and toss gently. Serve with hot cooked rice.

YIELD: 2 TO 4 SERVINGS

BROCCOLINI

Broccolini, a California native, is a delightful cross between broccoli and Chinese kale. The entire vegetable is edible, from the stem to the flowering bud, and the flavor has been described as slightly sweet and slightly bitter. Broccolini can be steamed, blanched, stir-fried, microwaved, or grilled, and always makes an attractive addition to the dinner table.

MARINATED SKIRT STEAK WITH BLACK BEAN CHILI

2 pounds skirt or flank steak
6 garlic cloves, pressed
2 teaspoons oregano

Salt and pepper to taste
$1/4$ cup vegetable oil
Black Bean Chili (below)

Rub the steak with the garlic, oregano, salt and pepper. Place in a shallow dish. Drizzle the oil over the steak. Turn the steak in the marinade several times. Let stand for 2 hours. Place on a grill rack. Grill over hot coals for 2 to 3 minutes on each side or to the desired degree of doneness. Serve over Black Bean Chili.

YIELD: 6 TO 8 SERVINGS

BLACK BEAN CHILI

4 cups dried black beans, sorted, soaked, drained
2 cups crushed tomatoes
2 large onions, chopped
$3/4$ cup coarsely chopped red bell pepper
$3/4$ cup coarsely chopped yellow bell pepper
$1/2$ cup vegetable oil

2 tablespoons cumin seeds
2 tablespoons oregano
$1/2$ teaspoon cayenne pepper
$1^1/2$ tablespoons paprika
$1/4$ cup chopped jalapeño chiles, peeled, seeded
2 garlic cloves, chopped
1 teaspoon salt

Combine the black beans, tomatoes, onions, bell peppers, oil, cumin seeds, oregano, cayenne pepper, paprika, jalapeño chiles, garlic and salt in a large saucepan. Cook over medium-low heat for 1¾ hours.

A full-bodied red wine, such as cabernet sauvignon or syrah, is a perfect accompaniment to this unusual entrée.

GUADALUPE FLANK STEAK

1¹/₂ **pounds flank steak**
¹/₂ **cup vegetable oil**
¹/₃ **cup minced onion**
¹/₄ **cup white vinegar**
¹/₄ **cup packed brown sugar**
3 **tablespoons Worcestershire
   sauce**

3 **tablespoons lemon juice**
1 **teaspoon pepper**
¹/₂ **teaspoon Tabasco sauce**
¹/₄ **teaspoon nutmeg**
¹/₄ **teaspoon salt**
¹/₈ **teaspoon ground cloves**

Place the steak in a shallow dish. Combine the remaining ingredients in a bowl and mix well. Pour over the steak. Marinate, covered, in the refrigerator for 4 hours or longer, turning the steak every hour. Drain the steak, reserving the marinade. Pour the reserved marinade into a saucepan. Boil for 2 to 3 minutes, stirring constantly. Place the steak on a grill rack. Grill over hot coals to the desired degree of doneness, basting with the cooked marinade and turning once. Remove to a serving platter. Cut diagonally into thin slices.

YIELD: 6 TO 8 SERVINGS

GRECIAN BEEF STEW

3 **pounds boneless beef chuck,
   trimmed, cut into 1-inch cubes**
1¹/₂ **tablespoons all-purpose flour**
1¹/₂ **teaspoons salt**
¹/₂ **teaspoon cinnamon**
2 **teaspoons mixed whole pickling
   spices**
3 **garlic cloves, minced**

2 **tablespoons dark raisins**
1 **tablespoon brown sugar**
2 **small onions, cut into 6 wedges
   each**
2 **cups dry red wine**
1 **(8-ounce) can tomato sauce**
3 **tablespoons red wine vinegar**
Minced fresh parsley to taste

Soak the top and bottom of a 3¹/₄-quart clay cooker in cold water for 15 minutes; drain. Coat the beef cubes in a mixture of the flour, salt and cinnamon. Place in the clay cooker. Tie the pickling spices in cheesecloth. Place in the center of the cooker. Sprinkle the beef with the garlic, raisins and brown sugar. Layer the onions over the top. Mix the wine, tomato sauce and vinegar in a bowl. Pour into the cooker. Place the covered cooker in a cold oven. Bake at 450 degrees for 1³/₄ hours or until the beef is tender, stirring once or twice and adding additional liquid if necessary. Sprinkle with parsley before serving.

YIELD: 4 TO 6 SERVINGS

GRADES OF BEEF

The three main grades of beef found in butcher shops and restaurants are *prime*, *choice*, and *select*. The beef is graded for quality, juiciness, flavor, and tenderness. *Prime* is the juiciest, due to the amount of fat marbling through the muscle. *Choice*, the most widely available, has less marbling than prime. *Select* is the leanest of the three grades, but also the least tender and juicy.

BLANQUETTE VEAL STEW

2 pounds boneless veal shoulder, cut into 1-inch cubes
8 ounces mushrooms, cut into quarters
1 medium onion, chopped
1/2 teaspoon tarragon
1/8 teaspoon nutmeg
1 teaspoon salt
1/4 teaspoon white pepper
1 tablespoon lemon juice
1 tablespoon Dijon mustard
1 cup dry white wine
1 cup whipping cream

Place ½ of the veal in a heavy 4-quart Dutch oven. Cover with the mushrooms and onion. Top with the remaining veal. Sprinkle with the tarragon, nutmeg, salt and white pepper. Stir the lemon juice gradually into the Dijon mustard in a small bowl until smooth. Stir in the wine. Pour over the layers. Bake, covered, at 375 degrees for 1½ hours or until the veal is tender, stirring several times. Remove the veal to a serving bowl and keep warm. Pour the cooking liquid into a large skillet. Add the cream. Bring to a boil. Cook until the mixture is reduced by about ⅓ and slightly thickened, stirring occasionally. Pour over the veal.

YIELD: 6 TO 8 SERVINGS

Osso Buco

6 veal shanks
1 cup all-purpose flour
Salt and white pepper to taste
1/4 cup olive oil
3 tablespoons butter
2 leek bulbs, thinly sliced

1 onion, chopped
1 cup white wine or vermouth
1 cup beef consommé or chicken
   broth
1/2 cup brandy
Gremolata (below)

Coat the veal with a mixture of the flour, salt and white pepper. Brown in the olive oil and butter in a skillet. Arrange in a single layer in a large baking dish. Sauté the leeks and onion in the skillet. Add to the veal. Pour the wine over the veal. Let stand for 15 minutes. Add the consommé. Bake, covered, at 350 degrees for 2 hours, basting every 30 minutes with the pan juices and adding additional consommé or warm water if needed. Remove the veal to a platter and keep warm, reserving the pan drippings. Make a sauce by adding more liquid and the brandy to the pan drippings. Pour over the veal. Sprinkle with Gremolata.

YIELD: 6 SERVINGS

This dish may be prepared the day before serving. Reheating it gives a thicker, richer flavor to the sauce. Be careful not to overcook.

Gremolata

Grated lemon zest
Finely chopped garlic
Finely chopped fresh parsley

Combine the lemon zest, garlic and parsley in a small bowl and mix well.

**Osso Buco
(AW-so-BOO-koh)**

Meaning "pierced bone" in Italian, osso buco traditionally consists of meaty veal shanks braised and simmered with white wine, stock, onions, tomatoes, garlic, carrots, celery, and seasonings until moist and succulent. Turkey or lamb can be substituted for the veal with surprisingly good results. Risotto is the recommended accompaniment.

Veal Croquettes with Lemon

12 slices white sandwich bread,
   crusts trimmed
1 cup milk
2 pounds veal, ground
4 eggs
1 cup freshly grated Parmesan
   cheese
2 tablespoons fresh lemon juice
1/4 teaspoon salt

1/2 teaspoon freshly ground
   white pepper
4 cups vegetable oil or shortening
   for frying
11/2 cups unbleached all-purpose
   flour
1/4 cup (1/2 stick) unsalted butter
2 tablespoons fresh lemon juice
1 cup drained large capers

Soak the bread in the milk in a large bowl for 30 minutes. Drain, discarding the milk. Squeeze the moisture from the bread. Combine the bread, veal, eggs, cheese, 2 tablespoons lemon juice, salt and white pepper in a large bowl and mix well. Heat the oil in a deep skillet to 375 degrees. Shape the veal mixture by 1/4 cupfuls into egg-shaped croquettes. The mixture will be very soft. Coat the croquettes in the flour. Fry in the hot oil in batches until golden brown. Drain on paper towels. You may prepare up to this point and store, covered, in the refrigerator for 24 hours. Bring to room temperature before baking.

Arrange the croquettes in a single layer in a shallow baking dish. Dot with the butter. Baste with 2 tablespoons lemon juice. Bake at 300 degrees for 5 minutes. Add the capers. Drizzle with the pan juices. Bake for 5 minutes longer or until heated through. Serve with the pan juices.

YIELD: 4 TO 6 SERVINGS

CACTUS ON FIRE
(NOPALITOS IN GREEN CHILE SAUCE WITH GROUND BEEF)

Gil Garcia

1 pound tomatillos
4 ounces serrano chiles
Chopped fresh cilantro
1 small red onion, chopped
1 teaspoon cumin
1 pound ground sirloin or ground turkey
1 teaspoon oregano
Salt to taste
1 (15-ounce) jar nopalitos (Dona Maria tender cactus)
2 teaspoons cumin

Remove the skin from the tomatillos and discard. Rinse the tomatillos. Rinse the serrano chiles and remove the stems. Combine the tomatillos and serrano chiles in a saucepan. Add enough water to cover. Bring to a boil; drain.

Process the serrano chiles, tomatillos, cilantro, red onion and 1 teaspoon cumin in a blender ½ at a time until puréed.

Brown the ground sirloin with the oregano and salt in a skillet, stirring until crumbly; drain. Add the green chile sauce and nopalitos and mix well. Season with 2 teaspoons cumin. Simmer for 15 minutes

YIELD: 4 TO 6 SERVINGS

Perfect for those who love food that ranks high on the hot and spicy scale.

NOPALITOS

Nopalitos are the "pads" of the prickly pear cactus. They are thought to be native to Mexico, where they've been eaten as a vegetable for many years. The Spanish explorers took the plant from Mexico to Europe, where the Moors discovered it and introduced it to North Africa. These tasty little "cactus pads" are a welcome addition to egg dishes, soups, chilies, and tortillas.

MEAT LOAF WITH BASIL AND PROVOLONE

¹/₂ cup sun-dried tomatoes
1 cup hot water
¹/₂ cup ketchup
1 cup seasoned bread crumbs
1 cup finely chopped onion
1 cup chopped fresh basil leaves
¹/₂ cup (2 ounces) shredded provolone cheese
2 eggs, beaten
2 tablespoons minced garlic, or to taste
1 pound lean ground beef
¹/₂ cup ketchup

Place the sun-dried tomatoes in the hot water in a bowl. Let stand for 30 minutes or until soft; drain. Chop the sun-dried tomatoes finely.

Combine ½ cup ketchup, the bread crumbs, onion, basil, cheese, eggs, garlic and ground beef in a large bowl and mix well. Add the sun-dried tomatoes and mix well. Shape into a loaf in a 5×9-inch loaf pan sprayed with nonstick cooking spray. Spread ½ cup ketchup over the top. Bake at 350 degrees for 1 hour or until a meat thermometer inserted in the center registers 160 degrees. Remove from the oven. Let stand for 10 minutes before slicing.

YIELD: 6 TO 8 SERVINGS

 A light-bodied red wine such as pinot noir or merlot gives class to a meat loaf dinner.

YOUR FAVORITE MEAT LOAF

1 tablespoon butter

1 cup minced scallions

3/4 cup minced white onion

3/4 cup minced carrots

1/2 cup minced celery

1/4 cup minced red bell pepper

1/4 cup minced green bell pepper

2 1/2 teaspoons minced garlic

3 eggs, beaten

1 teaspoon salt

1 teaspoon black pepper

1/2 teaspoon cayenne pepper

1/2 teaspoon nutmeg

1/2 teaspoon cumin

1/2 cup ketchup

1/2 cup half-and-half

1 1/2 pounds lean ground beef

8 ounces unseasoned lean ground
   pork sausage

3/4 cup bread crumbs

Heat the butter in a heavy skillet until melted. Add the scallions, white onion, carrots, celery, bell peppers and garlic. Sauté for 10 minutes or until the moisture has evaporated. Remove from the heat to cool. Combine the eggs, salt, black pepper, cayenne pepper, nutmeg and cumin in a large bowl and mix well. Add the ketchup and half-and-half and mix well. Add the ground beef, ground pork sausage, bread crumbs and vegetable mixture and mix well. Press into a greased 5×9-inch loaf pan. Place the loaf pan in a larger pan filled with 1 inch boiling water. Bake at 350 degrees for 45 to 60 minutes or until cooked through. Remove from the oven. Let stand for 10 minutes before serving.

YIELD: 6 SERVINGS

Depending on the spiciness of the pork sausage or the amount of pepper used, serve a pinot noir with the less spicy meat loaf or a zinfandel with the spicier rendition.

SPAGHETTI SAUCE

WINE GLASSES

Can the shape of the glass influence the flavor of the wine? Many experts believe that it does. Although you can enjoy your favorite wine out of a paper cup, following these guidelines will enhance the tasting experience. Choose glasses that are thin and clear and wider on the bottom. An inwardly curving rim makes it possible to swirl the wine and release more of the aroma.

2 pounds ground round
3 cups chopped onions
4 garlic cloves, minced
1 tablespoon salt
2 (8-ounce) cans tomato sauce
2 (16-ounce) cans chopped
   tomatoes
1 (6-ounce) can tomato paste
1 tablespoon Worcestershire sauce
1 tablespoon red wine vinegar
1 teaspoon Tabasco sauce

1 teaspoon basil
1½ teaspoons rosemary
1 teaspoon marjoram
1 tablespoon oregano
1 tablespoon chili powder
1 tablespoon paprika
1 tablespoon sugar
1 teaspoon pepper
3 bay leaves
3 cups minced green bell peppers
2 cups sliced fresh mushrooms

Brown the ground round, onions, garlic and salt in a large heavy skillet, stirring until the ground round is crumbly; drain. Combine the tomato sauce, tomatoes, tomato paste, Worcestershire sauce, red wine vinegar, Tabasco sauce, basil, rosemary, marjoram, oregano, chili powder, paprika, sugar, pepper, bay leaves, bell peppers and mushrooms in a large heavy stockpot and mix well. Add the ground round mixture and mix well. Bring to a boil and reduce the heat. Simmer for 5 to 6 hours. Discard the bay leaves before serving. You may freeze in tightly covered containers.

YIELD: 4 QUARTS

A full-bodied or hearty red wine such as zinfandel or merlot pairs well with this sauce.

RACK OF LAMB WITH CHERRY AND PEPPERCORN SAUCE

1 tablespoon butter
1/3 cup finely chopped shallots
1 tablespoon tomato paste
1 cup beef broth
1 1/2 cups chicken broth
1 1/2 cups dried cherries
1/2 cup ruby port
1/2 cup brandy
1/2 teaspoon chopped fresh
   rosemary
1/2 teaspoon chopped fresh
   marjoram

1/2 teaspoon chopped drained
   green peppercorns in brine
2 (1 1/2-pound) 8-rib racks of lamb
3 tablespoons chopped fresh
   parsley
3 tablespoons chopped fresh
   rosemary
3 tablespoons chopped fresh
   marjoram
Salt and pepper to taste
2 tablespoons olive oil

Melt the butter in a medium saucepan over medium heat. Add the shallots. Sauté for 2 minutes. Stir in the tomato paste. Add the beef broth and chicken broth. Boil for 25 minutes or until the mixture is reduced to 1¼ cups. Strain the sauce into a small saucepan, discarding the solids. Add the dried cherries, port, brandy, ½ teaspoon rosemary and ½ teaspoon marjoram. Boil for 15 minutes or until the mixture is reduced to 1 cup. Stir in the peppercorns. Remove from the heat.

Sprinkle each rack of lamb with 1½ tablespoons parsley, 1½ tablespoons rosemary and 1½ tablespoons marjoram and press to adhere. Sprinkle with salt and pepper. Heat the olive oil in a large skillet over high heat. Add 1 rack of lamb. Cook for 6 minutes or until brown on all sides. Arrange the rack of lamb meat side up in a baking pan. Repeat with the remaining rack of lamb. Bake at 425 degrees for 18 minutes or until a meat thermometer inserted into the center registers 130 degrees for medium-rare. Remove the racks of lamb to a carving board. Let stand for 10 minutes. Bring the cherry and peppercorn sauce to a simmer. Cut the lamb between the bones. Serve with the sauce.

YIELD: 4 SERVINGS

CRUSTED BUTTERFLIED LEG OF LAMB

1 (6-pound) butterflied leg of lamb,
  at room temperature
1 tablespoon olive oil
3 large garlic cloves, crushed
1/2 teaspoon oregano

1/2 teaspoon salt
Freshly ground pepper to taste
1/4 cup fresh lemon juice
Crust Topping (below)

Rub the lamb on both sides with the olive oil. Mix the garlic, oregano, salt, pepper and lemon juice in a small bowl. Rub on both sides of the lamb. Place the lamb in a shallow roasting pan. Bake at 450 degrees for 20 minutes. Reduce the oven temperature to 325 degrees. Bake for 30 minutes. Remove from the oven. Spread the Crust Topping over the lamb. Return to the oven. Bake for 15 minutes or until the topping is light brown but still soft.

YIELD: 8 SERVINGS

CRUST TOPPING

2 tablespoons butter or margarine
1 tablespoon olive oil
1 1/2 to 2 cups minced shallots
6 cups fresh bread crumbs

3/4 cup minced fresh Italian parsley
1 1/4 cups grated Parmesan cheese
3/4 to 1 cup broth
1 egg, lightly beaten

Heat the butter and olive oil in a large skillet until the butter is melted. Add the shallots. Sauté until softened. Combine with the bread crumbs, parsley and cheese in a large bowl and mix well. Stir in the broth and egg.

 A perfect accompaniment to this dish is a California zinfandel or California pinot noir.

SAVORY BARBECUED LEG OF LAMB

¹/₂ cup soy sauce	2 large garlic cloves, crushed
1 teaspoon molasses	1 (5-pound) butterflied boneless
³/₄ cup water	leg of lamb
¹/₄ cup lemon juice	¹/₂ cup tomato sauce
¹/₃ cup creamy peanut butter	Dash of Tabasco sauce, or to taste
¹/₂ teaspoon red pepper flakes	

Combine the soy sauce, molasses, water, lemon juice, peanut butter, red pepper flakes and garlic in a 1½-quart saucepan and mix well. Bring to a boil. Simmer for 30 minutes. Place the lamb in a sealable plastic bag. Add the soy sauce mixture and seal the bag. Marinate in the refrigerator for 2 hours or longer, turning the lamb frequently.

Drain the lamb, reserving the marinade. Pour the reserved marinade into a saucepan. Bring to a boil. Boil for 2 to 3 minutes, stirring constantly. Add the tomato sauce and Tabasco sauce and mix well. Arrange the lamb on a grill rack. Grill to 125 degrees on a meat thermometer for medium-rare or to 140 degrees for medium, basting frequently with the cooked marinade. Remove to a serving platter. Cut the lamb diagonally into slices. Serve with your favorite rice dish.

YIELD: 6 TO 8 SERVINGS

ROAST LEG OF LAMB WITH CURRANT SAUCE

1 (6- to 7-pound) leg of lamb	¹/₄ teaspoon pepper
1 jigger gin (3 to 4 tablespoons)	2 tablespoons all-purpose flour
2 tablespoons Dijon mustard	¹/₂ cup currant jelly
1 garlic clove, crushed	¹/₄ teaspoon salt
¹/₂ teaspoon rosemary	1¹/₄ cups water
1 teaspoon salt	¹/₄ cup gin

Pat the lamb dry. Arrange fat side up on a rack in a roasting pan. Combine 1 jigger gin, the Dijon mustard, garlic, rosemary, 1 teaspoon salt and pepper in a small bowl and blend to form a paste. Spread over the lamb. Bake at 325 degrees for 2 hours for rare or 2½ to 2¾ hours for medium to well done. Remove from the oven. Place the lamb on a platter and keep warm.

Pour the pan drippings into a saucepan. Stir in the flour. Bring to a boil and reduce the heat. Simmer for 3 minutes. Add the jelly. Cook until melted, stirring constantly. Blend in the remaining ingredients. Cook for 2 to 3 minutes or until thickened, stirring constantly. Serve with the lamb.

YIELD: 6 TO 8 SERVINGS

LEG OF LAMB

Here's a formula to help you pick the right size leg of lamb for your next dinner party. A six-pound leg will yield about four pounds of lamb, since one-third of the weight will be bone. If you leave the bone in, allow one-half to three-quarters of a pound per person. If the bone is removed, allow one-third to one-half pound of lamb per person.

BRAISED LAMB SHANKS MOROCCAN STYLE

Tom Meyer, Executive Chef, Los Olivos Café, Los Olivos, California

4 lamb fore shanks, at room temperature
Kosher salt and freshly ground black pepper to taste
$1/4$ cup olive oil
2 cups chopped onions
8 whole garlic cloves
1 cup chopped carrots
1 cup chopped celery
6 tomatoes, chopped
6 cups chicken stock

$1/4$ cup cumin
1 teaspoon cayenne pepper
1 tablespoon coriander
1 tablespoon ginger
1 teaspoon nutmeg
2 cups drained chick peas
2 cups chopped zucchini
2 cups chopped fresh cilantro
3 cups cooked couscous
Chopped fresh mint and chopped fresh cilantro to taste

Season the lamb with kosher salt and black pepper. Brown the lamb in the olive oil in a skillet. Arrange the lamb in a large baking dish. Add the onions, garlic, carrots, celery, tomatoes, stock, cumin, cayenne pepper, coriander, ginger and nutmeg. Bake, tightly covered, at 400 degrees for $2^{1}/_{2}$ hours or until tender. Add the chick peas, zucchini and 2 cups cilantro. Adjust the seasonings to taste. Serve with the couscous and sprinkle with chopped mint and cilantro to taste.

YIELD: 4 SERVINGS

 Serve with Bernat Vineyards and Winery syrah.

LAMB SHANKS WITH WINE AND HERBS

Photograph for this recipe is shown on page 184.

6 meaty lamb shanks
1 to 2 medium onions, sliced
3 garlic cloves, chopped
1/4 cup (or less) packed brown
   sugar
1 (14-ounce) can tomato sauce

1 tomato sauce can filled with
   white wine
1 tablespoon dill weed
1 tablespoon rosemary
Salt and pepper to taste

Brown the lamb in a Dutch oven. Add the onions, garlic, brown sugar, tomato sauce, wine, dill weed, rosemary, salt and pepper. Bake, covered, at 325 degrees for 3 hours. Bake, uncovered, for 30 minutes longer. Remove the lamb to a platter and keep warm. Skim the fat from the pan juices. Cook until reduced to a sauce consistency. Spoon over the lamb shanks. Serve topped with Gremolata (page 197).

YIELD: 6 SERVINGS

GRILLED LAMB CHOPS WITH MERLOT MARINADE

1 small onion, finely chopped
3 garlic cloves, finely chopped
2 sprigs of fresh rosemary,
   coarsely chopped

12 sage leaves, crushed
3/4 cup merlot
1/4 cup olive oil
8 lamb chops

Combine the onion, garlic, rosemary, sage, wine and olive oil in a noncorrosive bowl and mix well. Add the lamb chops. Marinate, covered, in the refrigerator for 8 to 12 hours. Drain the lamb chops, reserving the marinade. Pour the reserved marinade into a saucepan. Bring to a boil. Boil for 2 to 3 minutes. Arrange the lamb chops on a grill rack. Brush with the cooked marinade. Grill until the lamb chops are cooked through, basting occasionally with the cooked marinade. If sage or rosemary grow in your garden, cut a few sprigs to use as the marinade brush.

YIELD: 4 SERVINGS

ROSEMARY

Rosemary, a member of the mint family, is a sweet, fragrant herb native to the Mediterranean area. It has been used extensively since 500 B.C. and was once believed to be a cure for disorders of the nervous system. The slender, slightly curved grayish-green leaves resemble miniature pine needles.

PORK TENDERLOIN WITH ONION AND APPLE CREAM

PORK

This little piggy went to market, this little piggy stayed home...and this little piggy was served for breakfast, lunch, and dinner. Pork lends itself to a variety of flavors including classic French seasonings such as tarragon, fennel, and wine; Asian spices like soy, ginger, and teriyaki; and sweet additions like apples, cinnamon, cloves, and honey. And what would breakfast be without the cured and smoked cuts such as bacon, ham, and sausage?

6 tablespoons whipping cream	1 (12-ounce) whole pork tenderloin
2 tablespoons cream sherry	2 tablespoons butter
1 teaspoon Dijon mustard	1 large onion, thinly sliced
1/2 teaspoon prepared horseradish	1 small apple, thinly sliced
1/2 teaspoon salt	

Combine the whipping cream, sherry, Dijon mustard, horseradish and salt in a small bowl and stir to mix well. Arrange the pork on a rack in a roasting pan. Insert a meat thermometer into the thickest portion. Bake at 425 degrees for 25 to 30 minutes or until the meat thermometer registers 170 degrees, basting frequently with some of the cream mixture.

Melt the butter in a large skillet over medium heat. Add the onion and apple. Cook for 20 minutes or until limp and golden brown, stirring frequently. Add the remaining cream mixture. Bring to a boil. Spoon into a small bowl and keep warm.

Arrange the pork on a small serving platter. Garnish with sprigs of fresh parsley. Serve with the onion and apple cream.

YIELD: 2 SERVINGS

 Pair this entrée with either a full-bodied white wine such as a rich chardonnay, or a full-bodied red wine such as syrah or merlot.

ORANGE DIJON PORK MEDALLIONS

Photograph for this recipe is shown on page 184.

2 tablespoons olive oil	3 tablespoons orange marmalade
1¹/₂ pounds pork tenderloin	1 tablespoon Dijon mustard
Pepper to taste	1 tablespoon butter
¹/₂ cup white wine or apple juice	

Heat the olive oil in a deep 12-inch nonstick skillet over medium heat. Sprinkle the pork lightly with pepper. Cut the pork into slices ¼ inch thick. Some pieces will be very small. Add the pork to the skillet. Increase the heat to medium-high. Fry for 5 minutes on each side or until cooked through. Remove the pork to a platter and keep warm.

Return the skillet to medium heat. Add the wine, stirring to deglaze the skillet. Cook for 1 minute, stirring constantly. Add the marmalade and Dijon mustard and mix well. Remove from the heat. Add the butter and mix well. Drizzle over the pork.

YIELD: 4 SERVINGS

CITRUS ZEST

The zest of an orange or lemon is the colored rind, while the pith is the white section underneath. To "zest" the fruit, use a potato peeler, a grater, a special zester tool, or a sharp knife. One medium orange or one large lemon yields one to two tablespoons of zest.

OVEN-BARBECUED SPARERIBS WITH MAPLE TWIST

5 pounds pork spareribs	2 garlic cloves, minced
¹/₂ cup water	2 cups ketchup
2 tablespoons butter	1 cup maple syrup
1 medium onion, chopped	Grated zest of ¹/₂ lemon

Arrange the ribs on a rack in a shallow roasting pan. Pour the water into the pan. Cover tightly with foil. Bake at 350 degrees for 1 hour.

Melt the butter in a skillet. Add the onion and garlic. Sauté until tender. Add the ketchup, maple syrup and lemon zest. Simmer for 10 minutes.

Remove the foil from the ribs. Bake for 30 to 40 minutes longer, basting frequently with the sauce.

YIELD: 6 SERVINGS

BRANDIED PORK CHOPS

PUTTANESCA SAUCE
(POOT-TAH-**NEHS**-KAH)

Derived from the Italian
word *puttana*, meaning
"whore," puttanesca,
or alla puttanesca,
refers to a spicy sauce
made of tomatoes,
onions, capers, black
olives, anchovies,
oregano, and garlic.
Some believe the
sauce got its colorful
name because the
intense aroma was like
a siren's call to the
men who visited the
"ladies of the evening."

8 pork chops	1/2 cup chopped dried apricots
1 tablespoon butter	1/2 cup honey
5 Granny Smith apples, sliced	1/2 teaspoon cinnamon
1/2 cup golden raisins	1/2 cup brandy
1 cup chopped pecans	1/4 cup water

Brown the pork chops in the butter in a skillet. Combine the sliced unpeeled apples, raisins, pecans, apricots, honey and cinnamon in a bowl and toss to mix well. Layer 1/2 of the apple mixture in a buttered 4-quart baking dish. Arrange the pork chops over the apple mixture. Top with the remaining apple mixture. Sprinkle with a mixture of the brandy and water. Bake, covered, at 350 degrees for 1 hour or until the pork chops are cooked through.

YIELD: 6 TO 8 SERVINGS

PENNE PUTTANESCA WITH ITALIAN SAUSAGE

3 medium hot Italian sausage links, casings removed	2 tablespoons drained capers
	1/2 cup chopped kalamata olives
3 garlic cloves, sliced	1 teaspoon red pepper flakes
1 tablespoon extra-virgin olive oil	16 ounces uncooked penne
1 (16-ounce) can diced peeled tomatoes	Shredded mozzarella cheese to taste

Cook the sausage in a skillet for 10 minutes, stirring until brown and crumbly. Brown the garlic in the olive oil in a saucepan. Add the tomatoes, capers, olives and red pepper flakes. Bring to a boil. Reduce the heat to low. Simmer for 15 minutes. Add the sausage and mix well.

Cook the pasta using the package directions; drain. Spoon the sauce over the hot pasta. Sprinkle with mozzarella cheese.

YIELD: 4 SERVINGS

 Serve a bottle of Italian chianti or a California sangiovese to heighten the flavor of this robust Italian meal.

RABBIT WITH MUSTARD SAUCE

1 fresh rabbit, cut into serving pieces
1/2 cup honey mustard
Salt and pepper to taste
3 tablespoons grapeseed oil
1 tablespoon unsalted butter
1 bottle white wine
2 medium onions, sliced
1 tablespoon superfine all-purpose flour
1 teaspoon thyme
1 bay leaf
1/3 cup chopped fresh parsley

Brush 1 side of each piece of rabbit evenly with 1/2 of the honey mustard. Season generously with salt and pepper. Heat the grapeseed oil and butter in a large skillet over medium heat. Add the rabbit, coated side down. Cook for 10 minutes or until brown. Brush the top of the rabbit pieces with the remaining honey mustard and turn. Cook for 10 minutes or until brown. Remove the rabbit from the skillet to a warm platter. Add several tablespoons of the wine to the skillet, stirring to deglaze the skillet. Add the onions. Cook until golden brown, stirring constantly. Remove from the heat. Sprinkle with the flour. Stir in the remaining wine, thyme and bay leaf. Return the rabbit to the skillet. Simmer over medium heat for 1 hour or until the rabbit is tender and the sauce begins to thicken. Discard the bay leaf. Remove the rabbit to a serving platter. Spoon the sauce over the rabbit. Sprinkle with the parsley.

YIELD: 4 SERVINGS

 Serve with a red wine such as pinot noir or syrah.

RABBIT

The domesticated rabbit is plumper and less gamy than its wild relative. The most tender rabbits are young and weigh between two and two and one-half pounds. The meat is fine-textured and almost all white, and they are most flavorful when fried, grilled, or roasted. You'll be able to find whole or cut-up rabbit in either the fresh or frozen section of the supermarket.

SAVOR
THE SUNSET

desserts and sweets

ITALIAN CREAM CAKE

PETITE CHEESECAKE TARTS

LEMON DROPS

SNOWFLAKES

ZABAGLIONE RAMPONE

BISCOTTI WITH ALMONDS AND ANISE

APRICOT WALNUT BARS

YUM-YUMS

PECAN PIE SQUARES

(shown left to right)

Photograph © Michael Brown

Vineyard in Santa Rita Hills *Photograph © Kirk Irwin*

Bob and Jane Atwater, Barry and Norris Goss, Don and Rose Louie, Georgiana Nammack, Santa Barbara Bank and Trust

Berry-Glazed Cheesecake

3/4 cup coarsely ground pecans or walnuts	1 tablespoon fresh lemon juice
3/4 cup finely crushed graham crackers	2 teaspoons vanilla extract
3 tablespoons butter, melted	2 cups sour cream
32 ounces cream cheese, softened	1/4 cup sugar
4 eggs, at room temperature	1 teaspoon vanilla extract
1 1/4 cups sugar	1 quart medium strawberries or raspberries
	Raspberry Glaze (below)

Combine the pecans, graham cracker crumbs and butter in a bowl and mix well. Press into a lightly buttered 10-inch springform pan. Bake at 350 degrees for 10 minutes. Remove from the oven to a wire rack to cool completely. Beat the cream cheese in a large mixing bowl until smooth and creamy. Add the eggs, 1 1/4 cups sugar, lemon juice and 2 teaspoons vanilla and beat well. Spoon into the cooled prebaked crust. Arrange on a baking sheet and place on the center oven rack. Bake at 350 degrees for 40 to 45 minutes or until set. The cheesecake will rise slightly, crack in several areas, settle again and the cracks will minimize. Let stand at room temperature for 15 minutes to cool. Combine the sour cream, 1/4 cup sugar and 1 teaspoon vanilla in a bowl and mix well. Chill, covered, in the refrigerator until ready to use.

Spread the sour cream mixture over the cheesecake. Bake at 350 degrees for 5 minutes. Let stand at room temperature to cool. Chill, covered, for 2 to 3 days. Rinse the strawberries and pat dry. Arrange pointed end up on top of the cheesecake. Spoon the Raspberry Glaze over the top. Chill, covered, until the glaze is set.

YIELD: 16 SERVINGS

Raspberry Glaze

12 ounces seedless red raspberry jelly	1/4 cup peach schnapps
1 tablespoon cornstarch	1/4 cup water

Mix a small amount of the jelly and the cornstarch in a saucepan. Add the remaining jelly, schnapps and water and mix well. Cook over medium heat for 5 minutes or until thickened and clear, stirring constantly. Cool to lukewarm, stirring occasionally.

 Serve with a late harvest riesling or a late harvest gewürztraminer.

TIRAMISU

TIRAMISU

(TIH-RUH-MEE-SOO)

The traditional tiramisu is a light, delicate creation consisting of sponge cake or ladyfingers dipped in a coffee-marsala mixture and layered with mascarpone and grated chocolate. Chill, serve, and enjoy the applause.

4 eggs
1/4 cup brandy
1 pound mascarpone cheese
1/2 cup sugar
1 package dry ladyfingers
1/2 cup espresso or strong coffee
2 ounces semisweet chocolate, grated

Separate the eggs into 2 large bowls. Add the brandy to the egg yolks and stir until blended. Add the cheese and stir to mix well. Beat the egg whites until soft peaks form. Add the sugar gradually, beating constantly until stiff peaks form. Add 1/2 of the egg whites to the cheese mixture and blend well. Fold in the remaining egg whites gently.

Dip the ladyfingers quickly into the espresso; do not saturate. Arrange flat side down in a shallow 10-inch round dish. Layer the cheese mixture, 1/2 of the chocolate and the remaining ladyfingers in the prepared dish. Spread the remaining cheese mixture over the top. Sprinkle with the remaining chocolate. Chill, covered, for at least 8 to 12 hours before serving.

Note: Mascarpone cheese is an Italian cream cheese found in most large grocery stores.

YIELD: 6 SERVINGS

BAVARIAN APPLE TORTE

1/2 cup (1 stick) butter, softened
1/3 cup sugar
1/4 teaspoon vanilla extract
1 cup all-purpose flour
12 ounces cream cheese, softened
1/4 cup sugar
1 egg
1 teaspoon vanilla extract
1/3 cup sugar
1/2 teaspoon cinnamon
4 cups sliced peeled tart apples
1/4 cup slivered almonds
1 cup whipping cream, whipped

Cream the butter, 1/3 cup sugar and 1/4 teaspoon vanilla in a mixing bowl until light and fluffy. Beat in the flour until smooth. Spread over the bottom and 1 inch up the side of a 9-inch springform pan.

Beat the cream cheese and 1/4 cup sugar in a mixing bowl until smooth and creamy. Add the egg and 1 teaspoon vanilla and beat well. Pour into the prepared pan. Mix 1/3 cup sugar and the cinnamon in a bowl. Add the apples and toss to coat. Arrange a layer of apple slices in concentric circles over the cream cheese layer, avoiding spilling the juice on the pastry. Sprinkle with the slivered almonds.

Bake at 450 degrees for 10 minutes. Reduce the oven temperature to 400 degrees. Bake for 25 minutes. Remove from the oven. Let stand until cool. Release the side of the pan. Serve with the whipped cream.

YIELD: 8 SERVINGS

MASCARPONE CHEESE (MAHS-KAHR-POH-NEH)

A product of Italy's Lombardy region, mascarpone is the reigning king of dessert cheeses. It's a buttery, ultra-rich cream cheese with a light, delicate texture similar to soft butter. Due to their high moisture content, soft cheeses do not keep as long as firm ones, so refrigerate and expect a shelf life of seven to ten days.

Bittersweet Chocolate Torte with Raspberries

14 ounces semisweet chocolate, coarsely chopped
1/2 cup (1 stick) butter
1/2 cup milk
3 eggs
1 teaspoon vanilla extract
1/2 cup sugar
1/4 cup all-purpose flour
1/4 cup seedless raspberry jam
2 cups fresh raspberries

Combine the chocolate, butter and milk in a heavy medium saucepan. Cook over low heat until the butter and chocolate melt, stirring constantly. Remove from the heat to cool.

Beat the eggs and vanilla at low speed in a mixing bowl. Add the sugar and flour. Beat at high speed for 10 minutes. Stir in the chocolate mixture. Pour into a greased 8-inch springform pan. Bake at 325 degrees for 35 minutes. The torte will be slightly puffed on the outer edge and the center will look underbaked. Remove from the oven. Cool for 10 minutes. Loosen the side of the torte from the pan using a knife. Let stand until completely cooled. Remove the side of the pan. Chill, wrapped in foil, for 8 to 10 hours.

To serve, bring the torte to room temperature. Melt the raspberry jam in a small saucepan. Remove from the heat to cool. Spread over the torte. Cover with the fresh raspberries.

YIELD: 10 TO 12 SERVINGS

 A muscat wine is perfect with this rich chocolate torte or try a tawny port.

COFFEE TOFFEE WRAPS

$1/4$ cup chocolate sauce
4 (8-inch) flour or cocoa tortillas
$1/2$ cup chopped Heath bars
2 cups coffee ice cream

Spread 1 tablespoon chocolate sauce evenly over each tortilla, leaving at least a 1-inch border around the edge. Sprinkle with the chopped candy. Spread each tortilla with $1/2$ cup of the ice cream. Wrap to enclose the ice cream. Serve immediately or freeze for 1 hour before serving.

YIELD: 4 SERVINGS

FRIED ICE CREAM

2 cups packed brown sugar
1 cup (2 sticks) butter or margarine
5 cups cornflakes, crushed
1 cup nuts, chopped
$1/2$ gallon ice cream, slightly softened, cut into slices

Heat the brown sugar and butter in a saucepan until melted. Add the cornflakes and nuts and mix well. Reserve $1/4$ of the cornflake mixture. Press the remaining cornflake mixture into a 9×13-inch dish. Spread the softened ice cream on top. Sprinkle with the reserved cornflake mixture. Freeze, covered, until firm. You may serve with chocolate or caramel sauce if desired.

Note: Vanilla and orange ice cream is a good combination to use in this recipe.

YIELD: 14 TO 16 SERVINGS

PEANUTS

The peanut is not a member of the nut family but is actually a legume. The two popular varieties are Spanish and Virginia. Wrapped in a plastic bag and refrigerated, peanuts should keep their fresh flavor for up to six months. When chopping nuts in a blender, add a little sugar to keep the nuts from sticking together.

ORANGE ALMOND MOUSSE

1/3 cup water	1 cup fresh orange juice
1 cup sugar	1/4 cup fresh lemon juice
2 tablespoons grated orange zest	2 cups whipping cream, whipped
1 tablespoon unflavored gelatin (1 envelope)	1/2 cup glacé cherries, cut into quarters
1/4 cup cold water	1 cup chopped blanched almonds

Bring 1/3 cup water to a boil in a saucepan. Add the sugar and orange zest. Boil for 1 minute, stirring until the sugar is dissolved. Soften the gelatin in 1/4 cup cold water in a bowl for a few minutes. Add to the hot syrup. Stir until the gelatin is dissolved. Add the orange juice and lemon juice. Remove from the heat. Let stand until of a jelly consistency. Fold in the whipped cream, cherries and almonds. Spoon into a freezer container. Freeze until firm. Serve in sherbet glasses.

YIELD: 10 TO 12 SERVINGS

STRAWBERRIES ROMANOFF

1 1/2 quarts fresh strawberries, cut into halves	1 pint vanilla ice cream, softened
2 tablespoons sugar	1 cup whipping cream, whipped
2 tablespoons Cointreau	1/4 cup lemon juice
	2 tablespoons Cointreau

Place the strawberries in a serving bowl. Sprinkle with the sugar and 2 tablespoons Cointreau. Chill, covered, in the refrigerator.

Beat the ice cream in a bowl using a wooden spoon. Fold in the whipped cream, lemon juice and 2 tablespoons Cointreau. Pour over the strawberries and serve immediately.

YIELD: 4 SERVINGS

CITRUS GRANITA

2 cups water
3/4 cup sugar
1 cup fresh orange juice
Juice of 1 lemon

Bring the water and sugar to a boil in a saucepan over medium heat, stirring until the sugar dissolves. Boil for 5 minutes, beginning the timing when the mixture begins to boil. Remove from the heat. Cool to room temperature. Stir in the orange juice and lemon juice. Pour into nondivided ice cube trays or a similar shallow pan. Freeze until the texture of snow, stirring about every 30 minutes.

YIELD: 6 SERVINGS

RUBY RED SORBET

3 to 4 large red grapefruit
1 cup water
1 cup sugar
1¼ teaspoons tarragon

Squeeze enough juice from the grapefruit to measure 2 cups. Pour through a sieve into a large bowl, discarding the solids. Bring the water, sugar and tarragon to a boil in a saucepan, stirring until the sugar is dissolved. Simmer for 5 minutes. Whisk the syrup into the grapefruit juice. Chill, covered, in the refrigerator.

Pour into an ice cream freezer container. Freeze using the manufacturer's directions. Spoon into dessert dishes. Garnish with a sprig of fresh tarragon.

Note: You may store the sorbet in a tightly covered plastic container in the freezer for up to 1 week.

YIELD: 4 TO 6 SERVINGS

WINE LABELS

Wine labeling is strictly regulated by the Bureau of Alcohol, Tobacco, and Firearms, so labels must be legally correct as well as eye-catching. Artists endeavor to create a label that represents the philosophy of the winery, since labels can influence the buyer's attitude toward the wine. For example, a label with a picture of fine art suggests a fine wine.

221

Zabaglione Rampone (Italian Custard)

Photograph for this recipe is shown on page 212.

Photograph for this recipe is shown on page 212.

6 egg yolks, at room temperature
3/4 cup plus 1/4 teaspoon sugar
1/2 cup all-purpose flour
2 cups milk
1/3 cup cream sherry or marsala
1 cup whipping cream
1 (10-ounce) package frozen raspberries (rampone) in heavy syrup,
   thawed

Whisk the egg yolks, sugar, flour, milk and sherry in a heavy saucepan until blended. Cook over medium heat for 15 minutes or until the mixture comes to a boil and is thickened, stirring constantly. Reduce the heat to low. Cook for 2 minutes, stirring constantly. If lumps begin to form, whisk until smooth. Remove from the heat. Pour into a bowl and set in a larger bowl of ice water. Cool to room temperature, stirring occasionally. Beat the whipping cream at low speed in a mixing bowl until thick. Beat at medium speed until soft peaks form. Fold into the cooled custard.

Drain the raspberries, reserving 1/4 cup of the syrup. Process the raspberries and reserved syrup in a food processor fitted with a metal blade until puréed. Lift the bowl and scrape the bottom. Pour into a bowl. Stir in 1 cup of the golden custard.

To assemble, place 3 heaping tablespoons of the raspberry custard into each champagne goblet. Spoon a small amount of the remaining golden custard carefully into the center of the raspberry custard until each goblet is nearly full. Cover with plastic wrap, making sure the wrap covers the surface of the custard. Chill until ready to serve.

Note: You may prepare up to 24 hours in advance.

YIELD: 8 SERVINGS

Wine Bottle Sizes

Half bottle (split):
375 milliliters

Standard bottle:
750 milliliters

Magnum: 1.5 liters;
2 standard bottles

Jeroboam: 3.0 liters;
4 standard bottles, for
sparkling wine

4.5 liters; 6 standard
bottles, for red wine

Imperial: 6 liters; 8
standard bottles

Methuselah: Same
as Imperial, but
usually used for
sparkling wines

Salmanazar: 9 liters;
12 standard bottles

Balthazar: 12 liters;
16 standard bottles

Nebuchadnezzar:
15 liters; 20 standard
bottles

Hot Fudge Sauce

4 ounces bitter chocolate, melted
1¹/₂ cups sugar
3 tablespoons butter, softened

1 cup heavy cream
1 teaspoon vanilla extract

Melt the chocolate in a double boiler. Combine the chocolate, sugar, butter and cream in a medium saucepan and mix well. Bring to a boil over medium heat, stirring constantly. Boil for 7 minutes. Do not stir. Remove from the heat. Stir in the vanilla. Serve hot over ice cream.

YIELD: ABOUT 2 CUPS

Almond Cake

1 cup all-purpose flour
1¹/₂ teaspoons baking powder
¹/₄ teaspoon salt
1 cup almond paste
1¹/₄ cups sugar

1¹/₄ cups (2¹/₂ sticks) butter,
**   softened**
1 teaspoon vanilla extract
6 eggs

Sift the flour, baking powder and salt together. Combine the almond paste and sugar in a food processor and pulse until well blended. Add the butter and vanilla and pulse to mix well. Add the eggs 1 at a time, processing just until combined after each addition. Do not overmix. Add the flour mixture and pulse to mix well. Spoon into a greased and floured 9-inch springform pan. Place on a baking sheet. Bake at 325 degrees for 1 to 1¹/₂ hours or until golden brown on top and the edge begins to pull away from the side of the pan. Remove from the oven. Cool for 10 minutes. Release the side of the pan. Serve with vanilla ice cream and strawberries.

Note: You may sprinkle the cooled cake with confectioners' sugar.

YIELD: 8 TO 10 SERVINGS

WINE TASTING

The three basic elements of wine tasting are *appearance*, *aroma*, and *taste*. Begin by holding the glass at a forty-five degree angle and observing the color. A purple-red or pale white is likely to be younger and fruitier than a brown-red or golden-yellow wine. Next, swirl the glass and sniff the bouquet. Slowly sip the wine and hold it in your mouth for a moment. Notice the immediate impact, the subtle flavors, and the aftertaste.

APPLE DAPPLE CAKE

3 cups sifted all-purpose flour
1 teaspoon baking soda
1 teaspoon salt
1¹/₂ cups vegetable oil
3 eggs
2 cups sugar
1 teaspoon vanilla extract
1 teaspoon rum extract
3 cups chopped apples
1 cup chopped pecans
Brown Sugar Icing (below)

Sift the flour, baking soda and salt together. Combine the oil, eggs, sugar, vanilla and rum extract in a large bowl and mix well. Add the flour mixture and mix well. Fold in the apples and pecans. Spoon into a greased and floured bundt pan. Bake at 350 degrees for 1 hour. Remove from the oven. Poke holes in the hot cake. Pour the hot Brown Sugar Icing over the top. Let stand in the pan for 2 hours.

To serve, place in a warm oven to loosen the cake from the side of the pan. Invert onto a cake plate. Cut into slices to serve.

YIELD: 16 SERVINGS

BROWN SUGAR ICING

1 cup packed brown sugar
¹/₂ cup (1 stick) butter
¹/₄ cup evaporated milk

Combine the brown sugar, butter and evaporated milk in a saucepan. Cook for 3 minutes or until smooth, stirring constantly.

DOUBLE CHOCOLATE FUDGE CAKE

1 cup minus 1 tablespoon baking cocoa	2¼ teaspoons baking powder
1½ cups hot water	¾ teaspoon baking soda
3 eggs, at room temperature	½ teaspoon salt
½ teaspoon vanilla extract	1 cup (2 sticks) unsalted butter,
3 cups cake flour	softened
2 cups packed brown sugar	Chocolate Frosting (below)

Whisk the baking cocoa and hot water in a bowl until smooth. Cool to room temperature. Combine the eggs, ¼ of the cocoa mixture and vanilla in a bowl and mix lightly. Combine the cake flour, brown sugar, baking powder, baking soda and salt in a mixing bowl. Beat at low speed for 30 seconds. Add the butter and remaining cocoa mixture. Beat at low speed until the dry ingredients are moistened. Add the egg mixture ⅓ at a time, beating for 20 seconds after each addition. Pour into two 9-inch cake pans sprayed with nonstick cooking spray. Bake at 350 degrees for 20 to 30 minutes or until a wooden pick inserted in the center of each layer comes out clean. Cool in the pans for 10 minutes. Invert onto a wire rack to cool completely. Spread the Chocolate Frosting between the layers and over the top and side of the cake.

YIELD: 12 SERVINGS

CHOCOLATE FROSTING

1½ cups (9 ounces) milk
    chocolate chips
	2¼ cups (4½ sticks) unsalted
	    butter, softened

12 ounces semisweet chocolate, broken into pieces	

Combine the chocolate chips and semisweet chocolate in a double boiler. Simmer over hot water until smooth. Remove from the heat. Cool to room temperature. Place the butter in a mixing bowl. Beat at medium speed with an electric mixer fitted with a whisk attachment until light and fluffy. Add the cooled chocolate and beat for 3 minutes. Chill in the refrigerator for 10 minutes. Beat for 2 minutes or until fluffy.

Served for Elizabeth Taylor's 60th birthday celebration at Disneyland.

CHOCOLATE CURLS

Your cake may taste scrumptious, but garnishing it with chocolate curls will also make it attractive. To make curls, slightly soften a three- to four-inch bar of chocolate in a microwave at fifty percent power. Use a vegetable peeler to carve the curls, then chill until ready to use. To cut chocolate shavings, use a vegetable peeler or sharp knife.

FRUITCAKE BLANCO

1 (8-ounce) package pitted dates, cut into halves
1¹/₂ cups quartered dried figs
³/₄ cup golden raisins
¹/₂ cup quartered dried apricots
2 tablespoons Cognac
2¹/₂ cups all-purpose flour
2¹/₂ teaspoons baking powder
¹/₄ teaspoon salt

1 cup (2 sticks) unsalted butter, softened
1¹/₂ cups sugar
1 teaspoon vanilla extract
2 egg whites
1 cup milk
3 cups pecan halves
3 egg whites

Combine the dates, figs, raisins, apricots and Cognac in a large bowl and toss to mix well. Let stand, covered, for at least 1 hour or overnight.

Sift the flour, baking powder and salt together. Cream the butter, sugar and vanilla in a mixing bowl until light and fluffy. Add 2 egg whites and beat until smooth. Add the flour mixture alternately with the milk, beating well after each addition. Fold in the fruit mixture and pecans. Beat 3 egg whites in a mixing bowl until soft peaks form. Fold gently into the batter. Spoon into 2 greased and floured 5×9-inch loaf pans. Bake at 325 degrees for 1 hour and 15 minutes to 1 hour and 25 minutes or until the crust is golden brown and the loaves begin to pull from the sides of the pans. Remove from the oven. Cool in the pans for 10 minutes. Invert onto a wire rack to cool completely. To store, wrap in plastic wrap and then in foil.

YIELD: 2 LOAVES

desserts and sweets

ITALIAN CREAM CAKE

Photograph for this recipe is shown on page 212 and facing page.

1/2 cup (1 stick) butter or
   margarine, softened
1/2 cup shortening
2 cups sugar
5 eggs
2 cups all-purpose flour

1 teaspoon baking soda
1 cup buttermilk
2 cups flaked coconut
1 cup chopped pecans
1 teaspoon vanilla extract
Cream Cheese Frosting (below)

Cream the butter, shortening and sugar in a large mixing bowl until light and fluffy. Add the eggs 1 at a time, beating well after each addition. Add the flour and baking soda alternately with the buttermilk, mixing well after each addition. Stir in the coconut, pecans and vanilla. Pour into 3 greased and floured 8- or 9-inch cake pans. Bake at 325 degrees for 25 minutes. Remove from the oven. Cool on a wire rack for 15 minutes.

Spread Cream Cheese Frosting between the layers and over the top and side of the warm cake. Garnish with Jordan almonds.

Note: If you are going to transport the cake, it is better to take the cake unassembled and then frost at the destination.

YIELD: 12 SERVINGS

CREAM CHEESE FROSTING

1/2 cup (1 stick) butter or
   margarine, softened
8 ounces cream cheese, softened

1 (1-pound) package
   confectioners' sugar
1 teaspoon vanilla extract

Beat the butter and cream cheese in a mixing bowl until smooth and creamy. Add the confectioners' sugar gradually, beating until smooth after each addition. Stir in the vanilla.

CAKE PANS

Cakes will bake more evenly in round pans than in square ones. Crusts will be more tender if baked in a shiny pan, since it will reflect the heat. If you are using a glass dish, reduce the oven temperature by twenty-five degrees. Don't be afraid to grease pans generously to prevent cakes from sticking.

Lemon Pudding Cake

2 tablespoons all-purpose flour	2 egg yolks
$3/4$ cup sugar	$1/4$ cup fresh lemon juice
$1/4$ teaspoon salt	1 cup milk
1 tablespoon grated lemon zest	2 egg whites, stiffly beaten
1 tablespoon butter, softened	

Combine the flour, sugar, salt, lemon zest and butter in a bowl and mix well. Beat the egg yolks in a small mixing bowl until light and pale yellow. Add with the lemon juice and milk to the butter mixture and mix well. The mixture may have a curdled appearance, but this will not affect the texture. Fold in the egg whites gently. Spoon into a buttered 5×9-inch loaf pan. Place in a larger pan of hot water. Bake, uncovered, at 325 degrees for 40 to 45 minutes or until set. Remove from the oven. Cool to room temperature. Chill, covered, until ready to serve. Serve plain or with whipped cream.

YIELD: 6 SERVINGS

Heritage Oatmeal Cake

1 cup rolled oats	1 teaspoon cinnamon
$1/2$ cup (1 stick) butter, softened	$1/4$ teaspoon nutmeg
$1^1/2$ cups boiling water	$1/2$ cup evaporated milk
1 cup sugar	1 cup packed brown sugar
1 cup packed brown sugar	$1/2$ cup (1 stick) butter, softened
2 eggs	1 cup flaked coconut
$1^1/3$ cups all-purpose flour	1 cup coarsely chopped nuts

Combine the oats, $1/2$ cup butter and boiling water in a large bowl and mix well. Let stand for 20 minutes or until cool. Add the sugar, 1 cup brown sugar, eggs, flour, cinnamon and nutmeg and mix well. Pour into a greased and floured 9×11-inch cake pan. Bake at 350 degrees for 30 to 40 minutes or until the cake tests done.

Combine the evaporated milk, 1 cup brown sugar and $1/2$ cup butter in a saucepan. Heat until the brown sugar and butter melt, stirring frequently. Stir in the coconut and nuts. Spread over the warm cake. Broil until brown.

YIELD: 15 SERVINGS

COCONUTS

When shopping for a coconut, give it the shake test. If you don't hear the liquid inside, pick another one. The shell should be free of cracks and soft spots, and the "eyes" (the three small dimples at the pointed end) should be dry and clean. To remove the coconut water, pierce holes in the "eyes" with a hammer and nail and drain the liquid.

PUMPKIN ROULADE

3/4 cup all-purpose flour
1 1/2 teaspoons cinnamon
1 1/4 teaspoons ginger
1/4 teaspoon ground cloves
6 egg yolks
1/3 cup sugar
1/3 cup packed brown sugar

2/3 cup canned solid-pack pumpkin
6 egg whites
1/8 teaspoon salt
1 cup finely chopped pecans
Confectioners' sugar
Cream Cheese Filling (below)

Mix the flour, cinnamon, ginger and cloves together. Beat the egg yolks, sugar and brown sugar in a large mixing bowl until thick. Beat in the pumpkin at low speed. Add the flour mixture and beat at low speed until smooth. Beat the egg whites and salt in a mixing bowl until stiff peaks form. Fold into the batter gently. Pour into a 10×15-inch cake pan sprayed with nonstick cooking spray. Sprinkle with the pecans. Bake at 375 degrees for 15 minutes. Remove from the oven and cool slightly.

Place a smooth kitchen towel on a work surface. Do not use a terry cloth towel. Sprinkle with confectioners' sugar. Invert the warm cake onto the prepared towel. Roll the warm cake in the towel beginning at the long side. Cool on a wire rack for 1 hour. Unroll and remove the towel. Spread with Cream Cheese Filling and reroll. Place seam side down on a serving plate. Chill, covered, until ready to serve. Serve on warm caramel sauce with a dollop of sweetened whipped cream.

YIELD: 8 SERVINGS

CREAM CHEESE FILLING

8 ounces cream cheese, softened
1/4 cup (1/2 stick) unsalted butter,
    softened
1 cup confectioners' sugar

1/2 teaspoon vanilla extract
3 tablespoons minced candied
    ginger (optional)

Beat the cream cheese and butter in a mixing bowl until light and fluffy. Add the confectioners' sugar and vanilla and beat until smooth. Stir in the ginger.

 Serve with a late harvest sémillon or sauvignon blanc.

PUMPKIN PURÉE

For the freshest pumpkin pie, consider puréeing your own pumpkin rather than opening a can. Here's how: Roast the pumpkin on a baking sheet at 350 degrees for 1 1/2 hours. When cool, remove the seeds, scoop out the pulp and purée in a blender or food processor. Don't throw away those seeds! They make a great snack when sautéed in vegetable oil in a skillet until light brown and then baked on a baking sheet at 350 degrees for 10 minutes.

BLACK BOTTOM CUPCAKES

MACADAMIAS

(MAK-UH-DAY-MEE-UHS)

The macadamia tree, a native of Australia, is named for John McAdam, the chemist who first cultivated it. Hawaii is the largest exporter, but they are also grown commercially in California. The marble-sized nut has a hard, brown shell and creamy, white meat. Macadamias are very high in fat and turn rancid quickly, so refrigerate or freeze after opening.

1½ cups all-purpose flour	1 tablespoon vinegar
1 cup sugar	1 teaspoon vanilla extract
¼ cup baking cocoa	8 ounces cream cheese, softened
1 teaspoon baking soda	⅓ cup sugar
½ teaspoon salt	1 egg
1 cup water	1 cup (6 ounces) chocolate chips
5 tablespoons vegetable oil	

Sift the flour, 1 cup sugar, baking cocoa, baking soda and salt into a large mixing bowl. Mix the water, oil and vinegar in a small bowl. Add to the flour mixture and mix well. Stir in the vanilla.

Beat the cream cheese and ⅓ cup sugar in a mixing bowl until light and fluffy. Add the egg and mix well. Stir in the chocolate chips.

Fill paper-lined muffin cups ½ full with the chocolate batter. Top each with 1 tablespoon of the cream cheese mixture. Bake at 350 degrees for 25 to 30 minutes or until the cupcakes test done.

YIELD: 18 SERVINGS

MICROWAVE MACADAMIA BRITTLE

1 cup sugar	1 tablespoon butter
½ cup light corn syrup	1 teaspoon vanilla extract
⅛ teaspoon salt	1 teaspoon baking soda
1½ cups macadamia nuts, coarsely chopped	1 cup (6 ounces) semisweet chocolate chips, melted

Combine the sugar, corn syrup and salt in a 2-quart glass measure with a handle. Microwave on High for 5 minutes. Stir in the macadamia nuts. Microwave for 2 to 5 minutes or until the syrup and macadamia nuts are light brown, stirring after 2 and 4 minutes. Add the butter, vanilla and baking soda and stir until light and foamy and well mixed.

Spread ¼ inch thick on a buttered large baking sheet using the back of a spoon. Let stand until cool. Drizzle with the melted chocolate chips. Remove from the baking sheet and break into pieces.

Note: You may use other lightly salted roasted nuts, such as cashews, coarsely chopped almonds and peanuts.

YIELD: 16 (2½×3-INCH) PIECES

CHINESE FRIED WALNUTS

4 cups walnut halves
1/2 cup sugar
Vegetable oil for frying
Salt to taste

Boil the walnuts in water to cover in a saucepan for 2 to 3 minutes. Drain well on paper towels. Place in a large bowl. Sprinkle with the sugar and toss to coat. Fry the walnuts in 1/2 inch oil in a skillet until golden brown. Drain on waxed paper over newspaper. Sprinkle with salt while warm. Store in an airtight container.

YIELD: 4 CUPS

Wonderful for the holidays as a special gift from your kitchen.

SWEDISH NUTS

2 egg whites
1 cup sugar
Dash of salt
2 cups walnut halves
11/2 cups blanched almonds
1/2 cup (1 stick) butter

Beat the egg whites in a large mixing bowl until soft peaks form. Add the sugar and salt gradually, beating until stiff peaks form. Fold in the walnuts and almonds.

Melt the butter in a shallow baking pan. Spread the walnut mixture in the butter. Bake at 300 degrees until the butter is absorbed, stirring every 10 minutes. Remove from the oven to cool. Store in an airtight container.

YIELD: 6 CUPS

WALNUTS

A California crop for over a century, walnuts are a furrowed, double-lobed nut with a strong flavor. If you hear rattling when you shake a whole walnut, the nutmeat may be old and dry. Unshelled, they can be stored for up to three months, but once shelled they should be refrigerated. Walnuts are nutritious as well as delicious, due to their beneficial fatty acids, protein, and fiber.

Apricot Walnut Bars

Photograph for this recipe is shown on page 212.

Photograph for this recipe is shown on page 212.

³/₄ cup dried apricots

1 cup sifted all-purpose flour

¹/₄ cup sugar

¹/₂ cup (1 stick) butter

2 eggs, well beaten

1 cup packed brown sugar

¹/₃ cup sifted all-purpose flour

¹/₂ teaspoon baking powder

¹/₄ teaspoon salt

¹/₂ teaspoon vanilla extract

¹/₂ cup chopped walnuts

Cover the apricots with water in a saucepan. Bring to a boil and reduce the heat. Simmer for 10 minutes; drain. Let the apricots stand until cool. Chop the apricots.

Sift 1 cup flour and sugar into a bowl. Cut in the butter until crumbly using a pastry blender. Press into a 9×9-inch baking pan. Bake at 325 degrees for 25 minutes.

Combine the eggs and brown sugar in a bowl and mix well. Stir in ¹/₃ cup flour, the baking powder, salt, vanilla, walnuts and apricots. Spread over the baked layer. Bake for 35 minutes. Remove from the oven and cool in the pan. Cut into 16 large squares or 32 strips.

YIELD: 16 OR 32 SERVINGS

Biscotti with Almonds and Anise

Photograph for this recipe is shown on page 212.

Photograph for this recipe is shown on page 212.

1 cup (2 sticks) butter or
   margarine, softened

1¹/₂ cups sugar

4 eggs

¹/₂ teaspoon salt

1 tablespoon baking powder

1 tablespoon vanilla extract

1 tablespoon anise extract

3 cups all-purpose flour

1 cup chopped blanched almonds

Cream the butter and sugar in a mixing bowl until light and fluffy. Beat in the eggs, salt, baking powder, vanilla and anise extract. Add the flour and almonds and mix well. Shape into a ball. Divide the ball into 2 equal portions. Shape each portion into a loaf on a cookie sheet. Bake at 350 degrees for 25 to 30 minutes. Remove from the oven. Let stand until cool. Cut each loaf into slices. Arrange the slices on a cookie sheet. Bake at 350 degrees for 20 minutes or until toasted, turning once halfway through the baking time. Remove from the oven to cool. Serve as is or frost with your favorite confectioners' sugar frosting.

YIELD: 2 DOZEN

 Dip biscotti into a late-harvest muscat or sauternes for an exceptional finish to your meal.

CELEBRATION BUTTER COOKIES

1 cup (2 sticks) butter, softened	**1 teaspoon vanilla extract**
1 cup sugar	**2 cups all-purpose flour**
2 egg yolks	**Colored sugar**

Cream the butter and sugar in a mixing bowl until light and fluffy. Add the egg yolks 1 at a time, beating well after each addition. Add the vanilla and flour and mix well. Chill, covered, for 1 hour.

Roll a small amount of the dough at a time into a ball the size of a large marble. Arrange on a cookie sheet. Flatten with the palm of your hand as thin as possible. Sprinkle with colored sugar. Bake at 300 degrees for 10 to 15 minutes or until light brown. Remove to a wire rack to cool.

YIELD: 4 TO 5 SERVINGS

TO-DIE-FOR CHOCOLATE CHIP COOKIES

1^3/$_4$ cups vegetable oil	**2 teaspoons baking soda**
1^3/$_4$ cups sugar	**^{1}/$_2$ teaspoon salt**
2 cups packed brown sugar	**3 cups (18 ounces) chocolate**
4 eggs	**chips**
4 teaspoons vanilla extract	**1 cup chopped nuts (optional)**
4^1/$_2$ cups all-purpose flour	

Beat the oil, sugar, brown sugar and eggs in a mixing bowl until smooth. Add the vanilla, flour, baking soda and salt and mix well. Stir in the chocolate chips and nuts. Drop by tablespoonfuls 2 inches apart onto a nonstick cookie sheet. Bake at 350 degrees for 8 to 10 minutes or until golden brown. Remove to a wire rack to cool.

YIELD: 3 DOZEN

COOKIE BAKING TIPS

You can't unbake a cookie but you can remove a burned edge with the coarse side of a vegetable grater. To prevent sprinkles from scattering while decorating cookies, place the cookie cutter around the baked cookie to contain them. Cookie dough freezes well, so consider making a double batch and freezing half. That way the next time you crave a freshly baked cookie, you won't have to start from scratch.

CRESCENT COOKIES

1/2 cup (1 stick) butter, softened	1 teaspoon vanilla extract
3 tablespoons confectioners' sugar	1 cup pecan pieces
1 1/4 cups all-purpose flour	Confectioners' sugar for coating

Cream the butter and 3 tablespoons confectioners' sugar in a mixing bowl until light and fluffy. Add the flour, vanilla and pecans and mix well. Roll a small amount of the dough at a time in the palm of your hand to form an oval shape. Shape into a crescent. Arrange 2 inches apart on a lightly greased cookie sheet. Bake at 275 degrees for 20 minutes. Remove from the oven and cool slightly. Roll the warm cookies in confectioners' sugar. Place on a wire rack to cool completely. Roll in confectioners' sugar again if necessary.

YIELD: 1½ DOZEN

GINGER DROPS

3/4 cup shortening	1/2 teaspoon salt
1 cup sugar	1 teaspoon cinnamon
1/4 cup unsulfered molasses	3/4 teaspoon ground cloves
1 egg, beaten	3/4 teaspoon ginger
2 cups all-purpose flour	Sugar for coating
2 teaspoons baking soda	

Beat the shortening and 1 cup sugar in a mixing bowl until light and fluffy. Add the molasses and egg and mix well. Add the flour alternately with the baking soda, salt, cinnamon, cloves and ginger, mixing well after each addition. Roll into 1-inch balls. Dip in sugar. Arrange 2 inches apart on a nonstick cookie sheet. Press lightly to flatten with a fork dipped in sugar. Bake at 350 degrees for 10 to 12 minutes or until light brown. Cool on a wire rack.

YIELD: 3½ DOZEN

Lemon Drops

Photograph for this recipe is shown on page 212.

1¼ cups all-purpose flour
½ cup cornstarch
⅓ cup confectioners' sugar
¾ cup (1½ sticks) butter, softened
1 teaspoon lemon juice

2 teaspoons grated lemon zest
¾ cup confectioners' sugar
¼ cup (½ stick) butter, softened
1 teaspoon lemon juice
1 teaspoon grated lemon zest

Combine the flour, cornstarch, ⅓ cup confectioners' sugar, ¾ cup butter, 1 teaspoon lemon juice and 2 teaspoons lemon zest in a large mixing bowl. Beat at low speed for 2 to 3 minutes or until well mixed, scraping the bowl frequently. Divide the dough into 2 equal portions. Shape each portion into a 1×8-inch roll. Wrap in plastic wrap. Chill for 1 to 2 hours or until firm. Cut each roll into ¼-inch slices using a sharp knife. Arrange 2 inches apart on a nonstick cookie sheet. Bake at 350 degrees for 8 to 12 minutes or until set. The cookies will not brown. Remove to a wire rack to cool. Combine ¾ cup confectioners' sugar, ¼ cup butter, 1 teaspoon lemon juice and 1 teaspoon lemon zest in a small mixing bowl. Beat at medium speed for 1 to 2 minutes or until fluffy, scraping the bowl frequently. Spread over the cooled cookies.

YIELD: 4 DOZEN

Chewy Maple Cookies

1½ cups all-purpose flour
2 teaspoons baking powder
½ teaspoon salt
½ cup shortening
1 cup packed brown sugar

1 egg
½ cup pure maple syrup
½ teaspoon maple extract
1 cup flaked coconut

Mix the flour, baking powder and salt together. Cream the shortening and brown sugar in a large mixing bowl until fluffy. Add the egg, maple syrup and maple extract and beat well. Add the flour mixture and mix well. Stir in the coconut. Drop by tablespoonfuls 2 inches apart onto a greased cookie sheet. Bake at 375 degrees for 12 to 15 minutes or until golden brown. Cool on a wire rack.

YIELD: 3 DOZEN

Maple Syrup

The American Indians called it "sweetwater" and taught the Colonists how to tap the sap from the maple tree, then boil it until it became pure maple syrup. If all the liquid is evaporated after boiling, you'll have *maple sugar*. Maple-flavored syrup is a mixture of an inexpensive syrup and a little pure maple syrup, while *pancake syrup* is artificial maple extract added to corn syrup.

SNOWFLAKES

Photograph for this recipe is shown on pages 212 and 213.

4 egg whites
1 cup sugar
2 cups pecans, coarsely chopped

4 cups cornflakes, toasted
1 teaspoon vanilla extract

Beat the egg whites in a mixing bowl until stiff peaks form. Add the sugar gradually, beating constantly. Continue to beat for 1 minute. Add the pecans and cornflakes and mix well. Stir in the vanilla. Drop by teaspoonfuls 2 inches apart onto a buttered cookie sheet. Bake at 275 degrees for 20 minutes or until crisp and firm. Cool on a wire rack.

YIELD: ABOUT 2 DOZEN

Yes, we have snow in the mountains of Santa Barbara.

PECAN PIE SQUARES

Photograph for this recipe is shown on pages 212 and 213.

$1^1/_4$ cups all-purpose flour
$1/_3$ cup sugar
$1/_2$ cup (1 stick) butter or
   margarine
1 teaspoon vanilla extract
2 eggs, beaten
$2/_3$ cup sugar
$3/_4$ cup honey

2 teaspoons all-purpose flour
$1/_4$ teaspoon salt
2 tablespoons butter or margarine,
   melted
$1^1/_2$ teaspoons vanilla extract
1 cup chopped pecans
Confectioners' sugar

Mix $1^1/_4$ cups flour and $1/_3$ cup sugar in a bowl. Cut in $1/_2$ cup butter until crumbly. Add 1 teaspoon vanilla and mix well. Press evenly into a greased 9×9-inch baking pan. Bake at 375 degrees for 15 minutes. Remove from the oven. Reduce the oven temperature to 350 degrees.

Beat the eggs, $2/_3$ cup sugar, honey, 2 teaspoons flour, salt, 2 tablespoons butter and $1^1/_2$ teaspoons vanilla in a mixing bowl until smooth. Stir in the pecans. Pour over the crust. Bake at 350 degrees for 25 minutes or until firm. Cool in the pan on a wire rack. Cut into squares. Sprinkle with confectioners' sugar.

Note: This recipe may be doubled, but use a 12×15-inch baking pan.

YIELD: 3 DOZEN

LAYERED WALNUT SQUARES

½ cup (1 stick) butter, softened
1 cup sifted all-purpose flour
1½ cups packed brown sugar
¼ cup all-purpose flour
¼ teaspoon baking powder
½ teaspoon salt

2 eggs, lightly beaten
1½ teaspoons vanilla extract
1 cup chopped walnuts
½ cup shredded coconut
Orange Frosting (below)

Beat the butter, 1 cup flour and ¼ cup of the brown sugar in a mixing bowl until blended. Press firmly into a greased 9×9-inch baking pan. Bake at 350 degrees for 15 minutes.

Mix the remaining brown sugar, ¼ cup flour, baking powder and salt in a bowl. Add the eggs and vanilla and mix well. Stir in the walnuts and coconut. Spread over the baked layer. Bake at 350 degrees for 25 minutes. Cool on a wire rack. Spread Orange Frosting over the top.

YIELD: 32 TO 64 COOKIES

ORANGE FROSTING

1½ cups sifted confectioners'
   sugar
2 tablespoons butter, melted

2 tablespoons orange juice
2 teaspoons lemon juice

Combine the confectioners' sugar, butter, orange juice and lemon juice in a mixing bowl and beat until smooth.

YUM-YUMS

2¹/2 cups all-purpose flour
1 teaspoon baking soda
1 teaspoon cream of tartar
1/4 teaspoon salt
1 cup (2 sticks) butter or
    margarine, softened

1 teaspoon vanilla extract
2 cups sugar
3 egg yolks
Sugar

Mix the flour, baking soda, cream of tartar and salt together. Cream the butter and vanilla in a mixing bowl. Add 2 cups sugar gradually, beating constantly until light and fluffy. Add the egg yolks 1 at a time, beating well after each addition. Add the flour mixture and mix well. Shape the dough into 1-inch balls. Roll in sugar. Arrange 2 inches apart on a cookie sheet. Bake at 350 degrees for 10 to 15 minutes or until brown around the edges. Cool on a wire rack.

YIELD: 7 DOZEN

So easy, even the youngest of children can help with rolling the dough and coating with sugar.

SPIRITED CHOCOLATE PECAN PIE

3 eggs, lightly beaten
3/4 cup packed brown sugar
1/4 cup sugar
1 cup pure maple syrup
3 tablespoons butter, melted
2 tablespoons all-purpose flour
3 tablespoons Jack Daniel's
    whiskey

1 teaspoon vanilla extract
1 cup pecan halves
1 cup (6 ounces) semisweet
    chocolate chips
1 unbaked (9-inch) deep-dish pie
    shell

Combine the eggs, brown sugar, sugar, maple syrup, butter, flour, whiskey and vanilla in a large mixing bowl and mix well. Stir in the pecans. Scatter the chocolate chips in the pie shell. Pour the filling over the top. Bake at 350 degrees for 50 to 60 minutes or until the top is brown.

YIELD: 6 TO 8 SERVINGS

LEMON FROST PIE

1 cup sifted all-purpose flour	**²/₃ cup sugar**
2 tablespoons sugar	**2 teaspoons grated lemon zest**
¹/₄ teaspoon salt	**¹/₄ cup lemon juice**
¹/₂ cup (1 stick) butter	**5 drops of yellow food coloring**
2 egg whites	**1 cup whipping cream, whipped**

Mix the flour, 2 tablespoons sugar and the salt in a bowl. Cut in the butter until crumbly. Spread ¹/₃ cup of the mixture in a baking dish. Press the remaining mixture into a greased and floured 9-inch pie plate. Bake both at 375 degrees for 12 to 15 minutes or until golden brown. Remove from the oven to cool.

Beat the egg whites in a mixing bowl until soft peaks form. Add ²/₃ cup sugar, lemon zest, lemon juice and food coloring gradually, beating until stiff peaks form. Fold in the whipped cream gently. Spoon into the cooled piecrust. Sprinkle with the baked crumbs. Chill or freeze, covered, until ready to serve.

Note: To avoid raw eggs that may carry salmonella, we suggest using an equivalent amount of egg substitute.

YIELD: 6 TO 8 SERVINGS

SWEET LEMON AVOCADO PIE

2 ripe medium avocados	**1 (14-ounce) can sweetened**
3 ounces cream cheese, softened	**condensed milk**
¹/₄ cup fresh lemon juice	**1 (8-inch) graham cracker pie shell**

Combine the avocados, cream cheese, lemon juice and condensed milk in a mixing bowl and beat well. Spoon into the pie shell. Cover the surface with plastic wrap. Chill until ready to serve. Serve with whipped cream.

YIELD: 6 TO 8 SERVINGS

WHIPPED CREAM

To whip a firmer cream, add one tablespoon vanilla instant pudding mix or a pinch of unflavored gelatin while whipping. This should eliminate the liquid that accumulates at the bottom of the bowl. Also, shaking a little salt into the cream will reduce the whipping time. Since whipping cream doubles in volume, one cup will make two cups of whipped cream.

PEANUT BUTTER CREAM PIE

Chef Saturnina Mora, The Brewhouse, Santa Barbara, California

**1¹/₂ cups chocolate sandwich
    cookie crumbs**
¹/₄ cup creamy peanut butter
8 ounces cream cheese, softened

¹/₂ cup peanut butter
1³/₄ cups confectioners' sugar
3 cups whipping cream, whipped

Combine the cookie crumbs and ¼ cup peanut butter in a bowl and mix well. Press into a 9-inch pie plate. Bake at 350 degrees for 7 minutes or until set. Remove from the oven. Cool completely on a wire rack.

Beat the cream cheese, ½ cup peanut butter and confectioners' sugar in a mixing bowl until smooth. Fold in the whipped cream. Pour into the piecrust. Chill, covered, for 3 to 4 hours before serving.

YIELD: 6 TO 8 SERVINGS

NO-BAKE STRAWBERRY PIE

1¹/₂ cups fine vanilla wafer crumbs
¹/₃ cup butter, melted
**¹/₂ cup (1 stick) butter or
    margarine, softened**
**1¹/₂ cups sifted confectioners'
    sugar**

2 eggs, beaten
1 teaspoon vanilla extract
**1¹/₂ cups drained sweetened fresh
    or frozen strawberry slices**
**1 to 2 cups whipping cream,
    whipped**

Reserve 2 tablespoons of the vanilla wafer crumbs. Mix the remaining crumbs with ⅓ cup butter in a bowl. Press into a 9-inch pie plate. Chill, covered, until firm.

Cream ½ cup butter and the confectioners' sugar in a mixing bowl until smooth. Add the eggs and vanilla and beat until fluffy. Spoon into the prepared pie plate.

Fold the strawberries into the whipped cream in a bowl. Spread over the top. Sprinkle with the reserved vanilla wafer crumbs. Chill, covered, for 8 hours or until firm.

Note: To avoid raw eggs that may carry salmonella, we suggest using an equivalent amount of egg substitute.

YIELD: 6 TO 8 SERVINGS

STRAWBERRY TRIVIA

Every strawberry has approximately two hundred tiny seeds. The strawberry is the only fruit to have its seeds on the outside. If all of the strawberries grown in California in one year were placed side-by-side, they'd encircle the earth fifteen times. Eight medium-sized strawberries provide more vitamin C than an orange. The strawberry's flavor is influenced by soil, weather, moisture level, and ripeness when harvested, not size.

PETITE CHEESECAKE TARTS

Photograph for this recipe is shown on page 212.

1¼ cups graham cracker or
    chocolate sandwich cookie
    crumbs
¼ cup (½ stick) butter or
    margarine, melted
16 ounces cream cheese, softened

2 eggs
½ cup sugar
2 teaspoons vanilla extract
¾ cup currant jelly
Sliced fresh strawberries

Mix the graham cracker crumbs and butter in a bowl. Place 1 tablespoon of the mixture in paper-lined muffin cups and press down with a glass to flatten.

Beat the cream cheese, eggs, sugar and vanilla in a mixing bowl for 15 minutes or until smooth. Spoon into the prepared muffin cups. Bake at 375 degrees for 10 minutes. Remove from the oven to cool. Chill, covered, until ready to serve.

To serve, melt the jelly in a saucepan. Cook for 5 minutes, stirring constantly. Remove the tarts from the paper wrappers and arrange on a dessert tray. Top each with sliced strawberries. Brush with the melted jelly.

Note: You may also cover the tarts with chilled cherry, blueberry or peach pie filling.

YIELD: 20 SERVINGS

CRANBERRY TART

2 cups chopped cranberries
½ cup chopped walnuts
½ cup sugar
2 eggs
¾ cup (1½ sticks) butter, melted

1 cup sugar
1 cup all-purpose flour
¼ teaspoon salt
¼ teaspoon almond or vanilla
    extract

Mix the cranberries, walnuts and ½ cup sugar in a bowl. Press into a buttered tart pan with a removable bottom. Combine the eggs, butter, 1 cup sugar, flour, salt and almond extract in a mixing bowl and stir until smooth. Pour over the cranberry mixture. Place on the middle oven rack. Bake at 350 degrees for 40 minutes. Serve warm or cool with whipped cream or ice cream.

YIELD: 8 SERVINGS

SANTA BARBARA WINE COUNTRY

Winemaking was born in the area when Father Junipero Serra brought grapevine cuttings from Mexico in 1782. Today, there are over twenty-one thousand acres of vineyards and fifty-eight wineries in Santa Barbara County. The vintners enjoy an excellent reputation among wine enthusiasts and have won recognition on local, national, and international levels. Santa Barbara County is best known for fine chardonnay, pinot noir, syrah, sauvignon blanc, cabernet sauvignon, and riesling.

cookbook committee

CHAIRMAN:

Linda Hurst

RECIPES:

Rita Anderson

Marilyn Reginato

Nancy Waldron

RECIPE TESTING:

Peggy Hamilton

CHAPTERS:

Dianne Arguelles

Suzie Padrick

Lynn Wells

PHOTOGRAPHY:

Rose Louie

Charline Shook

Nancy Trotter

CELEBRITIES/CHEFS:

Pam Stoney

NON-RECIPE TEXT:

Susan Engles

Vickie Mahan

SPONSORS/PARTNERS:

Jane Atwater

ACCOUNTING/DISTRIBUTION:

Georgia Jameson

Ellie Starfas

MARKETING:

Sherry Hunt

Marilyn McLychok

Maureen Wilson

DAVID MUENCH:

David Muench is one of America's foremost photographers. His sensitivity to the spirit and beauty of the land has resulted in extensive publication of his artistic work in exhibit-format books, magazines, and wilderness materials as well as many exhibits. He currently resides in New Mexico.

MARC MUENCH:

Marc Muench photographs the landscape in his own dramatic style. His love for the out-doors and its natural beauty are evident in his landscape photographs, which are taken throughout the United States in all seasons. He resides in Santa Barbara, California.

KIRK IRWIN:

Kirk Irwin has turned his passions for fine photography and fine wine into a creative and successful career. He looks for scenes that capture the essence of the vineyard, looking for that special light that transforms the ordinary to the magical. Living in Santa Barbara, he also focuses his camera on the beauty of this coastal community.

MICHAEL BROWN: Food Photography—Santa Barbara, California.

CLAIRE STANCER: Food Stylist.

Acknowledgments

ASSISTANCE LEAGUE® of Santa Barbara expresses deep gratitude to our partners whose donations helped make this project possible. We "savor" your generosity.

CABERNET SAUVIGNON

Douglas and Francesca Deaver

Tom and Pat DeBerry

Yoshiharu and Yoshie Ohara

Nicholas and Sue Vincent

SYRAH

Bob and Jane Atwater

Thomas and Barbara Brashears

Barry and Norris Goss

LeRoy and Sherry Hunt

Don and Rose Louie

Muench Photography

Georgiana Nammack

Cap and Diane Price

John M. and Lorraine Rasmussen

Santa Barbara Bank & Trust

Marcia G. Vaile (In memory of all the members of the class of 1956)

MERLOT

Stanley W. Abbott,
Attorney

Maris and Patricia Andersons

Bernat Vineyards and
Winery, Sam Marmorstein—
Winemaker

George R. and
Marjorie K. Bliss

DB Club of Santa Barbara

Goleta National Bank

First American Title Company

Charles and Peggy Hamilton,
in memory of Marian E. Zuelch

Holmes & Holmes
Insurance Agency, Inc.

Jim and Linda Hurst

Elenore K. Johnson

Joan and Wayne Kidder

Montecito Bank & Trust

Mulligan Mamas

Barbara Offerman

Richard and Phyllis Pool

Mike Richardson Realtors

Jack and Maureen Wilson

ZINFANDEL

Stan and Lois Abbott

Marjorie Boyle

Jim and Susan Chapman

Hughes Automobile Company

Venard and Sally Kinney

Sona MacMillan

Terry and Linda Perkins

Gordon Hardey and Marilyn
Wankum, Prudential Realty

Robert and Patricia Reid

Scott and Barbara Schurmer

Edythe Sparks

Zaca Mesa Winery

contributors

Barbe Abbott
Lois Abbott
Kathleen Aguilera
Helen Nielsen Allen
Rita Anderson
Patricia Andersons
Dianne Arguelles
Carol Ashamalla
Jane Atwater
Margery Baragona
Tony Baragona
Virginia Barker
Patricia Barry
Shirley Bendix
Colleen Booth
Marjorie Boyle
Mary Lou Brace
Barbara Brashears
Patricia Brians
Gigi Brown
June Brusse
Ruby Buck
Margret Buelow
Heather Burris
Kathy Bush
W. Joe Bush
Jean Campbell
Mary Ann Campbell
Sandy Beste
    Campbell
David Michael Cane
Tis Carlson

Louise Casey
Doris Caswell
Sandy Catalana
Jeannie Cavender
Susan Chapman
Marian Christopher
Sherry Churchill
Edith Clark
Lenor Cooper
Mary Jane &
    Andrew Cooper
Jane Criswell
Chef Linda Crocker
Martha Daniel
Deanne Davis
Dianne Davis
Dorothy Davis
Jeanne Davis
Edwin Dawson
Judy Dawson
Deborah de Lambert
Francesca Deaver
Pat DeBerry
Jennifer Deming
Sue Deming
Shirley Dettmann
Alma Diaz
Chef Katherine
    Dittmann
Tom Dixon
Joyce Donald
Ann Donlon

Mary Jean Ducale
Wanda Duncan
Kathy Durkee
Joyce Eggers
Susan Engles
Barbara Eschbach
Albert Field
Kate C. Firestone
Chef Mark Fisher
Patty Fligsten
Chef Charles
    Fredericks
Julie Freedman
Jacque Gamberdella
Gilbert Garcia
Joy Gilles
Carol Goodell
Norris Goss
Jan Gould
Edna Gregory
Karen Gressingh
Judy Grover
Barbara Hagen
Fran Hamer
Peggy Hamilton
E. Lynn Handloser
Maura Harding
Krista Harris
Felicie Hartloff
Sue Hebert
Pat Heidner
Charlene Heinz

Anne Higgins
Ann Hiller
Sibyl Hilliard
Bob Hiltz
Wendy Hiltz
Cheri Holcombe
Penny Hoyt
Sherry Hunt
Linda Hurst
Georgia Jameson
Jim Jameson
Len Jarrott
Ellie Johnson
Judy Johnson
Obie Johnson
Susan Jordan
Patricia Just
Evelyn Kay
Courtney Kaylor
Dot Kelley
Emily Kerr
Juliana Kimball
Sally Kinney
June Kjaempe
Nancy Knight
Barbara Kucera
Sharon Larson
Ruth Leggett
Diann Lindblad
Rose Louie
Judy Love
Susan Love

Sona MacMillan
Camille Maertz
Vickie Mahan
Dorothy Mainz
Gerry Mason
Sally Matthews
Debby McCombs
Patti McCormack
Mary McDonald
Leslie McFadden
Natalie McFadden
David T. McKee,
  Ph.D.
Dorothy McKiddie
Madonna McKinnon
John McLychok
Marilyn McLychok
Michael McLychok
Annie and Robert
  McMillin
Rebecca McNeil
Betsy Meehan
Executive Chef
  Tom Meyer
Jenny Millan
Pat Miller
Peter Miller
Susan Miller
David Mirmoez
Marion Moore
Chef Saturnina Mora

Elaine Anderson
  Morello
DeEtta Nancarrow
Executive Chef
  Tim Neenan
Joan Nielsen
Terri O'Brien
Irene O'Connor
Dan O'Hare
Kelly O'Hare
Barbara Offerman
Yoshie Ohara
Joanne Oliver
Kelly Onnen
Suzie Padrick
Linda Perkins
Ruth Perry
Sheryl Pike
Judy Piper
Barbara Pollard
Phyllis Pool
Richard Pool
Diane Price
Lynn Rabinowitz
Nancy Ransohoff
Lorraine Rasmussen
Marilyn Reginato
Roxanne Reginato
Patti Reid
Victoria Ricci
Viola Richardson

Marlene & George
  Riemer
H. Douglas Roberts
Karen Roberts
William Rogers
Carolyn Rutherford
Eleanore & William
  Sanders
Elsie Schacht
Jim Schnarr
Kelly Schultz
Barbara Schurmer
Alice Scott
Nancy Seed
Patti Shaw
Charline Shook
Audrey Short
Brigitte Shrode
Lene Shutt
June Smith
Paula Smith
Sally Smith
Edythe Sparks
Imogine Spence
Ellie Starfas
Pat Sternberg
John Stoney
Pam Stoney
Jane Sutphen
Nancy Szulczewski
Jeanne Thornton

Ruth Topping
Cindie Trieger
Ethel Trione
Nancy Trotter
Hiro Tsuzuki
Carole Turner
Beverley Verkouteren
Sue Vincent
Nancy Waldron
Steve Ward
Gloria Wascher
Fitzie Waters
Joan Watson
Jo Ann Wayne
Lynn Wells
Lyn Westsmith
Mary Whalen
Diana White
Chef Eric Widmer
Jan Williams
Parmele Williams
Julie Willig
Caroline Willsie
Jack Wilson
Maureen Wilson
Marcy Wilson-Mann
B. J. Wittwer
Anne Wunsch
Holly Yee
Gayle Young
Jaime Zermeno

Bernat Vineyards and Winery

Zaca Mesa Winery

Photograph © Kirk Irwin

Bader, Dr. Myles H. *8001 Food Facts and Chef's Secrets.* Las Vegas: Northstar
    Publishing Co., 1997.

Fadiman, Clifton, and Aaron, Sam. *The Joys of Wine*.
    New York: Galahad Books, 1975.

Heloise. *In the Kitchen with Heloise*. New York: Berkley Publishing Group,
    a division of Penguin Putnam Inc., 2000.

Herbst, Sharon Tyler. *The Food Lover's Tiptionary*. New York: William Morrow
    and Company, Inc., 1994.

——. *Food Lover's Companion*. Hauppaugen, New York:
    Barron's Educational Series, Inc., 2001.

Johnson, Hugh, and Halliday, James. *The Vintner's Art*. New York: Simon and Schuster, 1992.

Rainbird, George. *An Illustrated Guide to Wine*. New York: Harmony Books,
    a division of Crown Publishers, Inc., 1983.

Rosso, Julee, and Lukins, Sheila. *The New Basics Cookbook*.
    New York: Workman Publishing Co., Inc., 1989.

Schmidt, Stephen. *Master Recipes*. New York: Ballantine Books,
    a division of Random House, Inc., 1987.

index

Savor Santa Barbara

Waterfront to Wine Country

A Collection of Recipes from ASSISTANCE LEAGUE® of Santa Barbara

P.O. Box 6061

Santa Barbara, California 93160

Phone & Fax 805-687-0204

Toll Free 877-687-0204

www.savorsantabarbara.com

YOUR ORDER	QUANTITY	TOTAL
Savor Santa Barbara at $27.95 per book		$
California residents add 7.75% sales tax		$
Postage and handling at $6.00 for first book; $2.00 for each additional book to the same address		$
	TOTAL	$

Name _____

Address _____

City _____ State _____ Zip _____

Telephone _____ Email _____

Method of Payment: [   ] MasterCard   [   ] VISA

[   ] Check payable to ASSISTANCE LEAGUE® of Santa Barbara —Cookbook

Account Number _____ Expiration Date _____

Signature _____

Photocopies will be accepted.